How to Use Computers

Second Edition

Visually *in* **Full Color**

Lisa Biow
Revisions by Bob Temple

SAMS

201 W. 103rd Street
Indianapolis, Indiana 46290

Contents at a Glance

How to Use Computers
Second Edition

International Standard Book Number: 0-672-32253-6

Library of Congress Catalog Card Number: 2001094224

04   03   02   01   4   3   2   1

Printed in the United States of America

First Printing: September 2001

Trademarks

Warning and Disclaimer

Acquisitions Editor
Betsy Brown

Development Editor
Jon Steever

Managing Editor
Charlotte Clapp

Project Editor
Carol Bowers

Copy Editors
Mike Henry
Rebecca Martin
Debra Sexton

Indexer
Kelly Castell

Technical Editor
Dallas Releford

Team Coordinator
Amy Patton

Cover Designers
Aren Howell
Nathan Clement

Interior Designers
Gary Adair

Page Layout
Lizbeth Patterson
Cheryl Lynch

About the Authors

Lisa Biow is a computer trainer and consultant to small- and medium-sized businesses in Oakland, California. She has taught everything from introductory computer classes to advanced database management courses on the college level. Lisa has authored several books on PC software, as well as the First and Bestseller's Edition of *How to Use Your Computer*.

Bob Temple is the president of Red Line Editorial, Inc., an editorial services and content services provider based in Minnesota. He is the author of six other computer books and 18 children's non-fiction titles.

Dedication

To my sister Cindy Shivers. —Lisa Biow

Acknowledgments

From Lisa Biow: Bob Temple updated much of the material in this edition of the book, including the chapter on Windows, with great care and fine writing. Acquisitions editor Betsy Brown kept the wheels well-greased and turning throughout the rewrite. My friends and colleagues Deborah Craig, Miriam Liskin, and Heidi Steele provided critical assistance and moral support on earlier versions of the book.

Thanks are also due to the friends who've loved and supported me through a bumpy few months, including Sue Scope, Suzanne Flint, Deborah Craig, Larry Ackley, Miriam Liskin, Harry Linkous, Maureen Elia, Vivian Dai, Kathleen Divney, Merle Yost, and my fabulous roommates Carol DeArment and Abbe Kalos. Thanks also to acupuncturist Mark Frost for his needles, herbs, and inspiration.

From Bob Temple: I'd like to thank Lisa Biow for doing such a great job on the earlier versions of this book. Having such a strong foundation to work from made performing this revision easy.

I'd also like to thank Betsy Brown for the opportunity to tackle this project, and for answering all my questions along the way.

Contents

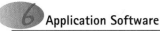

Introduction

Over the past 20 years, personal computers have moved from the hobbyist's basement to most of the offices, storefronts, factories, banks, supermarkets, farms, and classrooms in the United States. They've found their way into more than half of the homes as well. Given this fact, the question has become not whether you'll have to deal with computers, but whether you'll understand them when you do.

In most cases, the difference between someone who likes computers and someone who doesn't is a matter of knowledge. If you see the computer as a tool that can assist you in work or play, and that you can use for your own ends, you'll probably like it. On the other hand, if you see the computer as a mysterious contraption that you have to tolerate or appease in order to keep your job, you may need some time to warm up to it. This book is aimed at helping you turn the computers in your life from adversaries into willing helpmates.

I've written this book for four types of readers:

✓ People who have recently been confronted with a computer, either at work or at home.

✓ People who don't have a computer, but are either thinking about getting one or simply wondering what the fuss is about.

✓ People who've been using a computer for a while (a week, a month, three years) without ever feeling comfortable with it.

✓ People who are fairly proficient with one particular program or one particular area of computer use, but who want to round out their knowledge.

If you're totally new to computers, this book will tell you a little about everything you need to know. By the time you're through, you'll know what a computer is, what it's good for, and how it works in general. In short, you'll know the basic terms and concepts you'll need no matter how you plan to use your computer.

This book will also tell you enough about different ways of using computers to help you decide what areas you want to delve into further. When you're through, you may decide to learn all about spreadsheet programs so you can do your own financial projections. Or you may choose to wander the Internet in search of health tips, stock quotes, or new friends. In any case, you'll get enough of a background that you'll know where you want to head next. You'll also get the foundation you'll need for these further explorations. One of the hardest aspects of learning about computers is that most computer books and classes—even ones allegedly designed for beginners—assume that you already know the fundamentals. (As if people were born knowing the term "random access memory"!) By starting from the beginning, this book gives you the knowledge you need to use other resources such as books, classes, computer users' groups, and technical support staff. It will even enable you to converse with and understand computer sales-people and repair technicians.

If you're already using a computer, you can use this book to fill in the gaps in your knowledge. If you've spent years throwing around terms like memory, bits, and bytes without ever quite knowing what you're talking about, this is the book that will finally explain them to you. It will provide you with the concepts and skills you need to use your computer with more confidence and to move from knowing what keys to press to knowing what those key presses are doing (and what to do when they don't work).

How This Book Works

The heart of this book is pictures. Not just pictures of what a particular computer program or piece of equipment looks like, but pictures that illustrate concepts such as how the parts of a computer interact, or how information is organized inside a computer, or what you can do with a particular type of program.

Many of the pictures (and much of the text) draw analogies between computer components and things that are more familiar to you. You'll find parts of the computer compared to a set of mailboxes in a post office, for example, or to a sports stadium. You'll also find various computer components and programs personified in some of the pictures—not because I really believe there are little people in there, but because such images can help you visualize and remember the events taking place inside your computer.

This book focuses on IBM computers and compatibles, commonly known as PCs. If you have a Macintosh or other type of computer, you will find much of the material relevant, but will still probably want to purchase a book on your computer's operating system (the program that "makes it go"). I'll also be assuming that you are using, or plan to use, the Windows XP operating system. (You'll learn about operating systems in Chapter 1 and about Windows in particular in Chapter 5.) If you're using an older version of Windows, you will find much of the information is the same, it just looks different.

Tell Us What You Think!

As the reader of this book, *you* are our most important critic and commentator. We value your opinion and want to know what we're doing right, what we could do better, what areas you'd like to see us publish in, and any other words of wisdom you're willing to pass our way.

You can email or write me directly to let me know what you did or didn't like about this book—as well as what we can do to make our books stronger.

Please note that I cannot help you with technical problems related to the topic of this book, and that due to the high volume of mail I receive, I might not be able to reply to every message.

When you write, please be sure to include this book's title and author as well as your name and phone or fax number. I will carefully review your comments and share them with the author and editors who worked on the book.

E-mail: consumer@samspublishing.com

Mail: Mark Taber
            Associate Publisher
            Sams Publishing
            201 West 103rd Street
            Indianapolis, IN 46290 USA

Topic

The Basics

*L*earning to use computers is like learning a new language. Along with the new vocabulary and skills, you will inevitably acquire some new ways of thinking about and interacting with the world. Even if all you learn to do is plug in the computer and compose letters, the computer may change your writing process, by making it much easier to revise what you've written.

Learning about computers will also give you access to new ways of obtaining and working with information. After you know how to operate a computer, you can easily use it to chat with people across the country or the globe, about everything from international politics to recipes for bouillabaisse to Chinese word processing programs. If you have an office job, computer literacy may enable you to carry out some or all of your work from home—letting you communicate with the office computer using your own computer and a telephone. Finally, you may gain glimpses of what the future will be like, when computers are sure to be even more ubiquitous and more capable than they are today.

In short, learning about computers will probably change your life, at least a little. Consider it an adventure.

Computers Are Not Fragile

Before you start using your computer, you should know one critical thing. Contrary to popular opinion, computers are hard to break. There is no key or combination of keys that you can press that will damage the machine. Shy of dropping the computer on the ground or spilling soft drinks on it, there is little havoc you can wreak that is irreversible or even more than annoying.

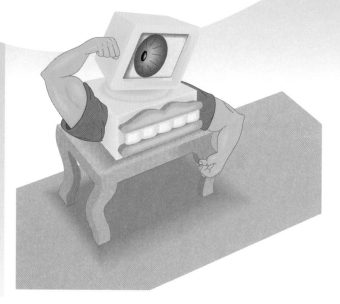

Begin

1 Protect Your Disks

The one fragile part of the whole setup is your computer's disks, which do not take kindly to vibration, dust, smoke, magnets, extreme heat, or spilled coffee. But for the most part, your computer is a sturdy object, without any auto-destruct sequence or ejector seat.

DON'T SPILL ON ME!

2 Most Mistakes Aren't Fatal

If you issue an instruction to your computer that doesn't make sense, it will usually let you know by displaying a message on the screen. As soon as you acknowledge the message (often by pressing another key), it disappears and the computer discards all knowledge of the misdeed.

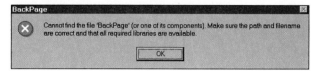

3 Fixing Mistakes

Computers are also very forgiving. Even if you blindly press every key in sight, the most likely result is that you will just delete some of the information you just entered. (Even this will take a little effort, and if you notice the mistake right away, it can often be corrected with a single command.)

If you see a button like this, you can click it to undo what you just did.

4 Try Again

You may inadvertently tell the computer to do something other than what you intended. After you notice the problem, you can almost always find a way to undo what you just did and then try again.

End

_____ *Notes*

Why Computers Break Down

I don't mean to imply that computers never break down. They do. But they break because of electronic or mechanical failure rather than because you pressed the wrong key at the wrong time.

How to Learn About Computers

The prospect of learning about computers can be intimidating for these reasons:

✓ People who already know about computers speak a dialect guaranteed to frighten off newcomers.

✓ It seems that everyone else, including every five-year-old on the block, already knows how to use computers.

✓ Maybe it's been awhile since you've explored such thoroughly new terrain.

For those of you who feel a little anxious or inadequate at the thought of "learning computers," here are some suggestions for approaching the learning process itself:

Begin

1 Assume That You Have the Capacity to Do This

Just about anyone can learn to use a computer. You don't need to be good at math or have mechanical aptitude. You don't need to be geared toward logical or linear thinking. You do, however, need some patience, self-confidence, and determination not to give up when something doesn't work the first (or even the second or third) time you try it.

2 Acquire New Knowledge in Bite-sized Pieces

Don't try to absorb everything at once. Learn only as much as you can comfortably assimilate in a single session, and then review and practice until you have mastered the material. Then go back and learn some more.

3 Make It Concrete

Whenever possible, put at least some of the information or skills you acquire to immediate use. Your new knowledge is much more likely to "stick" if you find some way to put it to work. When you read about computer equipment, see whether you can locate the various components in your own computer system. When you read about a particular type of computer program, imagine how you (or other people or businesses) might use such a program (or whether you'd have any use for it at all).

4 Cultivate Curiosity

The best way to get good at computers is to experiment, to question, to wonder if you can do x or what would happen if you did y. Don't just passively accept what you read here or in computer manuals. Try to figure out some things on your own.

5 Don't Try to Be Productive Immediately

If possible, keep the learning process free of deadline pressure. (Don't decide to learn how to produce a newsletter the day before the newsletter needs to be finished.) Try to make learning about computers a task in itself, not a means to an immediate end. Schedule plenty of time for the process and, if possible, work on something that interests or amuses you.

6 When in Doubt, Don't Panic

Your aim in learning about computers should be not to avoid mistakes, but to discover what to do when they happen. I'll give you lots of hints for what to consider when things go wrong, and suggestions about where to go for more help.

7 Avoid Bad Teachers

Thousands of people have learned to hate computers at the hands of well-meaning friends, relatives, and coworkers—someone who tries to tell them everything they need to know about computers in 15 minutes, or who forgets there was ever a time they didn't know what a CD-ROM drive was. If you feel stupid every time a certain someone tries to teach you about your computer, the problem probably lies in the teaching, not in you or the subject matter. If you want someone to hold your hand while you learn computers, choose someone you can ask "stupid questions," someone you don't need to impress—for most of us, this means avoiding a teacher who's either a boss or an employee, and quite possibly a spouse or child as well.

8 You Don't Need to Be a Computer Expert to Use a Computer

The purpose of the computer is to help you do something. You don't need a Ph.D. in electrical engineering to get some work done. Although you can make a career or a hobby out of learning about computers, it's fairly easy to do the basic things. If you just want to use your computer to compose and print simple letters, you can probably learn everything you need to know in an hour or two. To learn to produce a professional-looking newsletter, expect to spend weeks. (To learn to converse with computer salespeople, you may need months.) In any case, learning everything you want to know about computers may take awhile, but you can fairly quickly learn enough to get some work done.

9 Have Fun Whenever Possible!

If you merely relax and learn, you'll come to enjoy the many things your computer can do. Try not to stress about little problems or things you don't yet understand. Have fun!

End

Notes

Computers Are Literal

As you may have already heard or experienced, computers are completely and often maddeningly literal. There's an old phrase in computer lingo called GIGO: garbage in, garbage out. In some cases, if you spell something wrong or accidentally press the wrong key, the computer won't even *try* to guess what you mean. However, when you do everything correctly, computers provide immediate and decisive feedback. When you press the right keys, you get the right results; when you don't, you don't.

What Is a Computer?

A computer is a general-purpose machine for storing and manipulating information. Beyond this, there are two very different schools of thought: 1) Computers are dumb but very fast machines equivalent to extremely powerful calculators. 2) Computers are thinking machines capable of awe-inspiring, almost limitless feats of intelligence. Actually, both statements are true.

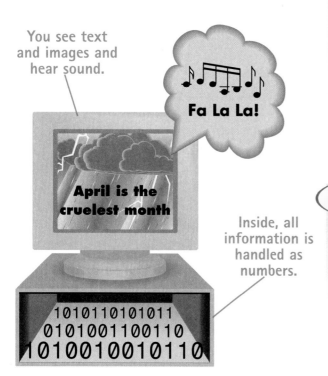

You see text and images and hear sound.

Fa La La!

April is the cruelest month

Inside, all information is handled as numbers.

Begin

1 How Computers Work

By themselves, computers have a very limited set of skills. They can add, compare, and store numbers. This probably seems very strange because the computers we see each day seem to do far more than this. They manipulate text, display graphical images, generate sounds, and do lots of other things that seem nonmathematical.

2 Information Is Numbers

Internally, the computer handles all information as numbers, and everything it does involves storing and manipulating those numbers. In this sense, computers are like fancy adding machines. But if you know how to "talk" to a computer in the language of numbers, as programmers do, you can get it to do some amazing things. Any kind of information that can be represented numerically—from music to photographs to motion picture videos—can be manipulated via a computer, assuming someone knows how to provide the computer with the proper instructions.

3 You Don't Need to Learn Programming

This does not mean that you need to know how to program computers (write your own instructions) to use them. You will buy and use programs that other people have created. You need to learn how to use those programs—a task that is far easier and less demanding than learning to write programs of your own.

4 Computers Are Everywhere

You probably deal with computers on a daily basis, whether you want to or not. Every time you use an ATM, or watch the checker scan the bar code on your milk carton into an electronic cash register, or use a hand-held calculator, you are using a computer. Some of those computers—such as the calculator—are designed to do a specific task, and the instructions for performing that task are built into the equipment itself. The type of computer you will be using at your home or office is probably more general purpose. It can do just about anything, provided it is given appropriate instructions.

5 Shapes and Sizes of Computers

Computers come in a multitude of shapes, sizes, and types, ranging from those that fit in the palm of your hand or hide in the corner of your microwave or VCR to those that occupy entire rooms; from ones generally used by one person at a time to those simultaneously used by dozens or even hundreds of people. This book is about personal computers—computers primarily designed for use by one person at a time.

6 Personal Computers

Personal computers are relative newcomers to the computer scene. Although the first computers were built in the 1940s, the first personal computers were only introduced in the 1970s and didn't come into widespread use until the 1980s. The speed and capacity of the machines has continued to increase almost as fast as their size and price shrinks, making them all the more practical and popular. Today's personal computers are hundreds of times more powerful than those sold 10 or 15 years ago, cost less, and can fit in packages the size of a notebook.

End

Notes

The First Friendly Computer

In 1984, Apple introduced the original Macintosh computer, specifically designed to be easy to learn, fun to use, and nonintimidating for the nontechnical user. Although not all this technology was original with Apple, this "user friendly" computer design has come to be the standard for most personal computers.

Computer Networks

Just because personal computers are "personal" doesn't mean they can't talk to each other. Computer networks are groups of computers that are linked together so they can share information, programs, and/or equipment. You'll learn more about networks in Chapter 7, "More About Hardware." Today, a PC can talk to millions of other computers over the Internet as well. You'll learn more about the Internet in Chapter 8, "Going Online."

The Two Personal Computing Camps

The majority of personal computers currently fall into two camps: IBM PCs/compatibles and Apple Macintosh computers (often referred to as "Macs"). Although at one time these types of computers were at opposite poles, in many ways they're growing more and more similar.

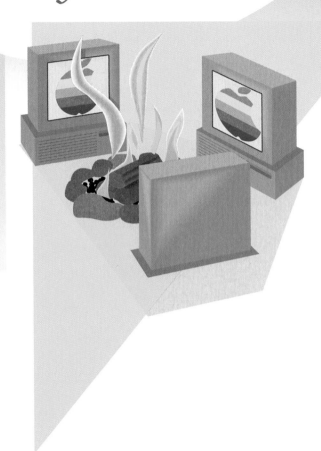

Begin

1 IBM Clones

The terms *IBM clone* and *IBM compatible* mean a computer that uses similar components and a similar design to IBM-manufactured PCs, and therefore can use the same type of programs as IBM computers. When it first created the PC, IBM decided to allow others to imitate its machines. The theory was that the more IBM imitations there were, the more likely it was that IBM-type systems and the software that runs on them would become the business standard. This strategy spurred the development of literally thousands of brands of IBM "workalikes" (a.k.a. *clones*).

2 User Interfaces

For a while, the main difference between PCs and Macs involved the *user interface*—the way they presented information on the screen and solicited and responded to your input. In general, Macs had a more playful, less intimidating interface, centered around pictures and *menus* (lists of options) on the screen. The PC interface tended to be starker and more text oriented. Today PCs employ a graphical user interface much like the Macs. (You'll learn all about this interface, called Windows, in Chapter 5, "Using Windows.")

3 How to Choose a Computer

If you are planning to buy a computer, one of your big decisions will be whether to get a Mac or a PC. If possible, try playing with both types of computers and see whether you prefer one of the two. See whether you can get a special deal on one type of computer through your school or job. Don't forget to consider whether all the applications you want are available for the platform you select.

4 Computers for Work and Home

If you use a computer at work and have any plans to bring work home, you might want to get the same type of computer you use at your job. If your friends are willing to help you learn about computers and ride to the rescue when something doesn't work, you may want to get the type of computer they use.

5 How Will You Use Your Computer?

If you plan to use your computer for a fairly specialized task—like editing video or managing an auto repair shop—start by selecting the program you want to use, and then choose the computer the program will run on. These days, many programs have both Mac and PC versions, but some will only work on one type of computer.

6 What Computers Are Used in Your Field?

Even if what you're doing is not all that specialized, you may want to find out what type of computer most people in your field are using. Most graphic designers use Macs; most tax and financial consultants use PCs. If you stick with the computer most of your colleagues are using, you're more likely to find a wide range of applicable programs, and people who know both your business and your computer, in case you need help.

End

Notes

What PC Means

Although the term *PC* (short for *Personal Computer*) was coined by IBM as the name for its first personal computer, its meaning has expanded over the years. Some people use *PC* to mean any personal computer. Others, including myself, use it to mean IBM-type computers, including IBM compatibles. In this book, *PC* means any computer designed to work like an IBM personal computer and able to run programs designed for such a computer.

What This Book Covers

When it comes to specific details about how computers work, this book covers PCs only. However, much of the general information applies to Macs and other personal computers as well.

Programs: The Wizard Behind the Curtain

People new to computers sometimes think that computers come ready and willing to do anything they want them to do, like electronic Wizards of Oz. Although computers can theoretically do just about anything, by themselves they do nothing at all. They are like VCRs without tapes. What allows your computer to actually do something is a *program*—that is, a set of instructions that tell the computer what to do and how to do it. A program is like the man behind the curtain, turning the knobs and pulling the levers, making your computer perform or seem to perform magic.

Begin

1 How Programs Work

For example, to use your computer to compose and print documents, you use a word processing program. The word processing program contains instructions that tell the computer what colors, characters, and images to display on your screen and how to respond to your actions (such as pressing various keys). When you run this program, your computer is temporarily transformed into an electronic typing and word processing machine. Your screen appears largely blank, the electronic equivalent of a blank sheet of typing paper. You will see a list of options at the top of the screen that enable you to perform word processing tasks, like setting margins, underlining, or adding footnotes.

2 "Playing" Programs

If you want to do something else with your computer—keep track of customers, for example, or play a game of solitaire—you need to find a program designed for that purpose. The computer is not "set up" to do that task, or any other task, on its own. In a sense, you could say that the basic function of a personal computer is to "play" different programs—just as VCRs are designed to play VCR tapes.

3 Using Multiple Programs

A single computer can, and usually does, hold several programs at once. In fact, these days you can run two, three, or more programs at once on your computer, and switch between them just by clicking with your mouse.

4 How Many Programs Can You Run?

The number of programs that you can run at once is limited only by the amount of "memory" your computer has. You'll learn the ins and outs of computer memory in Chapter 2, "Anatomy of a Computer." (In computer lingo, memory is often called RAM, for "random access memory.")

5 Installed Programs

When you buy a computer, it commonly comes with many programs already *installed*—that is, already on your computer and set up to work with your equipment. You can install new programs whenever you like, and after they are installed, they remain stored inside the computer, ready for you to use.

End

6 How Many Programs Can Your Computer Store?

The number of programs that you can store in a single computer is limited only by the amount of disk space you have. You will learn about disks and disk space in the next chapter.

Notes

Don't Open Too Many Programs at Once
Although most computers can now run several programs at the same time, it's better to run just the programs you are actually working with. Running lots of programs can make your computer run slowly. In Chapter 5, you'll learn how to switch between different programs that are running in Windows.

What You Can Do with a Computer

You can run dozens of types of programs on a personal computer, from ones that teach typing to ones that prepare your tax returns to ones that let you play video games. For now, we'll just outline some of the major categories. In Chapter 6, "Applications Software," you will learn more about the major types of programs, and how to select the right one for you.

1 Word Processing Programs

Word processing programs such as Microsoft Word let you use your computer to compose and print letters, papers, reports, and other types of documents. They offer much more extensive editing capabilities than typewriters—such as allowing you to insert new characters, delete existing ones, and move blocks of text from one part of the document to another without retyping. Most word processing programs have features for handling page numbers and footnotes. They also generally include a mail merge feature that enables you to generate personalized form letters by "merging" a letter with a set of names and addresses.

2 Desktop Publishing Programs

Desktop publishing (DTP) programs such as Quark enable you to combine text, pictures, graphics, tables, lines, boxes, and other design elements in a single document. They let you perform the type of page layout operations required to produce documents such as newsletters, books, and flyers—operations otherwise performed in a typesetting shop. These days, the most popular word processing programs include extensive desktop publishing capabilities.

3 Spreadsheet Programs

Spreadsheet programs such as Microsoft Excel are number crunchers. They let you perform almost any kind of mathematical calculation. Although they are most often used for financial calculations (budgeting, financial analysis, and forecasting), they can be used for scientific or engineering calculations and sorting other types of data as well. Besides the familiar ledger format, most have built-in graphics capabilities, permitting you to transform a set of numbers into a bar graph or pie chart, for example.

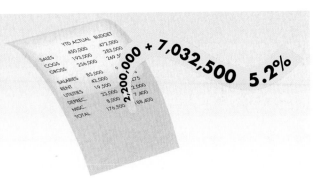

4 Accounting Programs

Accounting programs such as Quicken help you manage your money. They let you track and categorize income and expenses, reconcile your bank statements, and produce standard financial reports such as income statements and balance sheets. At one end of the spectrum are simple personal money management programs that let you balance your checkbook and track personal expenses. At the other end are sophisticated business accounting programs that generate extensive financial reports, produce invoices and statements to customers, handle accounts payable and receivable, print payroll checks and payroll reports, and track inventory.

Continues

5 Database Management Programs

Database management programs such as Microsoft Access let you store, retrieve, and manipulate large collections of information, such as mailing lists, inventories, student rosters, and library card catalogs. They enable you to keep your data up-to-date, sort it, generate statistics, print reports, and produce mailing labels. Database programs also let you extract portions of your data based on certain selection criteria—all your customers in Oregon with a credit limit over $100, for example, or all the inventory items of which there are fewer than three in stock.

6 Graphics Programs

Graphics programs such as Adobe Photoshop let you create pictures, slides, or designs to display onscreen or to print. This category includes painting and drawing programs that let you combine and modify existing pictures or construct your own. This category also includes programs that let you edit and enhance photographic images.

7 Browsers

Browsers such as Internet Explorer are programs that let you access and use the Internet. Most let you send and receive messages via electronic mail, as well as surf the World Wide Web for information on everything from politics to yoga, stock prices to recycling. (You can also use online services such as CompuServe and America Online to send and receive electronic mail.) You can access library card catalogs, locate airline schedules, and order products from the millions of companies that now sell their products online.

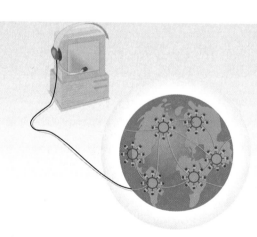

8 Presentation Programs

Presentation graphics programs such as PowerPoint create line graphs, pie graphs, organizational charts, and other types of diagrams, and, in many cases, combine these images into slideshows for use in business presentations.

9 Game Programs

Game, entertainment, and educational programs (sometimes called "edutainment programs") let you do everything from playing backgammon to doing battle with computer-generated dragons. There are programs that let you step inside detective and science fiction novels, work on your golf swing, and attempt to save the world from ecological disasters. There are also dozens of games for children, many of them educational, such as programs that "read" children's stories, highlighting each word on the screen while pronouncing it through the computer's speakers.

End

Notes

What Is the World Wide Web?

As you'll learn in Chapter 8, "Going Online," the *World Wide Web* is a collection of interlinked and interactive documents that is currently the most popular and most commercial part of the Internet.

Application Program Basics

Because there are literally thousands of applications programs available, this book won't explain how to use individual programs. Instead, I'll discuss in Chapter 6 how the major types of applications programs work, how to choose a program, and how to go about teaching yourself (including how to read computer manuals, locate good books, and obtain technical support).

Spreadsheet Versus Accounting Programs

Because spreadsheet programs are frequently used for financial calculations, many people have a hard time distinguishing them from accounting programs. Spreadsheets are completely open-ended: They can perform almost any calculation you can imagine, but only if you provide them with explicit instructions. Accounting programs, in contrast, already "know" how to handle accounting functions and generate standard accounting reports. All you need to do is type in your numbers.

Hardware Versus Software

Now that you know what a program is (a set of instructions), you are ready for your first two pieces of computer jargon. In computer terminology, all computer equipment is referred to as *hardware* and all computer programs are known as *software*. These two terms emphasize the fact that the equipment and program are two essential parts of a working computer system. Hardware is the machinery and its physical accoutrements, including the keyboard (the part that looks like a typewriter), the screen, and the printer. Software is the set of coded instructions that brings the machinery to life.

Begin

Hardware is the machinery and its physical accoutrements. It includes all parts of the computer system that you can touch.

1 Hardware Versus Software

Some people get a little confused about the difference between hardware and software. Part of this confusion has to do with the way software is packaged and sold.

2 What You Get When You Buy a Program

If you buy a new program, you get a box with one or more manuals explaining how the program works, plus either a CD-ROM or one or more floppy disks on which the program is stored.

3 Disks and CD-ROMs Are Hardware

When you get back to your home or office, you install the program by copying its instructions from the CD-ROM or floppy disks to your computer. As a result, many people think of disks as software. If you've never encountered *floppy disks*, they are round, flat wafers—kind of like small and flimsy records—that are encased in square plastic wrappers. They are used to store both programs and data.

Software is more elusive. It is like the music recorded on a CD rather than the CD itself. You can't touch it, you can only see or hear its results.

4 Software on CD-ROMs

Most programs are now available on CD-ROMs—special types of compact discs that are meant to be "played" on a computer. You'll learn all about floppy disks and CD-ROMs in Chapters 2 and 3.

Notes

Programs Are Software

From here on, I will be using the words *program* and *software* virtually interchangeably.

Hardware and Software Work Together

The terms *hardware* and *software* emphasize the fact that the equipment and program are two essential parts of a working computer system.

---

5 Hardware Rules

In fact, disks and CD-ROMs are hardware. The basic rule of thumb for determining whether something is hardware or software is whether you can touch it; and because disks and CD-ROMs can be touched, they're in the hardware camp. Software, on the other hand, is much more elusive. You can't touch, see, or taste it; you can only witness its results.

End

The Two Types of Software

As mentioned, the native language of computers consists solely of numbers. Because few of us are able (or patient enough) to speak to a computer in this language, we almost never interact with the computer directly. We always "speak" to the computer through an intermediary, namely, a program whose function (among other things) is to translate our requests to the computer. Programs enable the computer, by telling it how to display text or pictures on the screen, produce sounds, or print characters on paper, to "speak" back to us.

2 Operating Systems

Operating systems are programs that act as the intermediary between you and the hardware and, to some extent, between the hardware and the applications software. You'll learn a great deal about how to use one particular operating system, Windows, in Chapter 5. This book doesn't go into detail about DOS, or the Macintosh operating system.

3 Operating Systems Run Your Hardware

As you will learn in Chapter 5, operating systems serve several functions. For starters, the operating system controls various parts of the machine and allows them to talk to one another; in effect, it operates the hardware. Your operating system is the essential program that makes your computer "go."

Begin

1 Applications Software

There are actually two different types of software: applications software and operating systems. *Applications software* is the software that you use to actually perform your work. This includes the types of programs previously described under "What You Can Do with a Computer," such as word processing or spreadsheet programs.

4 What You Can Do with Your Operating System

Operating systems include various "housekeeping utilities" that allow you to find out what programs and data are stored on a disk, to copy programs and data to and from your computer, and to delete programs and data.

5 Starting Applications

The operating system allows you to start up application programs. If you want to play chess on your computer, for example, you issue a command that tells the operating system, "Go find the chess program and fire it up." Then the operating system acts as an intermediary between the applications and the hardware, by making sure they understand the requests they make of each other.

6 Different Operating Systems

Different operating systems are designed for different types of computers. If you are running a PC, you will probably use an operating system named Windows. The latest version of Windows is Windows XP. Depending on the age of your computer, you might be using Windows Me, Windows 2000, Windows NT, Windows 98, or Windows 95.

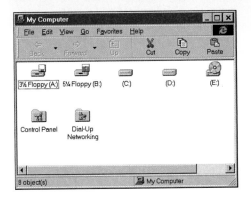

7 How DOS Worked

The Windows operating system employs pictures and menus to help you manage your application's programs and data. In contrast, DOS, which before the advent of Windows was the most common operating system on PCs, used a command-driven interface—whenever you wanted the computer to do something, you needed to type in a command. Because there were no visual cues on the screen, you needed to either memorize all the commands or look them up in a book as needed.

End

Topic

2

Anatomy of a Computer

In this chapter, you will learn the fundamentals of computer hardware—the essential parts of the machine and how they interact with each other. I will start with the core elements of the computer—the parts that let you store and manipulate information and communicate with your computer. Then I'll backtrack a bit and discuss the pieces that support and connect those core devices, turning the individual parts into a cohesive working system.

Probably the most important knowledge you will glean from this chapter concerns the way your computer stores information. By the time you finish this chapter, you will know the following:

- ✓ What happens when you load a program
- ✓ Where the data you type into your computer goes
- ✓ What happens when you save data (where the computer puts it, and how you get it back again)

Whenever possible, I'll use analogies to things you already know about, and for now, I'll give you just enough technical detail to get a feel for what's really going on inside your computer. You'll learn a bit more of the technical details in the next chapter and in Chapter 7, "More About Hardware."

Learning about hardware has an added purpose: It makes you feel more in control of your machine. The more you know about your computer's innards, the less likely you are to feel that there's an evil spirit in there, and the less fatalistic you're likely to be about hardware problems. ●

The Brains of the Computer

At the core of every computer is a device roughly the size of a large postage stamp. This device, known as the *central processing unit,* or *CPU,* is the "brain" of the computer; it reads and executes program instructions, performs calculations, and makes decisions. The CPU is responsible for storing and retrieving information on disks and other media. It also handles moving information from one part of the computer to another like a central switching station that directs the flow of traffic throughout the computer system.

1 Integrated Circuits and Transistors

In personal computers, the CPU (also known as the *microprocessor*) consists of a single integrated circuit. An *integrated circuit,* or *IC,* is a matrix of transistors and other electrical components embedded in a small slice of silicon. (*Transistors* are essentially microscopic electronic switches: tiny devices that can be turned on and off.)

2 Where the CPU Lives

Like the dozens of other integrated circuits that inhabit your computer, from the outside a CPU chip looks something like a square ceramic bug with little metal legs. These "legs" are designed to fasten the chip to a fiberglass circuit board that sits inside your computer and to carry electrical impulses into and out of the chip.

Begin

When placed under a microscope, a CPU chip resembles an aerial photograph of a city.

3 The Chip

Inside the ceramic case is the chip itself, a slice of silicon about the size of a fingernail. At first glance, it's hard to imagine how this tiny device can run your entire computer. But under a microscope, the slice of silicon reveals an electronic maze so complex that it resembles an aerial photograph of a city, complete with hundreds of intersecting streets and hundreds of thousands of minuscule houses. Most of the "houses" are transistors, and there are usually somewhere between a million and several million of them on a single CPU chip.

4 How Fast Is Your CPU?

The type of CPU that a computer contains determines its processing power—how fast it can execute various instructions. These days, most CPUs can execute on the order of millions of instructions per second. The type of CPU also determines the precise repertoire of instructions the computer understands and, therefore, which programs it can run.

5 Chip Models

In the PC world, people often categorize computers by the model of CPU chip they contain. The CPU chips most commonly used in new PCs are the Pentium III, the Celeron, and Pentium 4. These chips are all made by a company named Intel. Intel's main competitor is AMD, which makes a line of chips called Athlon.

6 The System Unit

The CPU resides inside a box known as the *system unit,* along with various support devices and tools for storing information. You will learn about these other residents of the system unit later in this chapter. For now, just think of the system unit as a container for the CPU. The system unit case—that is, the metal box itself—can either be wider than it is tall, in which case it usually sits on top of your desk, often underneath the screen, or it can be taller than it is wide, in which case it generally sits underneath your desk and is referred to as a *tower case.*

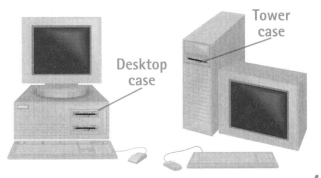

Tower case

Desktop case

End

Notes

Measuring CPU Speed

Within each class of CPU, speed is measured in terms of the cycle time at which the computer was designed to operate. All computers have built-in clocks that help regulate the flow of information from one part of the computer to another, rather like a metronome. Each pulse of this clock is known as a cycle, and a CPU can perform, at maximum, one operation per cycle. Every CPU is designed to work with a clock that "ticks" at a particular rate. A CPU may be designed to run at 800 megahertz (MHz) for example, meaning 800 million cycles per second.

TOPIC 2

Input and Output

The other parts of the computer system—that is, the parts outside the system unit—are primarily used as a means of communicating with the CPU, to send in instructions and data and get out information. Devices used to communicate with the CPU are known, collectively, as *input and output devices,* or *I/O devices.* Input devices are all those things that allow you to "talk" to your computer—to pose questions and issue commands. Output devices are what allow the computer to talk back, providing you with answers, asking you for additional information, or, at worst, informing you that it has no idea what you are talking about.

Begin

1 Keyboard

In personal computers, one of the two most common input devices is the keyboard. Using a keyboard, you can type text and issue commands.

2 Mouse

The other most common input device is a mouse. The mouse is a hand-held pointing device that allows you to point to words or objects on the computer screen. Pressing the buttons on the mouse (called pressing or clicking, depending on how fast you do it) lets you make selections on your screen. A mouse can also be used to move around items onscreen. You will learn more about using the mouse in Chapter 4, "Up and Running."

You can also communicate with your computer using an input device called a *trackball,* which is a pointing device that resembles a ball nestled in a square cradle and serves as an alternative to a mouse.

3 Scanner

Another input device is a scanner, which allows you to copy an image (such as a photograph, a drawing, or a page of text) into your computer, translating it into a form that the computer can store and manipulate.

4 Game Controllers

A number of different types of game controllers are commonly used. A joystick is an input device that lets you manipulate the various people, creatures, and machines that populate computer games. Other game controllers include game pads (similar to controllers for video game units) and steering wheel simulators.

5 Digital Camera

A digital camera lets you capture a photographic image in digital (that is, computer-readable) form and then lets you transfer that image directly from camera to computer. Digital video cameras allow you to do the same with video and sound.

6 Monitor

The most common output device is the monitor, which the computer uses to display instructions and present information. Computer monitors contain many types including LCD (liquid crystal display), and CRT (for cathode ray tube, the technology used in most desktop computer screens).

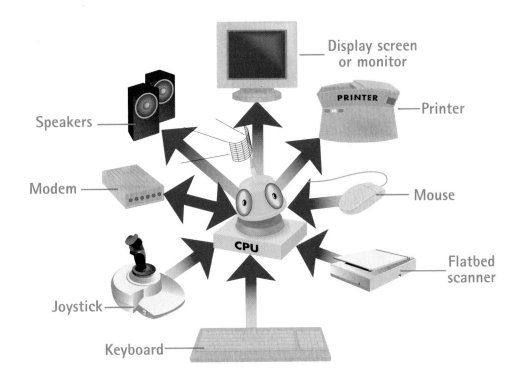

Display screen or monitor

Printer

Speakers

Modem

Mouse

Joystick

Flatbed scanner

Keyboard

CPU

7 Printer

A printer generates paper copies of your data. Like monitors, printers come in many shapes and sizes and generate output ranging from the old grainy-looking computer printouts to color printouts that rival the clarity of offset printing.

8 Speakers

These days, many computers also come equipped with a *sound board*—a device that resides inside the system unit and allows your computer to generate sounds and music. Most computers have some kind of speakers, which are the ouput device for the sound board.

9 Modems

A modem serves as both an input and an output device. A *modem* allows computers to communicate with each other over wires, such as phone lines. You can use modems both to send data and messages to other computers and to tap into the Internet information and online services such as AOL. Most modems have fax capabilities built in. Some modems are separate devices that plug into the system unit; others reside inside the system unit. You'll learn more about monitors, printers, sound boards, speakers, and modems in Chapter 7.

End

Notes

What Are Peripherals?

You may also hear the term *peripherals* applied to I/O devices. Technically, the term *peripheral* means everything outside the CPU (including I/O devices).

Storing Information

Now you know a little about the CPU of the computer and the devices that you use to communicate with that "brain." There is still one large gap in our image of a computer system, however—storage space.

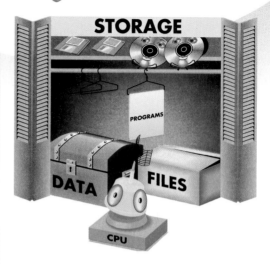

1 What Is Storage?

Although the CPU is terrific at manipulating data and following instructions, it has almost no capacity for storing information. (Think of it as a brilliant but extremely absent-minded professor.) Your computer needs a place to store both programs (the instructions that tell the CPU what to do) and data. You need, in other words, the electronic equivalent of a closet or filing cabinet.

2 Disks

In most computers, the primary storage places are disks—which are flat, circular wafers. (You may be used to thinking of computer disks as square because they are always housed inside square plastic jackets, but the disks themselves are round.)

3 Disk Drives

Like compact discs, these computer disks store information that can be "played" by devices known as *disk drives*. They are in several respects the equivalent of CD players. Like CD players, disk drives have components designed to access the information on a specific area of the disk. These parts are called *read/write heads* and are equivalent to the laser in a CD player. Disk drives spin the disk so different parts of the surface pass underneath the read/write heads. Most disk drives have at least two read/write heads—one for each side of the disk.

4 Reading and Writing to Disks

Unlike record players or CD players, however, disk drives can record new information on disks as well as play existing information. (In this sense, they're more like cassette tapes than music CDs.) In computer terminology, the process of playing a disk is called *reading* and the process of recording onto a disk is called *writing*. (Hence the term read/write head.)

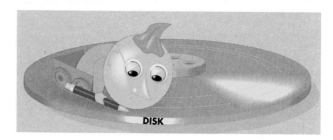

5 Types of Disks

Computer disks come in three basic types: floppy, CD-ROM, and hard. Floppy disks generally hold less information and are slower than hard disks. They can also be removed from their disk drives, so you can "play" different floppy disks in the same drive by removing one and inserting another. CD-ROM disks are similar to floppies in that they are portable. However, CDs hold many times more data than floppies.

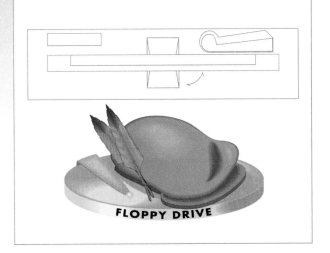

FLOPPY DRIVE

Inside the floppy disk's jacket is the floppy itself: a very thin piece of plastic.

6 Floppy Disks

The word *floppy* refers to the disk itself, which is a thin, round piece of plastic on which information is magnetically recorded (much as music is recorded on the surface of plastic cassette tapes). This decidedly floppy disk is enclosed inside a sturdier, unfloppy plastic jacket to protect it. The disks used in personal computers are usually 3 1/2 inches in diameter.

Continues

Read/write heads

HARD DRIVE

7 Hard Disks and Drives

Hard disks hold more information and spin much faster than floppies. They are also permanently enclosed within their disk drives, so the disk and its drive are essentially a single unit. Contrary to what you may think, hard disks are not always larger than floppies; they're capable of packing information more tightly, and therefore can store more data in the same amount of space. Most hard drives contain multiple disks, often called *platters,* that are stacked vertically inside the drive. Typically, each disk has its own pair of read/write heads. Because you never remove hard disks, hard-disk drives do not contain doors or slots, as do their floppy counterparts. This means that the drive itself is completely invisible (and sometimes hard to locate) from outside the system unit.

End

Notes

What's Data?

In computerese, the term *data* refers to whatever type of information you are trying to manipulate. Data, therefore, includes far more than numbers; it includes any information that you type or otherwise input into the computer. You can also think of data as the raw material that is processed or manipulated by applications programs. If you are using a word processing program, data means the document (letter, memo, poem, novel, legal brief, whatever) you are typing or editing. If you are working with a database program, it may be a set of names and addresses you are adding to your company mailing list.

CD-ROM Drives and Other Drives

These days, most PCs have one hard-disk drive, one floppy disk drive, and a CD-ROM drive. In general, you'll use hard disks as the primary repository of data and programs—the place you store the information that you work with day to day. You'll use floppy drives mainly as a means of getting information into and out of your computer, by transferring information to and from floppy disks.

Most programs are also stored on CD-ROMs instead of floppy disks, and new computers generally come equipped with a CD-ROM drive. As mentioned, a CD-ROM is a type of compact disc that is meant to be "played" in a computer. CD-ROM stands for compact disc–read-only memory.

Begin

1 Installing Programs from CD-Roms or Floppies

When you purchase a new program, it is usually stored on CD-ROMs or floppies. You must copy the program to your hard disk before you can use it. This process of copying these disks to your hard disk is known as *installing*.

2 Backing Up Your Data

You can use floppy disks to make extra copies of programs or data for safekeeping by copying from the hard disk to floppies. This is known as *making backups*. If you are working on the great American novel, for example, you will keep your main, working copy on the hard disk but keep an extra copy on a floppy disk, in case there is a mechanical problem with the hard-disk drive or you accidentally erase the original. If you want to be completely safe, you might even keep this duplicate copy in a safe deposit box or a fireproof safe.

Continues

3 Archiving Data

You can use floppy disks to archive data that you don't use regularly (and therefore don't want taking up space on your hard disk) but that you don't want to discard altogether.

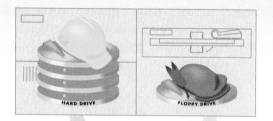

4 Transferring Data

You can use floppy disks to transfer data from one computer to another, by copying information from one computer's hard disk to a set of floppies, taking the floppies over to the other computer, and copying from those floppies onto the hard disk.

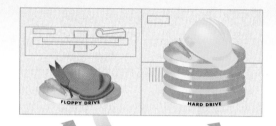

5 CD-ROMs Are Read-Only

You'll learn more about ROM (read-only memory) soon. For now, you just need to know that "read only" means that while you can "read" (access) the programs or data stored on CD-ROMs, you cannot easily "write" (store) your own data or programs on them using most CD-ROM drives. (Recording information on a CD-ROM requires a special type of drive.)

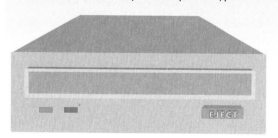

6 CD-ROMs Hold More Data

The reason that so many programs are now stored on CD-ROMs is that CD-ROMs can hold much more information than floppy disks: A single CD-ROM can hold more data than 300 floppies.

7 Internal CD-ROM Drives

You can only use CD-ROMs if your computer has a CD-ROM drive. Most CD-ROM drives sit inside the system unit and, from the outside, look pretty similar to floppy disk drives. These types of drives are known as internal CD-ROM drives.

8 External CD-ROM Drives

It's also possible to buy external CD-ROM drives. These drives work the same as the internal ones, but they come in their own little boxes, which sit outside the system unit and are attached to the system unit via a cable. You'll learn more about CD-ROM drives in Chapter 7.

9 CD-R and CD-RW Drives

Plain-vanilla CD-ROM drives are just one of many types of drives on the market these days. Special CD-ROM drives are called CD-Recordable (or CD-R) drives. What's special about these drives is that they are not read-only. That is, you can not only read information from the disks, but can write information to them as well. This feature makes these disks excellent for storage purposes. Another drive, called CD-RW (CD-Rewritable) allows you to write and rewrite to the same CD many times, making it the equivalent of a high-powered floppy disk. You'll learn more about CD-R drives, as well as a variety of other storage technologies, in Chapter 7.

Notes

Caring for Floppy Disks

You need to know several things to work with floppy disks, including how to determine which type will work in your disk drive, how to prepare them for use, how to insert and remove them, and how to care for them. You'll learn to do all these things in the next chapter.

Adding Hard Drives

Occasionally, people add more hard drives to their computers when the original hard drive fills up. It's often more cost-effective to add a second hard drive than to toss out the first computer and buy a new one with a larger capacity.

10 DVD Drives

DVD (Digital Video Discs) drives are similar to CD-ROM drives and can, in fact, be used to play CD-ROMs. However, they also allow you to play digital video, including DVD movies, on your computer.

End

Memory: The Electronic Desktop

Given what you've learned so far, you might assume that when you run a program, the CPU fetches instructions from the disk one at a time and executes them, returning to the disk drive every time it finishes a single step. If this were actually the way computers worked, they would be too slow to use.

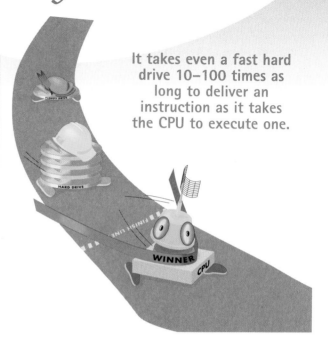

Begin

It takes even a fast hard drive 10–100 times as long to deliver an instruction as it takes the CPU to execute one.

1 CPU Speed Versus Disk Drive Speed

Left to their own devices, most personal computer CPUs are capable of executing between one million and one hundred million instructions per second. But because the disk drive is mechanical—that is, composed of moving parts—it cannot deliver program instructions anywhere near that fast. Reading an instruction from the disk involves rotating the disk so that the proper section is below one of the read/write heads and then moving the head closer to or farther from the center of the disk until it is positioned directly above the spot where the instruction is recorded. Even on a hard-disk drive, this process generally takes between 7 and 25 milliseconds (thousandths of a second). CD-ROM drives and floppy drives are slower still.

2 Random Access Memory (RAM)

For the computer to function efficiently, it needs some repository of information that is capable of keeping pace with the CPU. This extra piece is called *random access memory*, usually referred to as *RAM* or *memory* for short.

3 How RAM Works

Physically, RAM consists of a set of separate integrated circuits (each of which looks something like a small CPU chip) that are often mounted on fiberglass boards; in practice, however, memory is treated as a single, contiguous set of storage bins. One useful way to envision memory is as a set of mailboxes, like those inside a post office. Each mailbox holds a single character, and the entire collection of boxes is numbered sequentially. (In computer jargon, the mailboxes are called *bytes* and their numbers are known as *memory addresses*.)

MEMORY MAILBOXES

```
0   1   2   3   4
5   6   7   8   9
```

4 Memory Chips

Like the CPU chip, memory chips store and transmit information electronically. Sending an instruction from memory to the CPU is therefore a simple matter of transmitting electrical impulses. There is no waiting for a disk to spin or a read/write head to move to the proper position.

Memory is like an electronic desktop on which you can place the programs and other files you are working with at the moment.

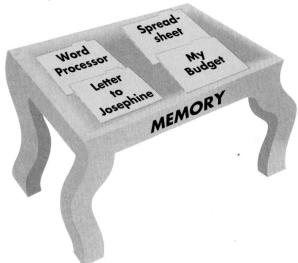

5 The Electronic Desktop

Because the CPU can move information into and out of memory so quickly, it uses memory as a kind of electronic desktop—the place it stores whatever it is working on this instant or plans to work with shortly. When you tell your computer that you want to use a particular program, for example, the first thing it does is find the program on your hard disk and copy it into memory. This process is known as *loading* a program. This gets the comparatively slow process of reading instructions from disk over with at the start. After the entire program has been loaded, the CPU can quickly read instructions from memory as needed.

End

Notes

Placing Programs in Memory

Although you can compare placing a program in memory to moving it from a file cabinet (the disk) to your desktop (memory), there is also one important difference: Placing something on your desktop entails removing it from its usual storage place in the file cabinet. In contrast, when you place a program in memory, you copy the program and place the copy in memory. The original program stays on the disk, ready to load again whenever you need it.

Loading a Program into Memory

The first program that is loaded into memory in every work session is the operating system. In fact, just about the first thing your CPU does when you turn on your computer is hunt for and load the operating system program. This program then remains in memory until you turn off your computer. When you load application programs, they always share the electronic desktop with the operating system, and, in fact, application programs need to have an operating system around to function. Loading an application program into memory involves several steps.

Begin

When you are using an **application** program, there **are three layers** of **information stored in memory.**

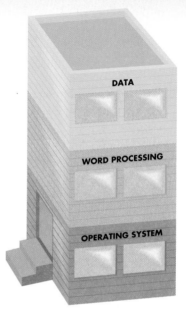

DATA

WORD PROCESSING

OPERATING SYSTEM

1 You Start the Program

You select an option from a menu (onscreen list), type a command, or double-click an icon (picture) to tell the CPU that you want to start the program.

2 The Read/Write Head Searches the Hard Disk

The read/write head finds your program on the hard disk.

WORD

HARD DRIVE

3 Your Computer Copies the Program into Memory

Your computer copies the program from disk into memory (alongside the operating system).

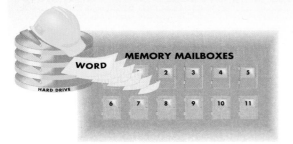

5 Entering Data

When you type in new data while working in an applications program or retrieve data from disk, the data is placed in memory as well, alongside the applications program and the operating system. The data remains in memory until you either issue a command to close the file (remove it from memory) or leave the application program. Whenever you leave an application program, both the program itself and any data that goes with it are removed from memory. The operating system stays put until you turn off your computer.

4 The Program Appears Onscreen

The program appears on your screen and you can start using it.

End

Notes

Layers of Information

You may find it helpful to think of these three different types of information as a set of layers, each of which depends on the one below. The operating system is the bottom layer, followed by the applications program, followed by the data. If you unload any one layer, the layers above are erased as well. If you unload the operating system—for example, by turning off or restarting your system—memory is completely erased. If you unload an application program from memory, by issuing that program's exit or quit command, both the program and the data you were working on inside that program are erased from memory. If you unload just the top layer—the data you are working with—by closing a particular word processing document, for example, both the application program (in this case, the word processing program) and the operating system remain loaded and ready to use.

Don't Confuse Memory with Disk Storage

Don't confuse erasing a program from memory with removing it from disk. Even if you erase an application program or a data file from memory, it should still be present on your hard disk (assuming you saved it there), and you can go back and retrieve it another time.

Saving Data

As you just learned, programs are not the only things that the CPU places in memory. It stores data there as well. As shown in this figure, each character that you enter, including any spaces, occupies a single "mailbox" of storage space.

Begin

Every character of data that you enter (including a space) occupies a single "mailbox" (byte) in memory.

MEMORY MAILBOXES

0 D	1 E	2 A	3 R	4	5 M
6 S	7 .	8	9 P	10 R	11 U
12 N	13 D	14 I	15 M	16 P	17 L
18 E	19 :	20	21 Y	22 O	23 U
24	25 H	26 A	27 V	28 E	29
30 W	31 O	32 N	33	34 T	35 E
36 N	37	38 T	39 R	40 I	41 L
42 L	43 I	44 O	45 N	46	47 D

1 Storing Data in Memory

There is one fundamental problem with housing data in memory: As soon as your computer is turned off, the contents of memory are erased. This means that if you accidentally kick your computer's power cord in the midst of typing a letter, for example, everything you have typed is lost. It also means that you can't rely on memory if you want to return to a piece of work the next day or next week, because you will undoubtedly turn off your computer in between.

2 Erasing Data from Memory

Data is also erased from memory whenever you leave an application program, because the CPU assumes you'll need to use the space for the next task you choose to tackle. If you are using a spreadsheet program, for example, the CPU erases the spreadsheet you were using from memory as soon as you exit that program, just as you might clear your desk when you finish a particular project.

OPERATING SYSTEM | APPLICATION APPI | DATA DAT...

CPU

3 Saving Your Data

To protect your work and to store it for use in future work sessions, you need to copy it from memory to a more secure storage place—namely, a disk. This process is known as *saving* your data. Don't worry about how, exactly, you tell your computer to save data; the procedure may vary from one application program to another or, at minimum, from operating system to operating system. For now, just focus on when you need to save and why.

4 When to Save

In general, you should save your data whenever you are done working with it and are ready to start on another project (if you finish typing one letter and want to start another one, for example). You should also save your data when you are ready to leave an application program.

MEMORY MAILBOXES

SAVE

HARD DRIVE

5 Saving Automatically

For your convenience, most programs automatically ask whether you want to save when you give the command to exit or to close a document. You should also save to disk whenever you have been working for a while and want to protect the work you have done so far. This protects your data against power failures, kicked power cords, or drastic mistakes.

6 Retrieving Data

After something is stored on disk, you can copy it back into memory when you want to use it again. This is known as retrieving data or opening a document or file. As soon as the data is copied back into memory, the data reappears on your screen and you can modify it if you like. In general, any data that appears onscreen while you're using an application program is currently in memory, although not all the data in memory may fit on your screen at one time.

End

Notes

Save Early, Save Often

How often should you save? A good rule of thumb is that you should save your work every time you'd be unhappy if you had to do it over again. For some people, this will be once an hour; for others, it will be every two minutes. Bear in mind that when you save something, you are not removing it from memory. You are making a copy and then storing that copy on disk. You can then continue modifying the original if you like.

When Not to Save

Occasionally, you will enter some data that you have no need or desire to save. For example, you may use a word processing program to type a short letter that you need to print but don't need to store for future reference. Or you may load your spreadsheet program to perform a few calculations and have no need to save the results. In such cases, you can close the document without saving your data and it won't take up space on your hard disk.

What's So Random About RAM?

As mentioned, the type of memory we have been discussing—that is, the memory used to temporarily house programs and data—is called random access memory, or RAM for short. To understand where this name comes from, you need to know more about how information is stored in memory.

Begin

1 Sequential Access

Remember, the CPU treats memory as a set of numbered storage bins, rather like a collection of mailboxes, each one of which holds a single character. In early computers, the CPU had to access the mailboxes (bytes) in numerical order, starting from the first mailbox and moving forward until it reached the one that actually contained the desired information. This is known as *sequential access*. With the development of random access memory, the CPU can go directly to whichever mailbox it is interested in.

With random access (CD-ROMs and disks), you can move directly to the information you want.

With sequential access (tape drives), you must start from the beginning and move forward one step at a time.

2 Random Access Versus Sequential Access

You can conceptualize the difference between random access memory and this older type of sequential access memory by comparing music CDs to cassette tapes. If you want to listen to the fifth song on a cassette tape (sequential access), you have to start at the beginning of the tape and move past the first four songs, even if you fast-forward the tape. With a music CD (random access), you can go directly to song five. Disks are random access devices, too. Rather than starting from the outside of the disk and reading inward, or from the inside and reading outward, the read/write head can jump directly to the spot where the desired data is stored.

3 What Is ROM?

There is actually a second type of memory used in personal computers, in addition to RAM. This second type of memory is named *read-only memory*, or *ROM* (rhymes with Tom). Unlike RAM chips, ROM chips have software (program instructions) etched into their circuitry. For this reason, ROM is often referred to as *firmware*—because it's kind of halfway between hardware and software.

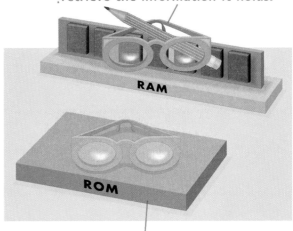

RAM is read/write memory. The CPU can store information in it as well as retrieve the information it holds.

ROM is read-only memory. The CPU cannot change its contents.

4 RAM Versus ROM

Both RAM and ROM allow random access. If the point is to distinguish RAM from ROM, then RAM would more properly be called read/write memory, meaning that you can both retrieve (read) information from RAM, and record (write) information to it. In contrast, with read-only memory (ROM), instructions are frozen into the circuitry. The feature that sets RAM apart from ROM is its changeability: the fact that you can alter its contents at will.

5 Short-term and Long-term Memory

The other difference between RAM and ROM is how long their memories last. RAM is short-term memory; it forgets everything it knows as soon as you turn off your computer. ROM is long-term memory; it remembers everything it has ever known as long as it lives. It's the elephant of the memory kingdom.

6 ROM Stores Part of the Operating System

In personal computers, ROM is generally used to store some part of the operating system. In IBM-type PCs, only a small part of the operating system is stored in ROM—just enough to get the hardware up and running and to tell the CPU how to locate and load the rest of the operating system from disk.

End

Notes

You Don't Have to Worry About ROM

ROM is changeable, but chances are you will never have to deal with it yourself. It's just another part of your computer to know about, even if you never need to see it, touch it, or think about it much at all. Don't worry about changing it unless a qualified technician informs you that it is necessary.

9

What's in a Byte: How Memory and Disks Are Measured

As mentioned, the term *byte* means the amount of space required to represent a single character—a letter, a number, or even a space. (In our mailboxes analogy, it's a single mailbox.) This term is used regardless of whether you're talking about space in memory, on a disk, or on any other storage medium. Because many, many bytes are often required to accommodate an entire word processing document, spreadsheet, database, or program, computerese includes terms for several larger units of measurement.

Begin

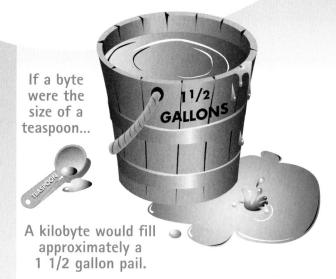

If a byte were the size of a teaspoon...

A kilobyte would fill approximately a 1 1/2 gallon pail.

1 Kilobyte

A *kilobyte* (often abbreviated as KB or K) is 1,024 bytes. To a computer's way of thinking, 1,024 is a nice round number. (Computers "think" in units of two, and 1,024 is 2 to the 10th power.) To us, however, it's a little unwieldy, so most people think of a kilobyte as "around 1,000" bytes. In other words, 100KB equals 100,000 characters.

2 Megabyte

The term *megabyte* (abbreviated as MB or meg) means a kilobyte squared (1,024 times 1,024), or approximately one million bytes. A floppy disk whose capacity is 1.44MB can hold 1,440,000 characters. (This is a standard capacity for high density 3 1/2-inch floppies.)

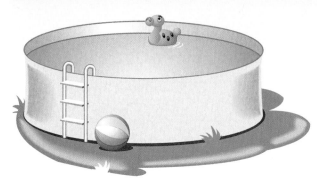

A megabyte would fill a small swimming pool (1500 gallons).

A gigabyte would fill an entire lake (1.5 million gallons).

3 Gigabyte and Terabyte

The term *gigabyte* (abbreviated GB or gig) means a kilobyte to the third power (1,024 times 1,024 times 1,024), or approximately one billion bytes. The term *terabyte* (abbreviated TB or T) means a kilobyte to the fourth power (1,024 times 1,024 times 1,024 times 1,024). Right now, there are no reasonably priced terabyte hard drives.

4 How Much Memory Is Enough?

Although a few years ago most computers had less than 1MB of RAM, these days most new computers have 128MB or more. Hard disks typically hold several gigabytes. Just to give you a measuring stick, a typical printed page of text, using single spacing, contains 2,500 to 3,000 characters. Therefore, 1MB holds close to 400 pages of single-spaced text.

5 Why Is Memory Important?

So why do you care how much memory your computer has? Because it determines what kinds of work you can do. The amount of memory in your computer dictates which programs you can run. Many Windows programs, for example, run best with 64MB or more of memory and cannot run at all on computers with less than 32MB.

6 Memory for Programs

The size of your hard disk is important because it defines how many programs and how much data you can store on your computer at once. In general, you will want enough room on your hard disk to accommodate all the programs and data that you work with regularly. Otherwise, you'll waste time copying data or programs to and from floppies. These days, each program you install requires 80MB or more of disk space, not including room for data. (Check the documentation that comes with the program if you're not sure.)

End

Notes

Memory and Hard Disk Space

You'll learn how to use Windows to find out how much room you have in memory and on your disk in Chapter 5, "Using Windows."

Upgrading Memory

Bear in mind that you can almost always add memory to your computer by buying additional memory chips and having them installed. If you are brave and have a good upgrading book, you may even be able to install the memory chips yourself. You can also add an additional hard drive if your current drive runs out of room.

Inside the System Unit

Now that you know what the CPU, memory chips, and disk drives do, you're ready to learn about where they reside and how they're connected. In most computer systems, all three of these components are housed inside the system unit. (Some computer systems have an external disk drive instead of, or in addition to, the ones inside the system unit.)

Begin

1 The Motherboard

The centerpiece of the system unit is a printed circuit board, known as the *motherboard*, which holds the CPU chip and its support circuitry. (You may also hear the motherboard referred to as the *system board*.) The motherboard generally lies face up at the bottom of the system unit.

2 Support Chips

The motherboard contains several other types of chips, in addition to the CPU, that help the CPU perform its job. One such support chip is the clock chip, which serves as the computer's metronome, setting the pace at which the various components function. There are also one or more ROM chips containing some part of the operating system software.

3 Memory Chips

Finally, the motherboard usually includes sockets for memory chips. In most cases, memory comes in the form of small, plug-in boards called SIMMs (single inline memory modules) or DIMMS, each of which includes eight or nine memory chips.

4 Disk Drives and the Power Supply

Aside from the motherboard, the system unit includes disk drives (usually one or two floppy drives and one hard drive) and a power supply. The power supply brings in power from the wall socket and supplies it to the motherboard. It also contains your computer's on/off switch and a place to attach the power cord that connects the system unit to a power outlet. The power supply unit usually contains a fan, to prevent the various chips from overheating. If your system includes an internal CD-ROM drive, modem, or tape drive, it probably resides in the system unit as well.

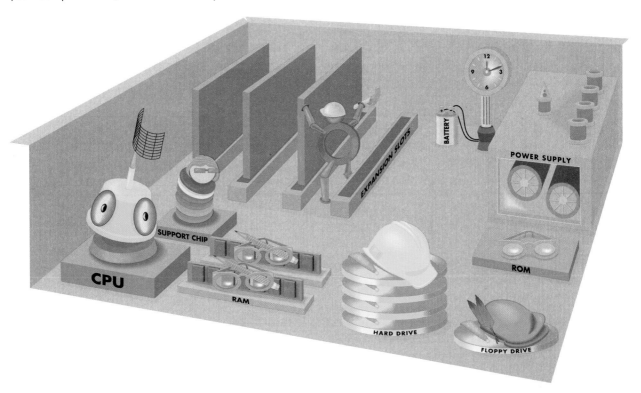

5 Expansion Boards

Most computers also contain additional circuit boards, commonly known as *expansion boards,* which fit into slots on the motherboard. (The slots themselves are known as *expansion slots;* think of them as parking spaces for circuit boards.) Expansion boards sit at the back of the system unit at a right angle to the motherboard itself. The purpose of most expansion boards is to allow an I/O (input/output) device—like a display monitor or a scanner—to communicate with the CPU.

Continues

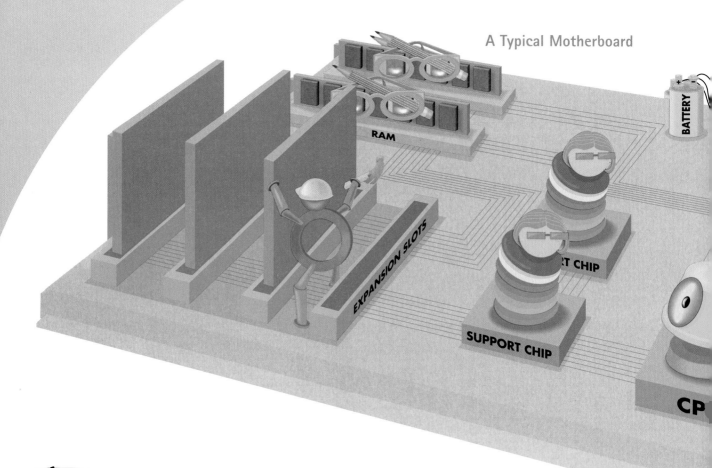

A Typical Motherboard

6 Ports

Expansion boards that are designed to serve as intermediaries between the CPU and some device outside the system unit have *ports* on one end. Ports are sockets that protrude from the back of the system unit. You can think of them as places where you can "dock" various external devices, plugging them into a circuit board that, in turn, connects them to the CPU. (Expansion boards that are designed for components inside the system unit—such as disk drives—do not include ports.) You'll learn about the various types of ports in Chapter 7.

7 The Bus

Finally, all motherboards contain a *bus:* a set of circuitry designed to carry data and instructions back and forth between various devices on the board itself. You might think of the bus as a collection of elaborate, high-speed conveyor belts. The bus not only carries data and instructions back and forth between the CPU and memory (both RAM and ROM), it also connects the CPU and memory to any expansion boards that are plugged into the motherboard.

End

ROM

Notes

Customizing Your System

The advantage of this design—a motherboard containing all the standard circuitry of the computer and a set of expansion slots that allow you to plug in additional circuitry as needed—is that it allows you to customize your system. Two people can buy essentially the same computer but add on different sets of peripherals. This design also allows you to easily add new parts to your computer as your needs change or as new forms of computer paraphernalia are invented.

Topic

Your Computer's Filing System

To use your computer effectively, you need to understand a bit about its filing system—namely, how it stores and organizes information on disks. This chapter begins by discussing files, the repositories of programs and data on disks, and other long-term storage media. You will learn about file formats used by various application programs, and about the organization of files into groups known as folders or subdirectories.

The second half of the chapter delves into detail about the disks themselves—the medium on which files are generally stored. By the time you're through, you will know how to choose the right type of disks for your floppy-disk drive(s), protect floppy disks from accidental damage, prepare new floppy disks for use, care for your hard disk, use CD-ROMs and Zip disks, and ward off computer viruses. ●

What Are Files?

All data on disks is stored in files. A *file* is a named collection of information stored on a disk. There are two basic types of files: *program files,* which contain instructions to your computer, and *data files,* which contain data that you enter through an application program. In Windows, data files are usually referred to as *documents,* regardless of their actual contents. A spreadsheet or mailing list file is considered to be as much a document as is a word processing file, for example.

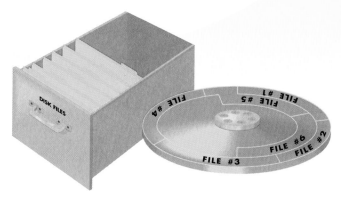

Begin

A file is a named collection of information stored on a disk.

1 Creating Data Files

Unless you delve into programming at some point, most of the files you create will be data files. Every time you enter data in an application program—be it text, numbers, pictures, or anything else—and then save it for the first time, you are creating a new data file. And, because all files, by definition, have names, the first thing the program asks you to do when you issue the command to save is assign a filename. (There are special rules for naming files and folders, which you'll learn more about in the "Rules for File and Folder Names" topic in Chapter 5, "Using Windows.")

2 Unique Filenames

In general, every file on a particular disk must have a unique name. (We'll explain the qualifications to this rule a little later in this chapter, after you learn about folders.) This way, when you tell your computer to find the file LETTER.DOC and copy it into memory, it knows exactly which file you mean. It doesn't need to determine *which* LETTER.DOC.

WHAT DO YOU WANT TO NAME THAT FILE?

3 Use Unique Filenames to Avoid Overwriting Files

You must keep this law of unique filenames in mind when copying files. If you copy a file named LETTER.DOC from disk 1 to disk 2, and disk 2 already has a file named LETTER.DOC, the old version of the letter is completely and permanently replaced by the new one. If you are using Windows, you will be asked to confirm that you want to replace the existing file.

4 Data Storage Formats

Most application programs have their own unique format for storing data, a format that only makes sense to that one program. For example, the format in which the Lotus 1-2-3 spreadsheet program stores data is not the same as the format used by the Excel spreadsheet. The format that the Microsoft Word word processing program uses is not the same as the format that WordPerfect uses.

5 File Formats

Special codes that tell the program how to arrange and format the data distinguish the file format used by one program from that used by another. A word processing program arranges data completely differently from a spreadsheet program, for example.

6 Looking at Files

In general, if you want to see what's inside a particular data file, you need to look at the file from inside the program in which it was created. For example, if you want to see what's inside an Excel spreadsheet file, you need to look at it from within the Excel program. If you try to look at it from within a word processing program or even from within another spreadsheet program, you will probably just see a lot of nonsense characters. Families of related programs (called "suites") such as Microsoft Office can generally read from each other. So, you can view an Excel spreadsheet from within Word.

Notes

Using Files in Other Formats

Many programs have commands for importing and exporting data in the formats used by other programs. Microsoft Word can import WordPerfect files, for example, translating all the WordPerfect formatting codes to their Word equivalents.

Saving Files in a Generic Format

Occasionally, a program is not capable of opening a file created by another program and interpreting the special codes that file contains. In this case, the file must be saved in a generic format, without any of the special formatting codes specific to one particular program. The most commonly used generic format is one known as ASCII or text-only. (ASCII stands for American Standard Code for Information Interchange and is a set of standardized codes used to represent all the characters you can produce on a typewriter, plus a few others.) After you have saved a file in ASCII or text-only format, you can open it in almost any other program, although you may need to specify the file format when you open the file or issue a special import command. Consult your program documentation for information on saving and using ASCII or text-only files.

I CAN'T READ THIS.

Saving, Retrieving, and Resaving Files

As you learned in Chapter 2, "Anatomy of a Computer," after something is stored, whether on your hard drive or on a floppy disk, you can always copy it back into memory when you want to use it again (just as you can fetch a particular document from your file cabinet). This is known as retrieving data or opening a file.

Begin

1 Retrieving Files

Just like when you load a program from your hard disk into memory, when you retrieve data from your hard disk or a floppy, the original copy of that data remains in place and intact on the disk. If you then change the copy in memory, you end up with two different versions: an older version on disk and a newer version in memory. The same situation occurs when you save a new document but continue working on it. You might, for example, get halfway through writing a letter, save your data to disk, and then continue with the letter. You then have two separate and independent versions of the same letter: one (the older one) on disk and another (the current one) in memory.

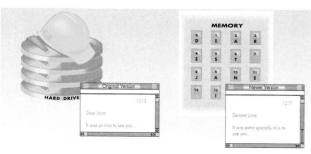

When you retrieve a file and then change it, the version in memory is newer than the version on disk.

2 Saving Your New Version

This has a couple of implications. First, if you like the new version better than the old one, you must remember to save it before you leave the application program. Otherwise, you'll have only the old version of the document (the one on disk) and your changes will be lost. (Most programs politely inquire whether you want to save if you try to close a file that you've modified since the last save.)

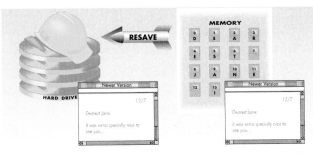

If you want to keep your changes, you need to save the revised file to disk again.

3 Closing Without Saving

Second, if you decide that you prefer the older version, you can close the document (remove it from memory) without saving it. When you do so, the version of the document currently in memory is erased. You can then retrieve the old version (the one on disk) and start amending it again. This can be extremely convenient when you completely bungle an edit and want to start all over.

4 Replacing the Old File with the New One

Whenever you want to save a file that has already been saved once, you need to decide whether to use the same filename as last time or a new filename. As mentioned, if you copy a file to a disk and the disk already contains a file of that name, the new one replaces the old one. The same issue arises when you resave a file. Suppose you create a budget in your spreadsheet program. Halfway through the process, you save your data; then you revise it and save it again. If you resave it under the original name, the new version will replace the old one. Most of the time, this is exactly what you want.

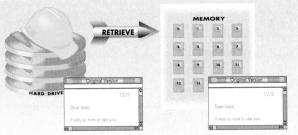

If you don't save the new version, you can retrieve the original from the hard drive.

5 Keeping the Old and the New Versions

In some cases, however, you'll want to keep both the old and the new versions of the file. If so, you need to resave the file with a new name or in a new location. If you regularly save multiple versions of files, developing some sort of system up front can ward off many migraines later down the line. You might want to save all the old versions in a separate directory, or save all the new versions with the word "new" or a number indicating which draft this is.

End

Notes

The Save and Save As Commands

In Windows, there are separate commands for resaving a document under its existing name (thus overwriting the previous version) and for saving a copy of the file under a new name. You use the **Save As** option on the **File** menu rather than the **Save** command when you want to save something under a new name.

Protection Against Overwriting Files

If you try to save a file with a name that's already in use, many application programs ask for confirmation to ensure that you don't accidentally overwrite the existing file.

Organizing a Hard Disk: Folders/ Subdirectories

Hard disks often hold thousands of files. Rather than piling this entire collection of files in a single and potentially massive heap, most people organize their files into groups. These groups are generally known as *folders* in Windows and as *directories* and *subdirectories* in DOS and older versions of Windows. You can think of folders/subdirectories as manila folders in a file drawer, each one of which can hold several individual documents (a.k.a. files).

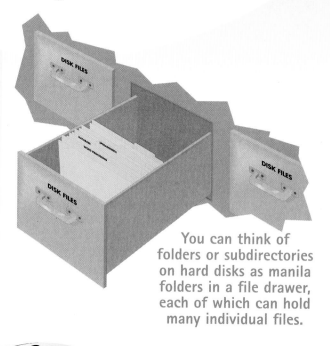

You can think of folders or subdirectories on hard disks as manila folders in a file drawer, each of which can hold many individual files.

1 Getting Organized

Just like setting up a manual filing system, when organizing a hard disk you must decide how many folders you need and what to store in each. Often you will place each application program and its associated files in a separate folder. For example, you might have one folder for your spreadsheet program, another for your word processing program, and a third for your database program.

2 Separating Programs and Files

Many people prefer to have two separate folders for each application—one to hold the program itself (this one is usually created automatically when you install the program) and another to hold the data files created in that program. You might, for example, have one folder for your word processing program and another for your word processing documents. Because it is fairly easy to copy all the files in a particular folder to a floppy disk or a Zip disk, storing nothing but data files in a folder makes it easy to create a backup copy of your data.

3 Folders for Different Types of Data

If you have many different types of data, you might also create a separate folder for each type. You might create one folder for business correspondence and another for letters to friends, or one for correspondence, another for reports, and a third for invoices. Each folder must have a unique name.

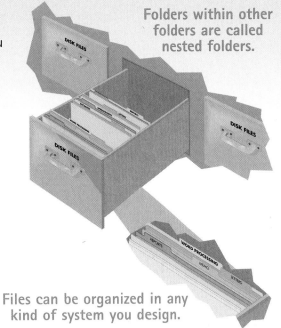

Folders within other folders are called nested folders.

Files can be organized in any kind of system you design.

4 Folders Within Folders

You can also create folders within folders if you like. (Folders within folders are sometimes called *nested folders.*) For example, you might create a word processing folder and then, within that folder, create other folders for different types of documents—such as reports, memos, and letters—you have created and saved.

5 Your Filing System Should Work for You

In other words, the filing system you create on a disk is as individual as the one you create in a filing cabinet. You can have your system as orderly or as freeform as you like, as long as it works for you and makes it easy for you to find the information you need.

End

Notes

Files in Different Folders Can Have the Same Name

Now that you know about folders, we can modify an earlier rule: Files in the same folder must have unique names. You can, however, have files of the same name in two different folders on the same disk.

Don't Nest Folders too Deeply

You can nest folders as deeply as you like. But bear in mind that it's easier to track down files if your folders aren't nested too deeply.

Working with Floppy Disks

Floppy disks can be used for a variety of reasons: to move data from one computer to another, to back up small amounts of data, or to pass a file or two to another person. Here you'll learn the ins and outs of floppy disks. Zip disks are similar to floppies, although they hold 70 times more data and require a separate Zip drive. Zip disks are a bulk option for backup and file storage because of the amount of storage space they offer.

Begin

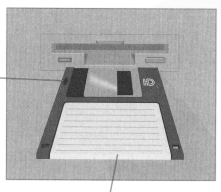

Arrow indicating proper way to insert disk

With 3 1/2-inch disks, the front side of the disk should face away from the disk eject button.

Notes

Formatting Disks

If you need to format a floppy disk—either because you bought unformatted disks or because you decide to reformat a floppy—the process is quite simple, but it may take a minute or two. In Windows, whenever you insert an unformatted disk, you're asked whether you'd like to format it. It's also simple to reformat a disk that's already formatted; you'll learn how to do this in the topic "Dealing with Disks in Windows" in Chapter 5.

Watch the Drive Light

When the read/write head is reading or writing to a disk, a small light on the front of the drive lights up. Do not remove the disk from the drive until this light goes off, indicating that the process is complete.

1 Your Disks Are Protected

You don't need to worry about accidentally touching or scratching the surface of 3 1/2-inch disks, because the disk remains protected until it is actually inserted into the drive. When you insert a 3 1/2-inch disk into a drive, the metal shutter is pushed to the side, exposing the disk's surface so the read/write heads can read and record information.

12/31/01

MY NOVEL

When you move this metal shutter you can see the disk inside.

2 Protect Your Disks from Magnets

With all floppy disks, you do need to be wary of magnets. Any exposure to magnets can scramble or erase the information recorded on the disk. Protecting your disk from magnets may take more vigilance than you realize. Magnets lurk in many un-suspected places, including many paper clip holders, some document holders, and various other office accessories. Because the coil for your telephone becomes magnetized every time your phone rings, it's wise to keep disks at least a few inches away from the phone.

3 Protect Your Disks from Heat

You should also avoid storing floppy disks in extreme heat. (Do not, for example, leave a disk on your dashboard on a hot summer day.)

5 Preformatted Disks

Most disks are preformatted for a particular type of computer and disk drive. (A number of years ago, you typically had to format all your floppy disks after you bought them—a rather rote and time-consuming process.) The only real reason to buy unformatted disks is if you have both a Mac and a PC and want to be able to use the disks in either machine.

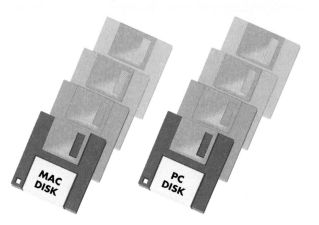

4 Write-protecting Floppy Disks

Occasionally, you may want to guard the files on a disk against accidental erasure or overwriting. You can do this by write-protecting the disk—making it impossible for anyone to copy new files onto the disk or erase files already on it. To write-protect a high-density 3 1/2-inch disk, you slide the tiny latch in the upper-right corner of the disk downward so a small window appears in the corner of the disk.

You can guard against accidental overwriting or erasure of data by write-protecting (or locking) a floppy disk.

End

The Care and Feeding of Hard Disks

Hard disks are not as vulnerable to dust and liquids as floppy disks are, because they are sealed inside metal cases. They are, however, far from indestructible. Knocking a computer off your desk or dropping it on the floor is a sure-fire way to lose some data, if not permanently damage the disk. Some hard disks are more sensitive than others and may respond poorly to being repeatedly moved from desk to desk.

Begin

1 Caring for Your Hard Disk

The basic rules of thumb for caring for a hard disk are

✓ Don't drop your computer.

✓ Unless you have a laptop or other computer designed for travel, don't move it any more often than you have to.

✓ If you're relocating to another office or building, try to pack the computer in its original packing materials to cushion it during the move.

✓ Most important, back up your data regularly. Operate on the assumption that sooner or later, your disk will fail (probably a day or two before some crucial deadline).

2 How Hard Drives Work

Most hard drives spin at thousands of revolutions per minute. While the disk is spinning, the read/write heads on hard disks hover above or below the disk's surface, at a distance of millionths of an inch. (To make it a little more concrete, the distance between the read/write heads and a spinning disk is less than half the width of a particle of smoke.) When your computer is turned off, the read/write heads do come to rest on the surface of the disk, but only within a specified parking area that is reserved for this purpose and is never used for storing information.

3 Hard Drive Malfunctions

If your hard drive malfunctions for some reason or you drop your computer on the floor, the read/write heads may fall onto the disk, permanently damaging it. This event, which is actually quite rare in modern-day hard drives, is known as a head crash. If someone tells you that their hard disk "crashed," they probably mean it underwent a head crash.

4 The Gap Between the Read/Write Head and the Disk

The small but essential gap that exists between the surface of the disk and the read/write heads explains why hard disks always live inside sealed containers, safe from such hazards as smoke, dust particles, and soda pop. Because the distance between the disk and the read/write head is half the size of a smoke particle, any encounter with such a particle would be like a high-speed go-cart running into a boulder.

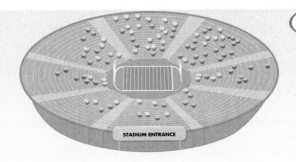

5 Fragmented Files

I've been representing each file as occupying a single discrete area of a disk. In reality, files are usually stored in segments scattered across the disk. The first part of a file may be wedged in between two other files, for example—perhaps in the space previously occupied by a file you later deleted. Because the whole file cannot fit in that space, your computer makes a note of where the next piece is stored (rather like the next clue in a treasure hunt). If there isn't enough room for the rest of the file in that second spot, your computer makes a note of where the third piece is stored, and so on. Files stored in this way are said to be fragmented.

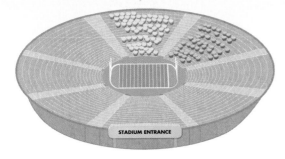

6 Defragmenting Your Hard Disk

Over time, your hard disk will accumulate many fragmented files (files stored in clusters scattered across the disk). Every time you load one of these files into memory, your computer has to jump from one part of the hard disk to another, collecting all the file's different pieces. You can improve your computer's efficiency by periodically *defragmenting* your hard disk—that is, running a special program that rearranges data so all the parts of each file occupy contiguous areas (clusters) on the disk. (You can compare this process to a bunch of people trading seats so a group of friends can sit together.)

Notes

The Disk Defragmenter Utility

Windows has built-in utilities for defragmenting a hard disk; look up defragment in the Help system for details. (You'll learn how to use the Windows Help system in Chapter 5.)

Using ScanDisk

Windows' ScanDisk utility allows you to search for and clean up errors on your hard disk that are causing problems or taking up space. ScanDisk is accessed from the Start menu's Accessories menu.

End

Using CD-ROMs

CD-ROM stands for compact disc–read-only memory. A CD-ROM is a CD designed to be "played" by a computer. Although CD-ROMs look just like audio CDs, they only work in a computer and, more specifically, in a CD-ROM drive that is either installed inside your system unit or attached to your system unit with a special cable. You can think of a CD-ROM drive as a computer-friendly version of a CD player. Unlike music CDs, which contain only audio information, CD-ROMs can hold graphics, text, sound, and full-motion video (movies). With today's CD-RW (compact disc rewritable) drives, you can make your own CDs easily and inexpensively.

Begin

1 CD-ROMs Can Store Lots of Information

CD-ROMs have become increasingly popular in the last few years for a simple reason: they pack a huge amount of information into a small space at a low cost. A single CD-ROM can contain up to 660MB of data, enough to comfortably house an entire encyclopedia.

2 What CD-ROMs Are Good For

Because they can accommodate so much data, CD-ROMs are ideal for storing multimedia applications, which tend to take up a lot of space—often more space than you might have to spare on your hard disk. CD-ROMs are also a popular way of distributing large applications that you will actually copy to your hard disk. An application that might fill 10 or even 20 floppy disks will fit easily on a single CD-ROM, and installing it from a CD-ROM will take a lot less time (not to mention sparing you the bother of changing disks 10 or 20 times).

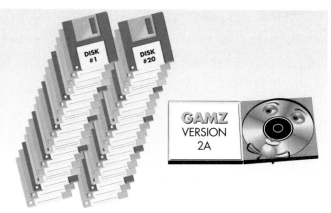

3 What Read-Only Means

As their name implies, standard CD-ROMs are read-only—you can copy files from CD-ROMs to your hard disk, but not the other way around. You can also load programs from a CD-ROM into your computer's memory, but not save the contents of memory back to the disc. (Certain specialized CD-ROM drives allow you to write information to CDs; you'll learn about these in Chapter 7, "More About Hardware.")

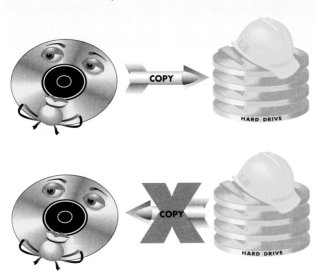

4 Internal and External CD-ROM Drives

CD-ROM drives come in two basic flavors: internal and external. The only difference between the two is their location: Internal drives fit into your computer's system unit and external ones sit in their own little boxes, which are connected to the system unit with cables. Internal drives are more common and slightly less expensive.

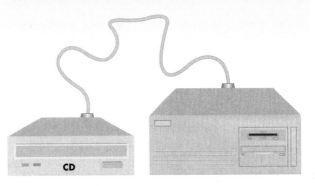

5 CD-ROM Speed

CD-ROM drives are generally categorized by speed: quad-speed, 6X, 8X, 10X, 12X, 24X, 32X and 48X. The first CD-ROM drives spun exactly as fast as a stereo's CD player. This tempo turned out to be a bit slow for running programs, however, so manufacturers created double-speed CD-ROM drives, which transfer data from the CD-ROM to your computer twice as fast. As of this writing, they've started manufacturing 48X drives, which transfer data 48 times as fast as the original CD-ROM drives.

6 Choosing a CD-ROM Speed

Which CD-ROM speed is right for you depends on your needs and budget. If you're buying a drive mainly to install new software and to look up things in an encyclopedia on occasion, 16X may be sufficient. Playing games is another story, however. If you spend hours on your computer playing graphics-intensive games, go for at least a 24X drive.

Continues

7 Handle CD-ROMs with Care

Because information is recorded on CD-ROMs using light rather than magnetic read/write heads, CD-ROMs, unlike floppy disks, are not sensitive to magnets or magnetic fields. They are susceptible to other hazards, however, such as dust, fingerprints, and soda pop. This means you need to take special care not to touch the surface of the disc, especially the part near the middle that contains the data and programs. Be particularly leery of touching the unlabeled side of the disc; that's where the CD-ROM drive reads the data. Instead, hold the disc by the edges or put your finger through the hole in the middle.

8 Handling Dirty or Damaged CDs

If one of your CD-ROMs becomes dusty, wipe the disc from the center out to the sides using a clean, soft cotton cloth. If the disc is actually dirty or you've spilled something on it, try either plain water or CD-ROM cleaner. If your CD-ROM gets scratched, try one of the products designed to repair scratches on audio CDs. Make sure the disc dries completely before you insert it in your CD-ROM drive. If you can't repair the disc, contact the company that produced it. Many CD-ROM publishers will send you a replacement disc in exchange for the damaged CD and a small fee.

9 Using a CD-ROM Drive

To use your CD-ROM drive, you press the open/close button on the front of the drive to elicit a plastic or metal tray. Place the disc on the tray and press the button again to cause both disc and plate to withdraw into the drive. To eject the disc, press the open/eject button again.

10 Using a CD-RW Drive

CD-RW drives have come down in cost so that they are now accessible to the average consumer. Many people use them to create their own music CDs, but they are also valuable as a means to back up data or exchange large quantities of data with others. Because the discs themselves are so inexpensive, CD-RWs are now in mainstream use.

End

Notes

The Data Transfer Rate

The speed at which the CD-ROM drive can read information from the disc and transfer it to your computer is known as its *data transfer rate*. The data transfer rate is 150KB per second for single-speed drives, 300KB for double-speed drives, 450KB for triple-speed drives, and so on. The other important benchmark for CD-ROM drives is access speed—the number of milliseconds (ms) it takes for the drive to locate a piece of data on a disc. When shopping for a CD-ROM drive, don't confuse the access speed with the data transfer rate. Data transfer rate is always measured in kilobytes or megabytes, because it refers to the amount of data that can be transferred in a second; access speed is measured in milliseconds.

What to Do If Your Disc Gets Stuck in the Drive

If your disc gets stuck in the drive (nothing happens when you press the eject button), check the drive's documentation to see whether your drive has an emergency eject hole. If it does, turn off the power to the drive. (If you have an internal drive, this means turning off the computer.) Then insert the tip of a paper clip into the emergency eject hole. If that doesn't work, contact a computer repair person or at least a technical-minded friend. If you do manage to get the tray out of the drive, make sure there's nothing wrong with it before you use it again.

Using Multimedia CD-ROMs

Most multimedia CD-ROMs feature sound as well as pictures. To fully enjoy such CD-ROMs, you'll need a sound card and a set of speakers as well as a CD-ROM drive. You'll learn more about sound cards, speakers, and multimedia in Chapter 7.

Computer Viruses

Even people who've never touched a computer have heard ominous tales about computer viruses. A *virus* is a program, generally designed by a bright but maladjusted computer nerd, that in one way or another interrupts or undermines the normal workings of your computer. Viruses work by copying themselves into legitimate files, called *hosts*. From there, they often branch out, replicating themselves in more and more files on the disk. Although some viruses infect almost every file in sight, others are pickier: Some viruses only infect application programs, others infect data files, and still others invade the operating system itself.

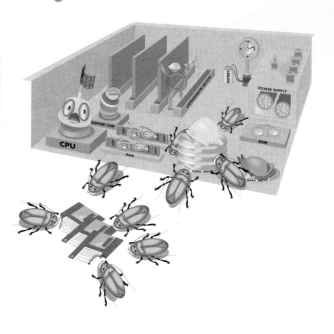

1 What Viruses Can Do

The level of destructiveness of viruses varies widely. Some viruses display pictures or messages on the screen periodically. Others erase or destroy programs and data. They also wreak havoc at different speeds: Some viruses spread through your system fairly quickly but don't actually do anything for days or even months. Macro viruses are a relatively new form of virus that currently affect only documents created in Microsoft Word and Excel.

2 How You Get a Virus

Viruses are often passed via disk: You buy or are given a disk that already has the virus on it. Some PC viruses are only passed if you boot (start your computer) from an infected disk—turning your computer on with the disk already in the floppy drive. Others can infect your system when you copy a file from an infected disk or even when you attempt to erase an infected disk. Viruses can also be passed when you use a modem to download (copy) a file from the Internet or access data or programs on a network. Many viruses also arrive in files attached to emails. The chances of contracting a virus are small if you only install commercially available, shrink-wrapped programs and rarely exchange disks with anyone else. The more computers your system comes in contact with—via the Internet or via floppy disks—the greater your risk.

3 Make Regular Backups

There are several steps you can take to protect your system from viruses: For starters, you should back up your data religiously, and don't discard or overwrite all your older backups. (You'll learn more about backups in Chapter 7.) It may take you days or weeks to notice and diagnose a virus, and many of your files may be damaged in the meantime. If you back up your data every day, you may just be backing up damaged files. What you need is an older copy of the data, one made before your computer was infected.

5 Use Antivirus Programs

In addition, you should use antivirus programs. The program will check your hard disk for viruses as soon as you turn on your computer, as well as scoping out any floppy disks you use over the course of the day.

End

4 Write-protect Your Floppy Disks

You should also write-protect floppy disks whenever possible. Because viruses cannot infect write-protected (locked) disks, you should write-protect any disks that you don't need to copy files to—in particular, your original copies of unprotected program disks—before you insert them into your computer. That way, if you install the program and the copy that resides on your hard disk becomes infected, you can always reinstall from your write-protected floppy disks.

6 Viruses Don't Cause All Computer Problems

Now that you know what viruses are, don't start blaming them for everything that goes wrong with your computer. Most problems you encounter on computers will be due to hardware problems, program bugs (mistakes within the program), or typos and other "user errors." If your computer starts displaying odd messages or if you keep encountering little happy faces in your word processing documents, by all means, investigate virus protection programs. But consider some of the other possibilities first.

Notes

Antivirus Programs May Conflict with Other Programs

If you install an anti-virus program and then start experiencing problems with other programs, see if uninstalling the antivirus program solves the problem.

Popular Antivirus Programs

The most popular antivirus programs are Norton Anti-Virus (produced by a company named Symantec), and McAfee's VirusScan.

Watch Emails Carefully

Never open or activate any file that is attached to an email unless you have a virus-protection program running. Many viruses are spread through email, sometimes inadvertently by people you know.

Topic

Up and Running

*T*his chapter discusses several things that are essential to know before you can operate your computer. Much of the information you'll learn here—such as how to turn the machine on and off and how to find your way around the keyboard—may seem obvious to those of you with even a small amount of computer experience. At the same time, these pages might reveal some new twist that you didn't know about, such as a new keyboard strategy for getting yourself out of trouble.

First, you'll learn what exactly happens when you turn on your computer—how to decode some of the sounds you'll hear and messages you'll see. Then you'll get some in-depth information about keyboards and keyboard layouts. You'll find out how to make your way around with the cursor movement keys. You'll also learn the ins and outs of some special keys, particularly the Delete and Backspace keys. In addition, you'll discover how and when to use the function keys, either by themselves or in combination with modifier keys such as Ctrl and Shift. As you'll see, you can enter numbers speedily with the numeric keypad, which can typically double as a set of extra cursor movement keys as well. Some of the most valuable keys and key combinations you'll discover are those that help you get unstuck.

You can also communicate with and control your computer via the mouse or its stand-ins: the trackball or touch pad. In this chapter, you'll learn the full variety of mousing techniques. After that, you will find out the proper way to turn off your computer. Finally, you'll learn some tips for arranging the different parts of your computer system for maximum comfort and minimum back, wrist, and eye strain.

What Happens When You Turn On Your Computer

Many personal computer systems are set up so that all the components, including the system unit and the monitor, are plugged into a single power strip. In this case, you turn on your computer (and everything else in sight) by throwing the switch on the power strip itself. If you don't have a power strip, you'll have to turn on the components one at a time. As you'll learn here, a whole sequence of events happens next.

Begin

1 What Happens First

As you learned in Chapter 1, "The Basics," your computer hardware can't do much of anything without instructions. When you turn on a computer, the first thing it does is go searching for a program that can tell it what to do next.

2 The Boot Program

The program the CPU is looking for is a very small part of the operating system known as the *boot program*. This program is stored in ROM and is known as the boot program because it essentially helps the computer "pull itself up by its own boot-straps," by loading (*booting*) the rest of the operating system into memory. The BIOS (basic input/output system) is part of the operating system that is stored in ROM. It runs the basic startup tests for your computer.

The CPU makes sure the disk drives and other components are working.

3 The Power-On Self Test

Under the direction of this boot program, the CPU performs what is known as a *Power-On Self Test* (*POST* for short). During this stage, the CPU tests to see whether the various parts of the system are still alive and well. You will see a progress report during this phase. At a minimum, you will probably notice the computer counting up its memory. You may also see messages as the CPU checks out various peripherals, and little lights on your keyboard and printer may turn on and off. Finally, a beep will indicate that everything seems to be okay.

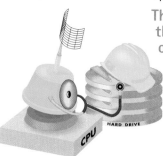

The CPU takes an inventory of memory.

4 Searching for the Operating System

After the CPU has finished its internal inventory, it goes hunting for the rest of the operating system: the part that is stored on disk. The first place it looks is in the floppy disk drive. (If you have a PC with two floppy disk drives, it looks to the one named drive A—which is usually the leftmost or uppermost drive.) If the floppy disk drive is empty, the CPU continues its search on the hard drive.

The read/write head, under instructions from the CPU, locates the operating system on the hard disk.

5 If You Have a Disk in the Floppy Disk Drive

If there is a disk in the floppy disk drive, your computer checks whether it contains the operating system. If it doesn't, the computer informs you that you have an invalid system disk or a non-system disk or disk error. Just open the floppy disk-drive door or eject the disk and then press any key on your keyboard to have the CPU resume hunting for the operating system on your hard drive. (The moral of this story is that if you plan to work with a floppy disk, postpone inserting it until your system is done booting.)

6 When Windows Starts

As soon as the CPU locates the operating system, it loads it into memory. If you are running Windows XP, you'll see the message **Starting Windows XP** and then the Microsoft Windows XP logo. (If you are running another version of Windows, you will see that version's logo and name at this point.) If you are not part of a network, you'll probably go immediately to a screen known as the Windows desktop. (You'll learn all about the desktop in Chapter 5, "Using Windows.")

7 Logging in to a Network

If you are on a network you'll need to enter your name and password before you arrive at the desktop. This process is known as *logging in*. (For more information on networks, see Chapter 7, "More About Hardware.")

End

Keyboards and Keyboard Layouts

Before you can use your computer effectively, you need to know your way around the keyboard. Your computer keyboard is very sensitive; you don't need to bang or lean on the keys, placing unnecessary stress on both your own wrists and the keyboard's innards; your computer recognizes and responds to the lightest key press. If you hold down a key for more than a second, your computer will respond as though you had pressed it several times in rapid succession. The effect will depend on what that key actually does in the program you are using, but it's unlikely to be the intended result. If you're not accustomed to typing at all, experiment to find the lightest touch that will work on your machine.

Begin

1 The Standard Keyboard

Close to a dozen different styles of computer keyboards are available. One of the most common keyboards is shown in the figure below. Although almost all keyboards have the letter and number keys in the same places, the location of other keys may vary.

2 The Feel of a Keyboard

Different brands of keyboards may also have a very different feel. On some, the keys click when you press them and on some they don't; the keys feel stiffer on some keyboards and looser on others. The nice part about this variety is that you can choose the feel and the layout you like. The unfortunate part is that if you switch computers at some point, you may need to spend some time getting used to the feel of the keyboard and searching for keys.

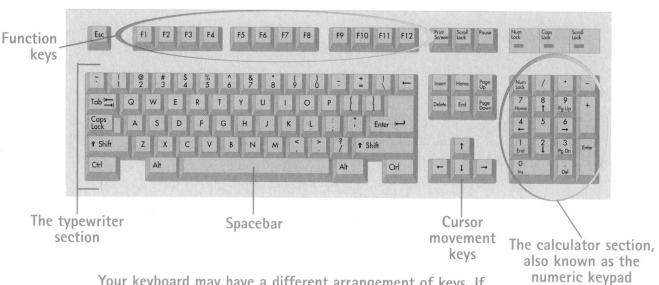

Function keys

The typewriter section

Spacebar

Cursor movement keys

The calculator section, also known as the numeric keypad

Your keyboard may have a different arrangement of keys. If you are using an older computer, or a laptop or notebook computer, you may have fewer keys altogether.

3 The Caps Lock Key

Caps Lock is what is known as a *toggle key*—a key you use to alternately enable and disable a particular feature. You press it once to turn the feature on and again to turn it off. Unlike the Shift Lock key on a typewriter, Caps Lock on a computer keyboard affects letters only. This means that typing a dollar sign requires holding down the Shift key while you press the 4 at the top of your keyboard, even if Caps Lock is on.

4 The Enter Key

If you first learned to type on a typewriter, you'll find that the Enter key works something like a carriage return: You press it to move to the next line when you get to the end of a paragraph. As you'll learn in Chapter 6, "Applications Software," however, you don't need to press Enter at the end of each line in word processing programs; the program automatically "word wraps" text to the next line when you reach the right margin. You still need to press Enter to force the cursor to a new line before you reach the right margin, however. You also sometimes use Enter to select options from a menu (onscreen list of options) or to indicate that you are done entering instructions or data and want the program to respond. (Not sure just what the *cursor* is? You'll learn in a moment.)

5 The Tab Key

On some older PC keyboards and many laptops, the Tab key doesn't actually say Tab. It just has two arrows pointing in opposite directions, like ←→. In some cases you get both the text and the arrows.

Notes

Different Names for the Enter Key

The Enter key is labeled Return on certain older PC keyboards. In addition, some keyboards label the Enter key with the ⏎ symbol. This symbol is used to indicate "Press the Enter key now" in many software manuals. Your keyboard may also have an additional Enter key, at the right of the numeric keypad, for entering numbers.

End

The Cursor Movement Keys

In most programs, a symbol indicates where you are on the screen at the moment—like a "you are here" indicator on a map for a park or shopping mall. When you are entering text in Windows, the "you are here" symbol is a blinking vertical line known as the *insertion point.* (Its DOS equivalent was the *cursor.*) On most keyboards, there are two groups of keys designed to move the cursor or insertion point around the screen: the arrow keys and another set of keys called Home, End, Page Up, and Page Down. You may also have a duplicate set of cursor movement keys on the numeric keypad. You can move the cursor or insertion point by using either the cursor movement keys or your mouse.

Begin

YOU ARE HERE

The insertion point or cursor indicates your current position on the screen.

1 The Arrow Keys

The arrow keys move the cursor/insertion point one character or one unit at a time in the direction of the arrow. To move one character to the left when you are entering text in a word processing program, for example, you press the left arrow key. On most keyboards, the arrows occupy keys by themselves.

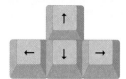

2 Additional Navigation Keys

The other cursor movement keys (Home, End, Page Up, and Page Down) let you make larger jumps across the screen. On some laptop keyboards, there are no separate cursor movement keys; they are always part of the numeric keypad (the calculator section). You'll discover how to use these dual-purpose keys when you learn about the numeric keypad.

3 The Home Key

The Home key is often used to move to the beginning of some set of data—such as the top of a document, the beginning of a line, or the upper-left corner of a spreadsheet.

4 The End Key

The End key is often used to move to the end of some set of data—such as the bottom of a document, the end of a line, or the last number or character in a particular block of data in a spreadsheet.

5 The Page Up Key

The Page Up key is usually used to move up one page or one screenful of data. (This key is often labeled PgUp.)

6 The Page Down Key

The Page Down key is usually used to move down one page or one screenful of data. (This key is often labeled PgDn.)

7 Moving the Insertion Point with the Mouse

You can also move the cursor or insertion point by using a mouse. Typically, you do this by clicking where you want the insertion point to go.

End

Notes

The Cursor

If you're still using DOS, the "you are here" symbol is a little blinking line or rectangle, known as a *cursor*. Keys for navigating in Windows programs are still called "cursor movement keys," even though they're actually moving the insertion point. You may occasionally see the insertion point referred to as the cursor.

The Cursor Versus the Insertion Point

You'll never have both a cursor and an insertion point. You always have one or the other, depending on the type of computer and the program you are using.

The Special Keys

The special keys include all the keys other than normal typewriter keys, cursor movement keys, the
numeric keypad (the set of keys resembling a calculator), and function keys. These keys are scattered
around the keyboard, and they generally perform
some operation other than displaying a particular
character on the screen.

Begin

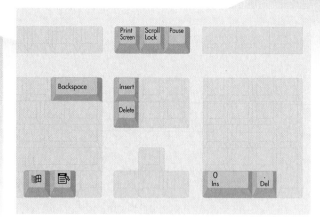

1 The Backspace and Delete Keys

Most PC keyboards include two keys for
erasing. The key labeled either Delete or Del generally
deletes the character immediately to the right of the
insertion point. The Backspace key deletes the character to the left of the insertion point. (On some keyboards, the key doesn't say "Backspace"; it shows a
left-pointing arrow.)

The Backspace
key gobbles
characters to the
left of the
cursor or
insertion point.

The Delete key
(sometimes
abbreviated Del)
gobbles characters
to the right of
the cursor or
insertion point.

2 Deleting Selected Text

In most programs, you can also select a group of characters to erase using either your keyboard or the mouse. Pressing either the Backspace or the Delete key will delete any currently selected characters. (In case you don't already know, you'll learn how to select shortly, under "Things You Can Do with a Mouse or Trackball.")

4 The Windows Logo Key

Some keyboards designed specifically to work with Windows contain two extra types of keys—Application keys and Windows Logo keys—that provide fast keyboard alternatives to many operations you'd usually perform with a mouse. For example, you can use the Windows Logo keys to open the Start menu, instead of clicking the Start button at the lower-left corner of the desktop.

3 The Insert Key

The Insert (or Ins) key is a toggle that determines what happens when you type new characters within existing text or numbers. If the Insert feature is on and you type new characters in the middle of a paragraph, for example, the old characters are pushed to the right to make room for the new ones. With Insert off, the new characters replace the old ones. In most programs, Insert may be set on by default, so you don't accidentally overtype what you've already entered. On some keyboards, Insert shares a key with the number 0 on the numeric keypad.

5 The Application Key

You can use the Application key to bring up a shortcut menu relevant to what you're doing at the moment (it's the equivalent of right-clicking). If you're not sure whether your keyboard contains these keys, look a bit to the left and right of the spacebar. The Windows Logo keys contain the Windows logo (surprise). The Application key looks like a menu with an arrow pointing to it.

Notes

Backspace Versus Left Arrow

Don't confuse the Backspace key and the Left Arrow key. Both of these keys contain left-pointing arrows. Although both of these keys move the insertion point to the left, the Left Arrow (like all arrow keys) doesn't change anything. In contrast, the Backspace key moves and erases at the same time. Every time you press the key, the character to the left of the insertion point is deleted and the insertion point moves left one space to take up the slack.

End

The Modifier and Function Keys

All PC keyboards contain three types of special keys that you use almost exclusively in combination with other keys. They don't do anything by themselves. (Many keyboards contain two keys of each type—two Shift keys, two Control keys, and so on.) This book will refer to these special keys as *modifier keys*. Occasionally, the modifier keys are used with a row of keys called *function keys*—labeled F1, F2, and so on—that you'll probably find across the top of your keyboard.

Begin

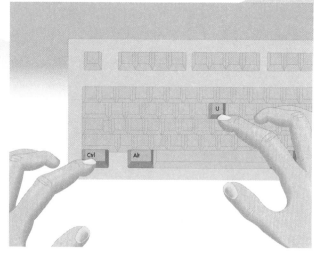

When you use key combinations, you always press the modifier key (in this case Ctrl) first and hold it down while you press the other key.

1 Modifier Keys

For those of you who've used typewriters, the Shift key on a typewriter is an example of a modifier key. Pressing the Shift key by itself does nothing. But if you hold down Shift while pressing the letter *A*, you get an uppercase *A* instead of the lowercase *a* you get by pressing the *A* key by itself.

2 The Shift, Control, and Alt Modifier Keys

Similarly, on a PC keyboard, nothing happens when you press Shift, Control (Ctrl), or Alternate (Alt). But in many application programs, holding down a modifier key while pressing another key is a way of issuing a command. In some word processing programs, for example, holding down the Ctrl key while pressing *U* issues the command to underline any currently selected text (while pressing *U* by itself would generate a letter *U* and pressing Ctrl by itself would do nothing). These key combinations are often called "hot keys" or "keyboard shortcuts."

3 Using Modifier Keys with Cursor Movement Keys

Often you can also modify the way the cursor movement keys work by using them in combination with one of the modifier keys. For example, in Microsoft Word, pressing Home moves the insertion point to the beginning of the current line, whereas pressing Ctrl+Home moves the insertion point to the beginning of the document. Shift+Home selects a block of text from the beginning of the paragraph to the insertion point.

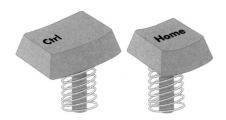

4 What Is a Key Combination?

A *key combination* is a combination of two or more keys (at least one of which is a modifier key) to perform an operation. To use a key combination, you press the modifier key first and hold it down while you press the other key. Don't try to press both keys at once; you might press the second key slightly before you press the modifier key, which has the effect of pressing that second key by itself.

5 How Key Combinations Are Notated

When computer books or manuals refer to key combinations, they sometimes combine the names of the keys with commas, hyphens, or plus signs. In other words, if you're supposed to hold down Alt while you press the Backspace key, you might see Alt,Backspace, Alt-Backspace, or Alt+Backspace.

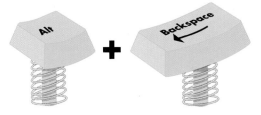

6 Function Keys

The function keys are the keys labeled F1 through either F10 or F12 and are usually located at the top of the keyboard. In many application programs, function keys are used to issue commands. For example, F1 frequently invokes an application's Help system, which provides you with information on how to use the program. F10 sometimes activates the program's menu system. Surprisingly, in many programs many of the function keys have no function at all.

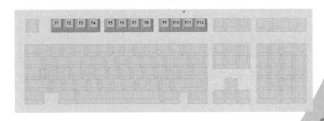

Notes

Function and Modifier Keys Together
The function keys are sometimes used in combination with the modifier keys. For example, in a number of word processing programs, pressing Shift+F7 invokes the thesaurus.

End

The Numeric Keypad

Currently, two basic layouts exist for PC keyboards: one, often called the *extended keyboard,* for desktop PCs, and another for laptops. The main difference is that most desktop keyboards have both a numeric keypad and separate groups of cursor movement keys, while most laptops have a numeric keypad that doubles as a set of cursor movement keys.

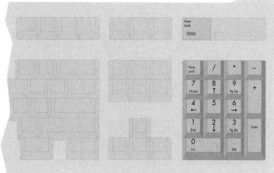

Begin

You can use the numeric keypad either for typing numbers or moving around the screen, depending on the current status of the Num Lock setting.

1 The Two Ways to Use the Numeric Keypad

On all keyboards, you can use the numeric keypad for either of two functions: typing numbers or moving around on the screen. The status of the Num Lock (number lock) setting—which you control by pressing the Num Lock key—determines the function.

2 The Num Lock Key

Num Lock is a toggle key: Each time you press it, the status of the Num Lock feature changes, from off to on or on to off. When Num Lock is on, the keys on the numeric keypad generate numbers. When Num Lock is off, they change to cursor movement keys. The 7 key acts like a Home key, for example, and the 8 key serves as an Up Arrow key. The function of each key is spelled out on the key itself. (The effect of the cursor movement keys was covered earlier in this chapter.)

3 Other Keys on the Numeric Keypad

The keys other than the Num Lock key around the outside of the numeric keypad work the same regardless of the Num Lock setting. You can use them to enter mathematical symbols such as + and -. (In a number of applications, the / symbolizes division and the * symbolizes multiplication.)

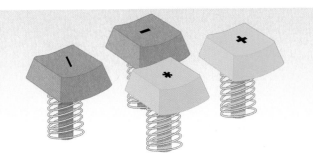

4 The Enter, Insert, and Delete Keys on the Numeric Keypad

The Enter key on the numeric keypad works just like the Enter key in the main section of the keyboard. (If you're typing lots of numbers, you might want to use this Enter key rather than the one that's in with the typewriter keys.) The Ins and Del keys work just like the Insert and Delete keys typically found to the left of the Home and End keys.

5 How to Tell Whether Num Lock Is On

You can usually determine whether Num Lock is on in several ways. On most keyboards, there is a little light on the key itself or a light labeled Num Lock above the key. If the light is on, the feature is on. Many application programs also display the words *Num Lock* or *Num* on the screen when Num Lock is on. If needed, you can check by pressing one of the arrow keys and see whether the cursor moves or a number is generated.

6 Turning Off Num Lock

Why would you want to turn off Num Lock? On many laptops, there is no separate set of arrow keys; you have to choose between using the cursor movement keys and using the numeric keypad to type numbers. If you don't need to do a lot of moving around at the moment, you might turn Num Lock on temporarily to enter a set of numbers, particularly if you're a touch-typing wiz on calculators. Otherwise, leave Num Lock off and use the number keys at the top of the keyboard to enter numbers.

End

Notes

Entering Arithmetic Operators from the Numeric Keypad

It's often easier to type arithmetic operators (like + and *) using keys at the side of the numeric keypad rather than keys at the top of the keyboard. If you use the keys at the top, you need to remember to hold down the Shift key, or you'll get = when you mean + or 8 when you mean *.

Options for Navigating

The Num Lock key was carried over to the newer keyboards primarily to accommodate people who were already used to navigating with keys on the numeric keypad. Some people also prefer the layout of arrow keys on the numeric keypad (with the Up Arrow key above the Left Arrow and Right Arrow keys).

What to Do When You Get Stuck

Never turn off your computer in the middle of an application if you can avoid it. (Turning off your computer is covered later in this chapter.) It can damage data and, at the least, cause you to lose any unsaved data in memory. Occasionally, however, you may just get stuck. There may be a "bug" (glitch) in the program you are using, causing an error message that won't go away; or the program may stop responding to your commands. Here are some techniques to try if you do get stuck, listed from the least drastic to the most.

Begin

1 The Escape Key

In many application programs, the Escape (or Esc) key is a general-purpose "get me out of here" key—used to cancel or back up a step in the current operation.

2 The Break Key

If the Escape key doesn't solve your problem, you can try the Break key. On most keyboards, either the Scroll Lock or Pause key doubles as a Break key. (You should see the word *Break* either on top of the key or on its front edge. If you don't find *Break* on either key, you can use Scroll Lock for this purpose.) By itself, Break does nothing, but holding down a Ctrl key and pressing this key will interrupt some programs or commands. This key combination is referred to as Ctrl+Break (pronounced "Control Break").

3 Rebooting Your Machine

If neither of the preceding techniques works, you can *reboot* your computer by holding down the Ctrl and Alt keys and then tapping the Del key. This opens a window that allows you to close specific programs or to reboot the machine by pressing Ctrl+Alt+Del a second time. Rebooting erases memory and reloads the operating system; you lose any data currently in memory. In some programs, you may damage data as well, so only use this key combination when you can't think of any other solution. Although fairly drastic, rebooting is still a bit safer than the next two options.

4 The Reset Button

Many PCs have a Reset button that lets you restart your computer without actually flicking the power switch. The main power to the computer's components is not interrupted. This saves wear and tear. (Some, but not all, Reset buttons are actually labeled *Reset*. If you can't find yours, check in the documentation for your computer.)

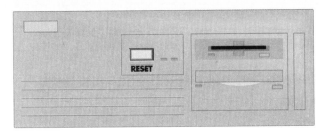

5 If All Else Fails

If all else fails and your computer does not have a Reset button, turn off the computer by switching off the power supply switch, wait at least 30 seconds, and then turn it on again.

End

Notes

Closing Programs and Rebooting in Windows

If you are using Windows, pressing Ctrl+Alt+Del invokes a Close Program dialog box. From there, you can select the program you suspect is causing the problem and click the End Task button. If that doesn't work, click the Shut Down button. If you still have no luck, press Ctrl+Alt+Del again.

Using a Mouse, Trackball, or Touch Pad

Keyboards are only one of the tools available for talking to your computer. The other main tool is a mouse or trackball. A mouse is a hand-held pointing device that lets you point to, select, and manipulate objects on the screen. As you move the mouse around on your desk, a special symbol, known as the *mouse pointer,* moves in an analogous direction on the screen. If you move the mouse forward and backward, the mouse pointer moves up and down on the screen; if you move the mouse left and right, the mouse pointer moves left and right. Although the mouse pointer most often looks like an arrow, it can assume many other shapes, depending on which program you are running and what operation you are performing.

Begin

1 Using the Mouse

You can hold the mouse in either hand. Most people prefer to use their dominant hand—the right if right-handed or left if left-handed. (Most computer stores offer left-handed mice.) Make sure the mouse cord is pointing away from you. Then just glide the mouse lightly over the surface of your desk or mouse pad.

2 Moving the Mouse

If you reach the edge of your desk or mouse pad before you reach the desired point on the screen, just lift your mouse up and move it. The mouse pointer only moves when the mouse is flat against a hard surface; the ball underneath rolls as you move the device. If you want to move the mouse pointer to the bottom of your screen, for example, and you reach the front edge of your desk when the mouse pointer is still an inch above the desired spot, just lift the mouse, move it up a few inches, put it back down again, and continue moving it down.

3 Using a Mouse Pad

If your computer didn't come with one, you will want to purchase a mouse pad, a rectangular piece of nylon-covered rubber that you place on your desk as a platform for your mouse. A mouse often gets better traction and therefore moves more smoothly on a pad than directly on a desk, particularly one with an uneven surface.

4 Trackballs

A trackball is essentially an upside-down mouse. Instead of having a ball on the bottom, it has a ball on the top, set inside a square cradle. Rolling this ball has the same effect as moving a mouse.

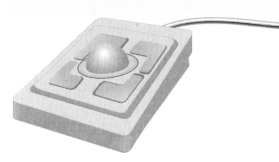

5 Pointing Sticks

Laptop computers sometimes sport yet another type of pointing device, known as a *pointing stick*. This is a small cylindrical piece of plastic that looks like the eraser on the end of a pencil. It is usually positioned in the center of the keyboard. By pushing the stick in various directions, you can control the movement of the mouse pointer on your screen. (The stick itself does not actually move when pushed, but it does respond to the pressure of your finger.) Computers with pointing sticks generally have two buttons near the bottom of the keyboard that you can press to simulate left and right mouse clicks.

6 Touch Pads

A *touch pad* is a small rectangular area on some keyboards. Moving your finger across the touch pad causes the pointer to move across the screen.

7 The Two Mouse Buttons

Many of the operations that you perform using a mouse, trackball, or touch pad involve pushing buttons. Mice designed for PCs typically have two buttons: a left button and a right button. The buttons on a trackball are usually positioned at the far end of the device. You can press them using either your thumb or forefinger. On a touch pad, you can click by either tapping the pad with your finger or pressing the left button.

8 Cleaning Your Mouse

If your mouse pointer starts moving in fits and starts or moves in one direction but not another, it's probably time for a mouse cleaning. Turn the mouse upside down. Next, either slide the round lid down until it pops open or turn it counterclockwise until it reaches the open position. Drop the ball out into your palm. Clean the rollers inside the mouse using a cotton swab dipped in alcohol. Clean the ball using a soft, dry cloth. Replace the ball and the lid and you're ready to go. To reassemble a trackball after cleaning, place the ball in one hand, with your other hand, place the mouse part on top of it, and flip your hands over.

Notes

How Your Mouse Will Look

When using some programs, your mouse may behave differently than it would otherwise. (The mouse pointer may look like a hand instead of an arrow.) Chapter 5 covers this mouse behavior in detail.

The IntelliMouse

Microsoft makes a mouse called the IntelliMouse that has a small wheel between the left and right mouse buttons that you can use to scroll through data or text.

End

Things You Can Do with a Mouse or Trackball

Moving the mouse pointer where you want it is just the first step. After you've done so, you need to use one of the available buttons, depending on which type of action you want to carry out. When you read software manuals, you are likely to encounter the following terms for the various things you can do with a mouse or trackball.

Begin

1 Pointing

Point means position the mouse pointer over a particular word or object on the screen. If the mouse pointer looks like an arrow, you need to position the tip of the arrow over the desired object. Pointing is usually the precursor to actually doing anything by using one of the mouse buttons.

2 Pressing the Mouse Button

Press means press and hold down the mouse (or trackball) button. You need to press the mouse button in preparation for dragging, which is described in a moment.

3 Clicking

Click means tap the button—pressing it in and then releasing it quickly. The term *click* generally means click the left mouse button. *Right-click* means tap the right mouse button. Often you click to initiate some action, such as pulling down a menu of choices. In Windows, right-clicking typically displays a *shortcut menu* of choices relevant to the object you clicked.

4 Double-Clicking

Double-click means click the button twice in rapid succession. Double-clicking often initiates some action right away; for example, if you have a program icon on your desktop, double-clicking that icon will launch the program.

5 Dragging

Drag means move the mouse or trackball while holding down the button. (*Right-drag* means move the mouse or trackball while holding down the right button.) Dragging is frequently used to move or resize items on the screen, as well as to select text or other items. When you've dragged the item to its new location, you drop it by releasing the mouse button. This procedure is called "drag-and-drop."

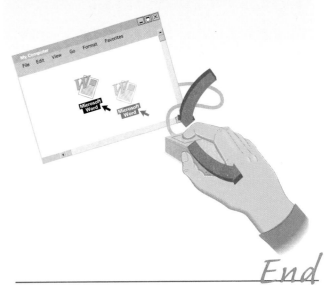

End

Notes

Click Means the Left Mouse Button

When you see instructions to press or click the mouse button, assume that you should use the left mouse button unless explicitly told otherwise. If you are supposed to click the right mouse button, for example, the instructions will say "right-click" or "click the right mouse button" rather than just "click."

How to Click the Mouse

To click the mouse in a particular spot, move the pointer to that spot and then, without moving the mouse, just use your index finger to press the mouse button. (Some beginners try to jab the mouse key from on high, which usually jettisons the mouse pointer away from its target.) If you're double-clicking, be sure to keep the mouse in the same spot between the first and second click.

Adjusting the Double-Click Speed

If every time you try to double-click, the computer responds as if you'd only clicked once, chances are you're waiting too long between the first and second click. If you're using Windows, you can adjust the double-click speed—that is, the amount of time you're allowed to leave between clicks. To do this, open the Start menu and select Control Panel. Then double-click the mouse icon, and you'll be there.

Turning Off Your Computer

The first thing to know about turning off your computer is not to do it too often. In general, you should turn it off only when you don't plan on using it again for several hours. If you're going to lunch, leaving the computer on causes less wear and tear than turning it off and then on again. (Some people even leave their computers on night and day, presumably with the thought that this is easier on the machine in the long run, even though it may not be easier on their electricity.) However, you may want to turn off your monitor temporarily, to protect the screen and to turn off the electromagnetic radiation. The monitor also consumes the most energy.

Begin

1 Saving Your Work

When you are done using your computer for the day, save any unsaved data that you want to be able to use in future work sessions.

2 If You Close Before You Save

If you are using Windows and forget to save something, the program double-checks with you before discarding your changes.

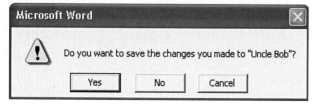

3 Shutting Down

After confirming your choices, click the **Start** button in the lower-left corner of the screen to display a Start menu. Click the **Turn off Computer** option.

4 Turning Off Your System

When Windows displays a box with the title Turn off Computer, click the button labeled **Turn off**. In a moment, you'll see the message `It's now safe to turn off your computer` and you can flip the on/off switch or press the power button.

5 Automatic Shut Down

Some laptops and desktops are smart enough to turn themselves off automatically. All you do is choose the Turn off Computer option; you don't need to flip an on/off switch or press a power button.

6 When You Can Turn Your Computer Back On

If you turn your computer off and then decide to turn it on again, wait for 30 seconds first to let all the electrical charges dissipate from the machine.

End

Notes

Shut Down

In versions of Windows before XP, the Turn off Computer sequence was known as Shut Down. If you are using Windows 98, for example, you will see Shut Down instead of Turn off Computer. The end result is the same either way.

Safe Mode

If you turn off your computer without shutting down properly in Windows, when you turn your computer on again you may see a message indicating that the computer is starting in "safe mode." If so, let the computer finish booting, and then shut it down properly. When you see the Turn off Computer dialog box, choose **Restart** and then click **OK**. When your computer restarts, it should be in regular (rather than safe) mode.

Ergonomics: Taking Care of Your Body While You Use a Computer

You'll never learn to love (or even tolerate) a computer if it causes you discomfort or pain. If you plan to spend hours at the keyboard, it's worth taking time to make the experience as comfortable as possible. Setting up your workstation properly isn't just about feeling good (although that's a worthy goal). It's also a way of preventing painful and potentially debilitating conditions like carpal tunnel syndrome, tendonitis, repetitive motion disorder, and chronic back pain. The figure shows how to arrange your computer to cause minimum wear and tear on your body. The basic rules of thumb are as given in the following paragraphs.

Begin

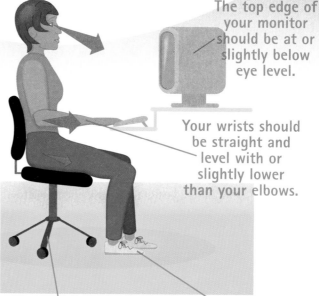

The top edge of your monitor should be at or slightly below eye level.

Your wrists should be straight and level with or slightly lower than your elbows.

Use a chair that provides good support for your back.

Your feet should be touching either the floor or a footrest.

1 Your Monitor

The top edge of your monitor should be at eye level or a little below, so you're looking down just slightly. (You may need to prop up the monitor with a large book or a monitor stand.) The front edge should be 20 to 30 inches from your eyes.

2 Desk Height and Posture

Your wrists should never be higher than your elbows. Ideally, your elbows should be bent at a 90-degree angle and your wrists should be straight, not flexed upward or bent downward. If you can't achieve this position using your desk, your desk is too high (or your chair seat too low). Try a typing desk or a keyboard drawer that allows the keyboard to sit lower than the desktop. Your feet should touch the floor or a footrest and the angle between your thighs and spine should be 90 degrees or a bit more.

3 Proper Mousing

Keep your mouse close to the keyboard so you don't have to reach far to use it. This will minimize strain on your shoulders. Also, try not to sit for hours with your hand on the mouse; let go of the mouse when you're not using it. If you use the mouse even more than the keyboard, put the mouse directly in front of you and the keyboard slightly off to the side. If you do start developing strain in your mouse arm or shoulder, consider using a touch pad.

4 Proper Wrist Position

One of the worst things you can do to your wrists is lean the heel of your hand on the desk with your wrist flexed backward as you type. Train yourself to hold your wrists up while you're typing (like your piano teacher taught you) or rest them on a wrist rest. Some mice conform to the shape of your hand and may result in less strain. You can also alleviate wrist strain by adjusting the angle of your keyboard. You can angle most keyboards so the back is slightly higher than the front.

5 Ergonomic Keyboards

Part of the problem with most computer keyboards is that they force you to hold your hands at an unnatural angle to your arms; your hands are both more horizontal to the desk than they'd like to be and rotated slightly outward at the wrist. Microsoft makes an ergonomic keyboard in which the left-hand and right-hand keys are slightly separated and angled outwards. (The angle between the keys cannot be adjusted.) There are similar keyboards available from third-party vendors.

6 Rest Your Eyes

Many people also experience some eye strain after staring at a computer screen for a few hours. The best approach here is to rest your eyes periodically by focusing on a distant object once in awhile, and blinking often. Also make sure you have proper lighting. Avoid overhead lights; they almost always reflect off your screen. The best source of lighting is probably a desk or floor lamp or track lights that are not directly aimed at your screen. Beautiful as it is, sunlight streaming in the windows usually leads to glare as well.

7 Find a Good Chair

Finally, if you have back problems (or want to avoid them), a good chair is essential. Look for one that provides support for your lower back and is fully adjustable. (You should be able to change both the height of the seat and the angle of the seat and the back.)

End

Notes

Breaks Are Important

One of the best ways to baby your body while using a computer is to take frequent and regular breaks. At least once an hour, take a minute or two to stand up, stretch your arms, turn your head from side to side, roll your shoulders around, and flex and extend your wrists.

Use a Glare Screen

If you're suffering from eye strain, you might want to try a glare screen. These screens, which you can buy for about $20, are usually made of very fine wire mesh, to fit over the front of your monitor—cutting down on glare and, in many cases, sharpening the contrast between light and dark.

Topic

5

Using Windows

*A*s you learned in Chapter 1, "The Basics," operating systems are programs that enable computers to operate. They help control the flow of information from one part of the computer to another, and serve as an intermediary between application programs and hardware. Learning at least a little bit about your operating system is an essential step in learning to use your computer. In fact, the more you learn about the operating system, the more you will understand both your hardware and the application programs that use the operating system as their base.

Windows is the most widely used operating system for PCs. This chapter introduces the Windows environment and explains how to load application programs within Windows and how to use Windows to perform disk housekeeping operations such as copying, renaming, and deleting files. It also explores many of the features common to Windows application programs as well as to Windows itself—things such as windows, dialog boxes, and menus.

Because virtually all PCs are now sold with Windows preinstalled, I will assume that Windows is already on your computer. If this is not the case, see the documentation that came with your copy of Windows for installation instructions.

This chapter covers Windows XP, the most recent version of Windows as of this writing. If you are using an older version of Windows such as Windows 98 or 95, you will notice a number of differences, both in appearance and functionality. In that case you should probably either buy a book (such as Sams Publishing's *How to Use Windows 98* or *How to Use Windows: Millennium Edition*) on your version of Windows or upgrade to XP. ●

What's So Great About Windows?

Windows is an operating environment created by Microsoft. It provides users of PCs with what's known as a *graphical user interface* (GUI)—that is, an environment based largely on pictures, buttons, and menu options on the screen rather than on typed commands. Issuing orders in Windows programs is a matter of clicking pictures on the screen or making selections from menus (onscreen lists of options). If you forget how to perform a particular task, you can often refresh your memory simply by poking around on the screen and seeing which choices are available.

2 Similar Commands and Menu Systems

Almost all Windows programs also feature similar menu systems and at least a few of the same commands. To leave most Windows applications, you choose the Exit option from a menu named File. After you have mastered one Windows program, it's fairly easy to learn the next.

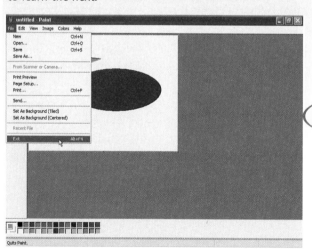

Begin

1 Windows Programs Look and Behave the Same

Most programs designed to run within Windows look and behave similarly. Windows application programs are populated with entities such as *icons* (pictures that represent data files, programs, or folders), *dialog boxes* (frames that display information and/or ask you questions), and, as you might guess, *windows* (frames in which programs and data are displayed).

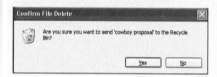

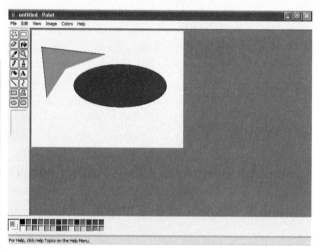

3 Running Several Programs at Once

Windows also enables you to run multiple programs at once. If you're just getting started with computers, this feature may seem of limited value: Why would you want to run two programs at once when you're still feeling overwhelmed by the first one? After you get a little more comfortable with your system, however, you may find this feature invaluable.

4 Switching Between Open Applications

Imagine getting a phone call about your latest sales figures when you're in the middle of typing a letter in your word processing program. If you are using Windows, you can easily open your spreadsheet program and find the necessary information without leaving your word processing program. When you're done, a single mouse click or keystroke will take you back to your word processing document, and you can pick up exactly where you left off.

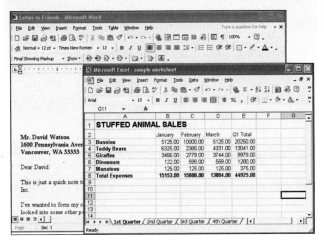

5 The Windows Clipboard

Windows also includes a feature known as the Clipboard that enables you to easily copy or move data from one program to another. (And, you can do this using the same Cut, Copy, and Paste commands in almost all Windows programs.) This means that you can copy those sales figures directly from your spreadsheet into your word processing document without having to use any special importing or exporting commands. You'll learn more about the Clipboard later in the chapter.

People multitask all the time: reading while watching television, talking on the phone while cooking dinner, chewing gum while jogging.

6 Multitasking: Doing Lots of Things at Once

Windows not only enables you to open two (or more) programs at once, it enables you to carry out work in both programs simultaneously. If you need to perform a time-consuming task in one program—such as copying a large file from the Internet—you can simply start the process and then switch to a different program. The first task will continue unattended while you work in the second. This capability to work on two or more things at once is called *multitasking*. It's the computer equivalent of patting your head while rubbing your stomach.

End

Notes

Equipment You Need to Run Windows

To run Windows XP, you need a fairly powerful PC, one with both a reasonably fast CPU (a 500MHz Pentium is recommended) and a substantial amount of memory (at least 64MB, although 128MB is better). You also need a monitor and video adapter card capable of displaying graphics. (A video card is an expansion board that enables your computer to "talk to" your monitor. You'll learn more about monitors and video adapter cards in Chapter 7, "More About Hardware.") Almost all new computers come with all the necessary horsepower, so if you bought your computer after 2000, it's probably Windows XP–capable. Windows XP comes preinstalled on most computers sold in the second half of 2001 and later.

The Windows Desktop

In the old days, a family computer could easily become a battleground. Mom would set things up just the way she liked them, only to have Junior come along and change all her settings. Then Dad would pop on and change the desktop image to something he liked, or perhaps even adjust the screen saver. Windows XP helps take the hassle out of shared computing by enabling the users of a particular computer to have their own accounts, with their own settings tailored to their preferences.

2 The Windows Desktop

After you've selected the user account you want, you arrive at a screen known as the Windows *desktop*. The desktop is a metaphor for your workspace—the surface on which you spread out any file folders, programs, and documents you want to use. Technically, the desktop is the area behind all the objects on the screen, including any windows that you open. A typical Windows desktop is populated with the little labeled pictures known as *icons*. Think of icons as doorways, each of which leads to a particular document, program, or folder. When you double-click an icon, you open it up into the rectangular frame called a window. (You only need to single-click if you've set up Windows to behave like a Web browser; you'll learn more about this in a moment.) The icons that appear on your desktop when you start Windows provide quick access to the "places" on your computer that you visit most often. (If they don't, you can add or subtract icons until your desktop suits you better.)

1 User Accounts

When you first start Windows XP, the program will ask you to create user accounts for everyone who will be using this computer. When this is complete, you'll be greeted by a screen with a list of user accounts each time you sign on to Windows. User accounts can be protected with passwords, so no one else can see your setup and files. Simply click the appropriate account name (and enter a password if required), and Windows will locate the settings for that account and open it up.

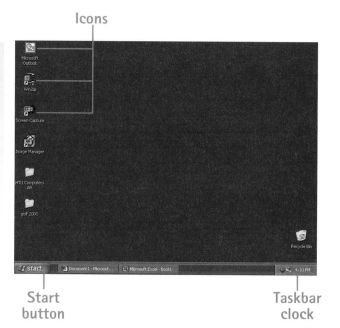

Icons

Start button

Taskbar clock

The desktop is your computerized workspace. It's where you put programs, file folders, and documents.

3 Folder Icons

Folder icons open into folder windows that reveal the contents of particular folders in your computerized filing system. (This window is currently displayed in standard view. If you display a window in Web-page view, it will contain a few additional elements.)

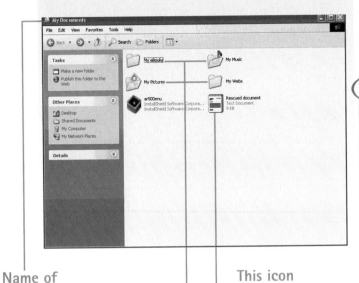

Name of folder.

This icon represents a file.

These icons represent folders.

4 Program Icons

Program icons open into application programs—that is, they load the associated programs into memory and start them running.

5 Document Icons

Document icons open into documents. When you double-click a document icon, Windows starts the application (word processing program, spreadsheet, database, or whatever) in which the document was created, and then opens the document (data file) itself.

6 Shortcut Icons

Shortcut icons provide alternative entryways to programs, documents, drives, and folders. Shortcut icons always have arrows on them, and their labels frequently contain the words "Shortcut to." You'll learn all about shortcuts and how they differ from other icons under "Creating and Using Shortcuts."

7 Special Icons

Your desktop may also contain a few specialized icons, including the Recycle Bin and possibly others. The Recycle Bin is discussed later in this chapter. See the Windows Help system for further details. (You'll learn to use the Help system later in this chapter.)

Notes

Launching Programs When You Turn On Your Computer

Windows can be configured to launch a particular program as soon as you reach the desktop. You can return to the desktop by minimizing or closing the application.

Your Welcome to Windows

You may also see a dialog box with the heading *Welcome to Windows XP*. If you grow tired of seeing this dialog box, uncheck the **Show this screen each time Windows starts** box by clicking it with your mouse.

Changing User Accounts

User accounts can be changed, users added and deleted, and so on, at any time. Simply open the Start menu, select Control Panels, and then open the User Accounts area and make the changes you need.

End

Making Your Desktop Behave Like a Web Page

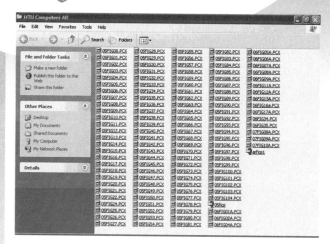

Begin

One of the nice things about Windows is that it enables you to make your desktop behave more like a Web page. (If you're not sure what the Web is or what Web pages are, you can read up on this topic in Chapter 8.) You can set up Windows to enable you to single-click instead of double-click icons to launch programs and open folders. You can also turn your desktop into an "active desktop" that can display active content from Web sites you choose. As just one example, you could have the weather report on your desktop, constantly updated so you're getting the current weather.

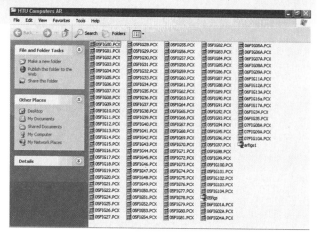

1 Turning on Single-Click Mode

If your mouse pointer looks like an arrow rather than a hand with the index finger extended when you point to items on the desktop or within a folder window, the single-click option is not turned on. To turn it on, choose My Computer from the **Start** menu. Open the Tools menu and choose **Folder Options** from the submenu. In the Folder Options dialog box, select the **General** tab, and click the button for "Single click to open an item." When you point to items on the desktop and in folder windows, the mouse pointer looks like a hand with an extended index figure. You can now single-click instead of double-click items. For example, you can click once on program icons on the desktop to launch those programs. Clicking once on documents within a folder window will open those files, as well as launch the appropriate application, if necessary.

2 Selecting Items When Single-Click Mode Is On

If you want to *select* an item on the desktop or within a folder window instead of opening it, just point to it. (Pointing to select an item is sometimes called *hovering*.) In a moment, it'll be selected—most likely it will be highlighted in blue. (Be careful: If you accidentally click items instead of pointing to them, you'll open the program, document, or folder you clicked, instead of just selecting it.) You'll learn more about selecting under "Selecting, Renaming, and Deleting Files and Folders."

3 Using the Forward and Back Buttons

The Standard Buttons toolbar displayed by default in folder windows and the Explorer includes Forward and Back buttons. (These buttons may not be available when you first open the window because you haven't "traveled" anywhere yet.) As in a browser, the Back button takes you to the previous folder window you were viewing, and, if you have clicked the Back button, the Forward button enables you to move forward through the sequence of windows.

4 The Back and Forward Button Drop-Down Lists

The Back and Forward buttons have associated drop-down lists that you can use if you've gone back or forward through several windows. For example, if you opened the My Computer window, opened a window for drive C, went to the Program Files folder, went to the Microsoft Office folder, and finally went to the Office folder, the Back drop-down list would look like this:

5 The Back Button Versus the Up Button

Don't confuse the Back button with the Up button on the Buttons toolbar. The Up button always moves you to the "parent" folder of the current folder (the folder one up in the folder hierarchy), whereas the Back button just moves you to whatever folder window you were in previously.

6 Maximizing a Window

When a window is maximized, it takes up the entire screen area. To maximize a window, you click the button directly to the left of the X in the upper-right corner. When a window is maximized, you see an additional menu on the left side of the folder, including shortcuts to the desktop, My Computer, and more. When you select a file, it also shows information and options for the file, such as renaming it, moving it, and the like. You also see information about the file, such as its size and the date it was modified.

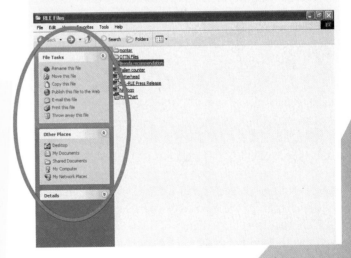

Notes

Switching Back to the Classic Desktop

If you're not used to the Web-page view desktop, you may have trouble adjusting to the new environment. You may accidentally open files when you mean to select them. To return to the original mouse behavior, open the **Start** menu, choose My Computer, and select **Folder Options** from the Tools menu. Then select the button for double-clicking to open the file, and click **OK.**

End

TOPIC 4

The Taskbar

Begin

The Windows taskbar is the bar with the word "Start" at the left end. It is usually located at the bottom of the desktop, but you can move it elsewhere. The taskbar is "control central" for Windows. Unless you go out of your way to hide it, the taskbar usually stays onscreen all the time, regardless of whether you're looking at the desktop or at an application program. It tells you which programs are currently running, which folder windows are open, and in most cases, what time it is. It also gives you access to a list of options known as the Start menu, which you can use to launch programs, find files, activate the Windows Help system, change the way Windows behaves, and shut down your computer.

These task buttons tell you that Microsoft Word and Microsoft Outlook are running.

1 The Start Button

The taskbar contains several sections. At the left edge is the Start button (the button with the word "Start" and the Windows logo). Clicking this button opens the Start menu, which you can use to start Windows applications, open documents, get help, and much more.

2 Task Buttons

In the center section of the taskbar, you will see one button for each program that your system is currently running, and one for every folder that's currently open on your desktop. This collection of buttons (known as *task buttons*) not only provides a running status report on your working environment, it gives you a quick means of switching from one folder or application to the next: Whenever you click a task button, Windows immediately activates the associated window or program. You can click the task button a second time to minimize the window you just activated.

3 Multiple Task Buttons

When you first start Windows, this middle section of the taskbar will probably be empty. As you begin opening folder windows and starting programs, however, the taskbar will grow a bit more crowded. When the taskbar becomes full, Windows combines similar task buttons every time you open a new folder window or application. So, if you have three different Microsoft Word documents open, you can access any one of them by clicking the Word task button, and selecting the filename from the pull-up list of files.

4 The Tray

The rightmost section of the taskbar is called the *tray*. It usually contains a clock that displays the current time (or at least the time your computer thinks it is). To display the current date, hold the mouse pointer over the clock for a moment. You can change the time or date by double-clicking the clock. As described in the Notes section, you can get rid of the clock altogether. The tray can also hold icons for various utility programs, such as the program that handles your connection to the Internet or the program that monitors the status of your battery on a laptop computer.

End

_____ *Notes*

What If You Don't See the Taskbar?

If you don't see the taskbar on your desktop, move the mouse pointer all the way to the edge of the screen (start by moving to the bottom) to see if one appears. If so, the taskbar's auto-hide feature was turned on to save room on the screen. To turn this feature on or off, right-click the taskbar, select **Properties**, and click the **Auto-hide the taskbar** check box to add or remove the check mark. Then click **OK** to close the dialog box and put your change into effect.

Expanding Your Taskbar

If your taskbar gets too crowded with task buttons, you can also expand it by dragging its innermost edge. (The innermost edge is the edge closest to the middle of the screen. If your taskbar is positioned at the bottom of the screen, as it usually is, the innermost edge is the top edge.) You can also make room by getting rid of the clock: Right-click the taskbar, choose **Properties**, click the box labeled **Show the clock** to remove the check mark inside the box, and select **OK**.

Working with Windows

The Windows program gets its name from its most ubiquitous feature: the rectangular frames, called *windows*, that you encounter at every turn. Just about everything that happens in the Windows environment takes place inside a window.

1 Application Windows and Document Windows

There are two types of windows in Windows. An *application window* houses either a program or a folder. A *document window* is a window that you open inside an application window. It contains data specific to that program.

Begin

These buttons affect the document windows.

These buttons affect the application windows.

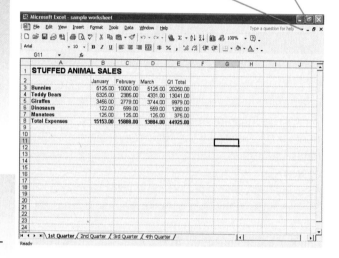

The application window for Microsoft Excel (a spreadsheet program), maximized.

2 Documents and Applications

If you load the word processing program Microsoft Word, for example, a Word application window appears on the screen. Then, every time you open or create a document in Word, it is displayed in its own document window within this main window. Document windows always reside inside application windows. If you close an application window, any document windows it contains are closed as well. (You can, however, close document windows without necessarily closing their application window.)

3 Maximized Windows

When document windows are maximized (as in the Excel document window shown in the previous figure), they fill the entire application window and are a little bit hard to distinguish from the application window. When they're not maximized, they have their own window frames and are much easier to make out. You can restore a document to maximized status by clicking the Restore Window button, which is in the upper-right corner and resembles an open window.

4 Arranging Your Desktop

Windows enables you to arrange your electronic desktop any way you like. You can work with one window at a time or several. You can move the windows around, shrink them, expand them, arrange them side by side, pile them on top of each other, and so on. In short, you can keep your electronic desktop as Spartan or as cluttered as your other desk. (As with a physical desk, however, the more chaotic your Windows desktop, the harder it becomes to find what you need when you need it.)

5 The Window with the "Focus"

Although most applications enable you to open multiple document windows at once, only one of those document windows can be active at any moment. This window is said to have *focus*. The document window with focus is the one that will respond to your next keystrokes or commands. Its title bar is always the same color as the title bar of its application window. (See the next section for information on title bars.) If the document windows overlap, the one with focus is always on top of the stack.

6 Jumping Off from a Window

Windows XP has added new functionality to most windows, including folder windows. There's a new menu down the left side of a maximized folder that gives options related to the folder itself, the files or programs within it. It enables users to have a quick jumping-off point to related topics, or to easily handle simple tasks, such as renaming a file.

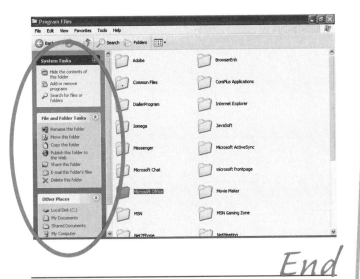

End

Notes

Arranging Windows on the Screen: Tiling and Cascading

Most application programs have several options in the Window menu that make it easy to arrange document windows. Options that refer to tiling will "tile" the currently open windows, reducing them in size and displaying them side by side. Options for "cascading" windows will display the open windows in an overlapping fashion, with the active window on top and all other windows with just their title bars showing.

Moving and Resizing Windows

In addition to tiling and cascading windows, there is a whole slew of strategies for moving and resizing the windows on your screen. You'll learn about many of these shortly, under "Having Your Way with Windows" and "Moving, Resizing, and Closing Windows."

Having Your Way with Windows

All the windows you'll encounter in Windows are very malleable: You can expand, shrink, push, pull, and rearrange them to your heart's content. When you first open a window, it may occupy less than the entire screen. If so, you can maximize the window to make it larger. If you instead need the window to be smaller, you can restore it to its previous size. If you want to reduce the window to the size of a small button, you can also minimize it.

Begin

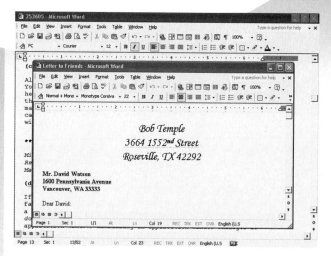

Resized window

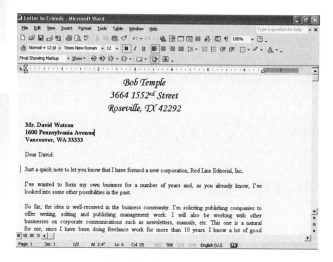

Maximized window

1 Maximizing Windows

If you want more room to work in, you can expand the window as far as possible by clicking its **Maximize** button, which looks like a tiny window with a title bar across the top. Maximizing the application window enlarges it so it fills the entire screen.

2 Restoring Windows

After you have maximized a window, the Maximize button itself is replaced by a **Restore** button, which contains a picture of two overlapping windows. Clicking this button restores the window to its previous size—that is, the size it was just before you maximized it.

3 Minimizing Windows

To minimize a window, click its **Minimize** button. This is the button to the left of the Maximize/Restore button that looks like a little dash.

4 Restoring a Minimized Document or Application

When you minimize an application window, it disappears from the screen, but its task button remains on the taskbar. You can restore the window at any time by clicking once on this task button. You can minimize it once more by clicking its taskbar button a second time. In some programs, you can also minimize just a document, while leaving the application window on screen. When you do this, the minimized document usually becomes a small box in the lower-left corner of the application window.

Minimized applications in the taskbar

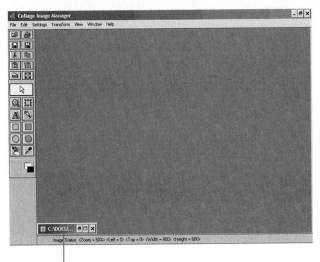

Minimized document in an application

5 Managing Your Desktop

Minimizing a window is rather like placing it on a corner of your desk. You're not putting it away completely; you're just removing it from the center of your attention, with the aim of returning to it later. (In more technical terms, when you minimize a window, you shrink it on the screen but leave it in memory.)

End

Notes

When Document Windows Are Maximized

When you maximize a document window, its title bar merges with that of the application window, and the title reflects both the program and document names. You also get two sets of Control menu icons and two sets of sizing buttons, which can be a little confusing. The Control menu icon and sizing buttons at opposite ends of the title bar affect the application window. The ones on the next row, to the left and right of the menu bar, control the document window. In many applications, document windows are maximized by default.

Another Way to Maximize and Restore Windows

Another way to maximize and restore windows is by double-clicking their title bars. If the window is not maximized, double-clicking its title bar expands it to full screen; if it's already maximized, double-clicking the title bar restores it to its previous size. (You have to double-click in this case, regardless of whether you have enabled single-clicking.)

7

Moving, Resizing, and Closing Windows

Not only can you minimize, maximize, and restore windows, you can also fine-tune a window's size by dragging its borders with the mouse. You can also use the mouse to change the location of nonmaximized windows. Finally, there are several simple ways of closing windows that you don't need to work with any longer.

Begin

1 Moving Windows

You can move a window on the screen (if it isn't maximized) by dragging its title bar with the mouse.

2 Resizing Windows

You also use your mouse to resize a window (again, if it isn't maximized). Start by slowly moving the mouse pointer across the border until the pointer changes into a double-headed arrow. Then press the left mouse button and hold it down as you drag the border of the window. When the window is the desired size, release the mouse button. If you want to change both the height and width of a window, drag one of its corners.

To move a window, drag its title bar.

To widen or narrow a window, drag its right or left border.

To expand or shrink a window in both directions, drag on a corner.

To make a window taller or shorter, drag its bottom or top border.

3 Another Way to Resize Windows

Some windows even have a special border in the lower-right corner that makes it easier to resize them. Just drag this border to resize the window's height and width at the same time. Even if the window doesn't have the special border, however, it can usually be resized by clicking in the very bottom-right corner.

4 Closing Windows

To close a window, you can click the Close (X) button in the window's upper-right corner.

5 Using the Control Menu

You can also manipulate windows via their Control menus—a menu that appears when you click the Control menu icon in the window's upper-left corner. To close a window, just select the **Close** option from the Control menu. In many cases, the Control menu will contain options for moving, resizing, minimizing, and maximizing the window.

6 Closing Windows with Key Combinations

You can also close windows using key combinations. To close a document window, press Ctrl+F4. To close an application window (including a folder window), press Alt+F4. (Remember, with key combinations, you hold down the first key while pressing and then releasing the second key.)

8 Closing Minimized Applications

If a file or application is minimized, you can even close it without restoring it first. Just right-click its icon in the taskbar, and select Close from the menu that appears.

End

7 Closing Windows with the File Menu

Finally, you can close an application window by opening the File menu and selecting the last option. (You'll learn to work with menus shortly.) This option will be named Close if you're in a folder window; otherwise, it will be called Exit. You can close a document window by opening the **File** menu and choosing **Close**.

Notes

What It Means to Close a Window

Bear in mind that closing a window means removing its contents from memory. In the case of document windows, this just means removing data from memory and from the screen. (Assuming that you've saved the document, the saved copy remains on the disk.) In the case of application windows, closing a window means leaving the program.

Getting Some Practice

If you want to try manipulating a window for practice, just double-click the **My Computer** icon in the Start menu to open a folder window. (You can single-click if you're using Web-page view.) Then try dragging the folder window around the screen, resizing it, maximizing it, minimizing it (notice that it disappears from the screen and appears as a button on the taskbar), restoring it (by clicking the button on the taskbar), and then closing it.

Working with Menus

As you have seen, you can perform many operations in Windows just by clicking, double-clicking, or dragging with your mouse, but other tasks require you to work with menus, telling the computer what you want it to do by selecting options from onscreen lists. There are four main types of menus in Windows and in most Windows applications: menu bars, pull-down menus, submenus, and context menus.

Begin

1 The Menu Bar

Most application windows (including folder windows) sport menu bars just below their title bars. The menu bar generally looks like a set of words, such as File, Edit, View, and Help, laid out horizontally starting at the left edge of the screen. If you'd like to see one now, click the **My Computer** icon from the Start menu and note the words near the top of the My Computer window.

2 Selecting Menu Options

To select an option from a menu bar, you can click the option with your mouse. For example, to select File and thereby open the File menu, you simply click the word **File** in the menu bar. You can also hold down the Alt key and press the underlined letter in the option name. To select File, for instance, you would press Alt+F. To then select an option from the menu, just point to it and click. Note that if you start to select either a menu option or a button on the screen and then change your mind, move the mouse pointer to a blank area of the screen before you release the mouse button.

3 Submenus

In some cases, selecting an option from one menu evokes another menu with a more specific set of options. (Menu options that lead to submenus typically have arrows to their right.) Whenever you point to a menu option that leads to a submenu, the menu automatically appears to the right of the current menu; if there is no room to the right, the submenu will appear to the left.

4 Selecting from a Submenu

To select an option from that submenu, slide your mouse pointer directly to the right (or left if the submenu is to the left). Then, when your pointer is positioned on the submenu, move up or down as necessary to point to the desired option, and click the option to select it. You can also select options from pull-down or submenus by using the Up Arrow or Down Arrow key to highlight the option and then pressing Enter, or typing the underlined letter in the option name.

5 Closing a Menu

To close a pull-down menu without making any selections, click anywhere outside the menu. If you prefer using the keyboard, you can either press Alt once or press Esc twice. To close a submenu, point to another option on the menu to its left or press Esc.

6 Shortcut Keys

Many menus have the names of keys or key combinations displayed to the right of some menu options. You can use these keys, known as *hot keys* or *shortcut keys,* as an alternative to using the menu system—pressing the accelerator key has exactly the same effect as selecting the associated menu option. Three of the most useful accelerator keys are Ctrl+C (equivalent to opening the Edit menu and choosing the Copy option), Ctrl+X (equivalent to choosing the Cut option from the Edit menu), and Ctrl+V (equivalent to choosing the Paste option from the Edit menu).

7 Other Menu Conventions

Several other conventions are used in Windows menus to convey information about particular menu options. As mentioned, menu options that lead to submenus have arrows to their right. Check marks or black circles (typically to the left of the option name) indicate that the option is in effect. These are often called toggle switches or buttons; choosing them once turns them on and choosing them again turns them off. Options followed by ellipses (...) lead to dialog boxes, which you'll learn about next. Finally, in some Windows programs, when you point to an option on a pull-down menu or submenu, a short description of that option appears in the status bar at the bottom of the window.

8 Context Menus

Context menus appear when you right-click an object on the screen. (Such menus are sometimes called *object menus* or *shortcut menus* as well.) Each context menu is essentially a list of the operations you can perform. The content of the menu therefore varies from one type of object to the next. If you right-click a folder icon, for example, you'll see a menu with options such as Open, Copy, Delete, and Rename. If you right-click the icon for a floppy disk, you'll get a context menu that includes Copy Disk and Format. Most Windows applications employ context menus as well. If you right-click text in Word, you'll see a context menu for altering the selected text.

End

Talking to Dialog Boxes

Dialog boxes are special windows that appear when a program needs more information before it can complete an operation you've requested. (Think of them as computerized questionnaires.) Sometimes expressing your preferences in a dialog box is a simple matter of clicking command buttons labeled Yes, No, OK, or Cancel. Other times, it involves stating your preferences via onscreen devices such as list boxes, drop-down list boxes (also known as combo boxes), check boxes, spinners, text fields, sliders, and radio buttons (also known as option buttons). Most of these items are shown in the following figure.

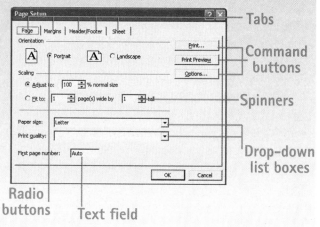

Radio buttons   Text field

Tabs
Command buttons
Spinners
Drop-down list boxes

Begin

1 Radio Buttons

Radio buttons are sometimes called option buttons. Clicking one button selects that option (the button becomes dark) and deselects any other selected option button in the group. In other words, the options are mutually exclusive.

2 Check Boxes

Check boxes are boxes that you can click to select or deselect. (Selected check boxes usually display an *X* or a check mark.) Often these options are not mutually exclusive—that is, you can select more than one of them.

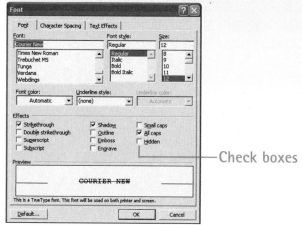

Check boxes

3 Spinners

With spinners, you can click the up arrow to increase the value or the down arrow to decrease it. (Spinners are sometimes called *spin boxes.*) You can also type values in the associated text field if that seems easier.

4 Text Fields

You can enter text or numbers in text fields. For example, you could type **10** in the **First Page Number** text field to have 10 be the first page number.

5 Drop-Down Lists

In drop-down list boxes, you can click the downward-pointing arrow to display a drop-down list box of options from which you can choose. Regular list boxes are similar but show more than one option at a time.

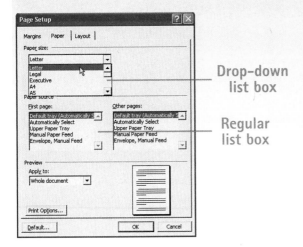

Drop-down list box

Regular list box

6 Command Buttons

You click command buttons to carry out an action or to display another dialog box. Command buttons that lead to dialog boxes have ellipses after their names, much like menu items that lead to dialog boxes.

7 Tabs

Some dialog boxes feature tabs, much like the plastic tabs in many notebooks. For example, the dialog box in the figure at the beginning of this topic has four tabs: Page, Margins, Header/Footer, and Sheet. You can switch from one of these "pages" of options to another page, with a whole new set of options, by clicking the appropriate tab.

8 Leaving a Dialog Box

When you're done with a dialog box, you usually both leave it and put your changes into effect by clicking a button labeled either **OK** or **Close**. If you decide to cancel the operation the dialog box is asking you about, click the button labeled **Cancel**, press Esc, or click the **Close (X)** button in the window's upper-right corner. In many cases, the OK button will be the default command button, so you can select it just by pressing Enter. (You can tell which button is the default because it has a darker border than the other buttons and may have a rectangle of dots surrounding its label.)

End

Getting to Work

Windows' main purpose is to serve as a platform for applications software, a launch pad for more goal-oriented word processing, database, and spreadsheet programs (among others). There are two approaches to getting to work in Windows: 1) You can open an existing document or create a new document from the desktop, and Windows will automatically launch the appropriate application. If you open a document created in a particular word processing program, for example, Windows will launch that program and then open the specified document. 2) You can start the program you want to use and then either open an existing document or create a new one.

Begin

1 Creating Documents

Not all applications require or even allow you to create documents. For example, playing a game or using the Windows calculator does not involve creating a document. In both cases, you'll always start the program directly, but much of your work will involve creating documents (data files). You may find it more intuitive to open a particular document and let Windows worry about which program you used to create the document.

2 Opening an Existing Document

To get to work by opening an existing document, you can locate the icon for the document you want to use—in a folder window, in the Windows Explorer (which you'll learn about shortly), or on the desktop itself—and double-click it. (Remember, you only need to single-click if you've set up Windows to behave like a browser.)

3 Opening an Office Document

If you are using Microsoft Office, open the **Start** menu, select All Programs, and choose **Open Office Document** from the menu. You'll soon see a dialog box you can use to search for and select the desired document. (See the program documentation for details.)

4 Creating a New Document

To create a new document, you can right-click the desktop or an empty area in a folder window and choose **New**. You will see a menu that includes options for creating folders, shortcuts, and a variety of different document types. As soon as you pick one, Windows creates a new icon for the document. You can name it just by typing something else. However, don't change the file extension at the end of the filename; doing so might inhibit your ability to use the file.

5 Creating Microsoft Office Documents

If you are using Microsoft Office, another way to create a new document is to open the **Start** menu, select **All Programs**, and choose **New Office Document**. You'll see a dialog box in which you can specify the type of document you'd like to create. Later, when you save the document, you'll get to specify both a name and a location for the file.

6 Starting Programs

When you open the **Start** menu, you'll see programs listed on the left side. The top two programs are your Internet browser and e-mail program (by default). The next six programs are the ones you've used most in the last couple of weeks. If the program you want to open is listed there, just click its name. If not, select **All Programs**, and then select the program you want to use. The other option is to locate the icon for the program you want to use—in a folder window, in the Windows Explorer, or on the desktop—and double-click it.

7 Using Shortcuts to Open Documents and Applications

Windows also enables you to create special icons, known as shortcuts, that allow you easy access to a frequently used program or document. To use a shortcut, you double-click the icon. Although you can place shortcuts in folder windows, they're usually placed on the desktop itself (because the whole point is to spare you the trouble of hunting around in folders or on menus). You'll learn to make your own shortcuts in "Creating and Using Shortcuts" later in this chapter.

8 Switching Applications with the Taskbar Button

Whenever you run more than one application at a time, you'll need a method of switching from one to the next. One infallible way to switch to another open application is to click the application's button on the taskbar.

Continues

9 Switching Applications by Clicking the Application Window

If any part of the other program's application window is visible, you can click anywhere in that window to switch to that application.

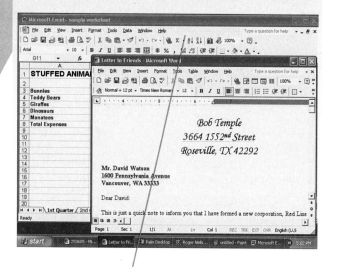

You can click anywhere in a window to activate it.

10 Switching Applications by Pressing Alt+Tab

You can also press Alt+Tab to switch between applications. When you do this, Windows displays a window in the center of the screen that contains icons representing each program you're running. If you hold down Alt and continue to press Tab, Windows cycles through the programs, enclosing one after another within a box, and listing its name at the bottom of the window. When the program you want is selected, release both keys to switch to that program.

End

Notes

The Minimize All Windows Command

Another way to quickly view the desktop again is to right-click a part of the taskbar that isn't covered by a task button and choose **Minimize All Windows** from the context menu. If you go this route, be sure to right-click the taskbar, which is usually located all the way at the bottom of the screen, rather than the status bar of your application program, which may appear just above the taskbar. If you want to "unminimize" the windows you minimized, just right-click the taskbar again and choose **Undo Minimize All**.

Active Program

As mentioned, one of the benefits of using Windows is that you can run several applications at once. No matter how many applications you open, however, only one of them is active at one time. The active program is the one that is affected by any commands you issue or data you enter. It is sometimes called the *foreground* application, because it always sits on top of the stack of application windows—in front of all the others. (Depending on whether the window is maximized, you may or may not see part of the other application windows underneath.) The foreground application is also the one that receives most of your CPU's attention. Other open applications are said to be running in the background, meaning that they continue to plod along at any tasks you have assigned to them, but they do so slowly because they are receiving a relatively small part of your CPU's brain power.

11

Working with Folder Windows

Folders are the building blocks of your computerized filing system. High-level folders called My Computer (which contains all the drives on your local computer) and, if you're part of a network, My Network Places (which provides access to drives on your network) are the foundation. Those folders contain folders for individual disk and CD-ROM drives. Those drive folders, in turn, contain file folders and individual files. The filing system can continue indefinitely—folders can contain folders, that can contain additional folders, and so on. The figure shows the basic structure of the filing system on most standalone (nonnetworked) PCs.

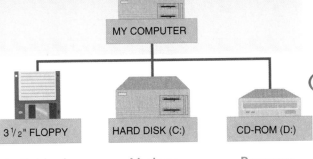

MY COMPUTER

3¹/₂" FLOPPY   HARD DISK (C:)   CD-ROM (D:)

| Individual documents and program files | Various folders containing programs, documents, and other folders | Program files, documents, and possibly folders |

Begin

1 The My Computer Folder

The My Computer folder serves as the point of entry into your computer's filing system. It is the first folder you'll open and, usually, the last one you'll close. (If you're part of a network, you'll use My Network Places to enter the network server's filing system.)

2 Opening a Folder Window

You can open a folder window by double-clicking a folder icon. If the folder you want is more than one level down in the folder hierarchy (anywhere below the My Computer or My Network Places level), you'll need to open two or more folder windows to get there—rather like those Russian nesting dolls in which one doll contains another, which contains another, and so on.

3 Parent and Child Windows

When you open one folder window from inside another, the first window (often called the parent window) usually disappears and the newly opened child window takes its place. You can get back to the parent window by using either the Up or Back button.

4 Creating a New Folder

You can create new folders by right-clicking a blank spot on the desktop or within a folder window and selecting New from the context menu. You can also open the folder window's **File** menu and select **New**, then **Folder**. Windows will create a new folder icon with the label New Folder. To rename the folder, type the name you want and press Enter.

5 Folder Options

You can change folder options for how folders look, whether you need to single- or double-click to open them, and other preferences by opening the Tools menu in any folder and selecting **Folder Options**. For example, if you want a new child window to open separate from the parent window, you would select **Open each folder in its own window** on the **General** tab.

Notes

Refreshing Folder Windows

If you insert a disk or CD into a drive while a folder window for that drive is open, you need to select **View** and choose **Refresh** to see the contents of the newly inserted disk.

End

Rules for File and Folder Names

As you learned in Chapter 4, "Up and Running," all files and folders must have names. These names should be chosen carefully. You'll want to use names that are easy to remember or at least to decipher; names that are neither so short that they're cryptic nor so long that they're tedious to read or type. You also need to be sure that your file and folder names don't include any "illegal" characters.

Begin

1 File-Naming Conventions

In Windows, the names you assign to files and folders can be up to 255 characters long. They can include spaces and periods, but there are a few characters that file and folder names cannot include:

* | < > ? / " :

2 Extensions

The names for most files include short last names known as *extensions* that are usually used to identify the file type. (Extensions can be anywhere from one to three characters long.) Programs that use extensions add them to your filenames automatically. If you name a file "Letter to Friends" in Word for Windows, for example, the full filename becomes Letter to Friends.doc. (The period and the doc extension are added by the program itself.) Here are some examples of common file extensions:

.doc	.tif
.xls	.tmp
.pcx	

4 Seeing the Extensions

If you prefer to see the extensions, open the **View** menu, and choose **Folder Options**. Select the **View** tab in the resulting dialog box, deselect the check box labeled **Hide extensions for known file types**, and click **OK**. This change applies to all folder and Explorer windows, not just the one that's active at the moment.

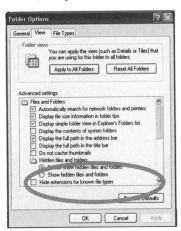

3 Some Extensions Aren't Displayed

Windows maintains its own Registry of file types and the associated extensions. By default, Windows does not display any extensions it recognizes. This means that even though your full filename is **Letter to Friends.doc**, it appears as **Letter to Friends** in folder and Explorer windows.

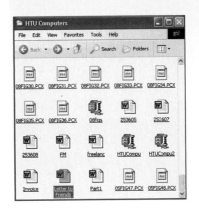

End

Changing Your View of a Folder Window

Windows provides five ways of representing the items in a folder window. By default, the items in a folder window are usually displayed in what's known as the Icons view. You can change to a different view, using the View option on the window's menu bar. In the View menu, you'll see options for Thumbnails, Tiles, Icons, List, and Details.

Begin

1 Thumbnails View

In Thumbnails view, each drive, folder, or file is shown as a large icon that looks like a small version of the opened file. Some programs don't allow thumbnails, however, so not all files will be seen this way.

2 Tiles View

In Tiles view, each drive, folder, or file is shown as a large icon with a name and description to its right. In this view, the items are arranged vertically.

3 Icons View

In Icons view, each drive, folder or file is shown as a large icon with the name beneath it. The files are arranged horizontally.

4 List View

In List view, each drive, folder or file is shown as a small icon with the name to the right, and the icons are arranged vertically.

5 Details View

Details view gives you more information, displaying not only item names, but also each item's size, type (folder or file type), and the date the item was last modified. You can change column widths in Details view by dragging the borders between the column headings.

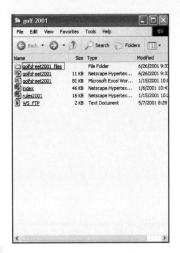

6 Sorting Icons

To sort icons, open the **View** menu and choose **Arrange Icons By**. Then you can sort by name, type, size, or date last modified.

7 Sorting Files in Details View

To sort the items in Details view, click a column heading. Clicking **Size** sorts the list by file size. Clicking **Name** sorts it alphabetically by filename. (Clicking the column heading again reverses the sort order; for example, if the names were sorted from A to Z, clicking the Name column again would sort the names from Z to A.)

8 Arranging Icons

If you want Windows to automatically preserve a particular arrangement within a view, open the **View** menu, choose **Arrange Icons By**, and select **Auto Arrange**. After Auto Arrange is turned on, any new items you add to the folder are instantly escorted to their proper place in the order you've specified. If you drag an icon out of position, it snaps right back. If you delete an icon, the remaining ones immediately close ranks. The advantage of leaving Auto Arrange off is that you may create your own clusters of icons within a folder window.

Notes

Additional File Information

The Details view tells you when a file was last modified. To find out when it was created or last opened, right-click the filename or icon and choose **Properties** from the context menu.

How Files Are Sorted

The sort order you establish in Details view carries over to any other view you choose. If you sort items by size in Details view, for example, they remain sorted by size when you switch to Large Icons view.

End

Selecting, Renaming, and Deleting Files and Folders

The more you use your computer, the more files and folders you are likely to accumulate. Learning to handle these files and folders is an essential part of using your computer well. There are actually two environments in which you can carry out file system maintenance in Windows. For now, we'll focus on using folder windows. Later, you'll learn to perform the same operations using the Windows Explorer.

Notes

Undo

If you delete one or more files and then change your mind before you've deleted, copied, renamed, or created any other file, you can reverse the deletion by right-clicking a blank spot on the desktop or in a folder window and selecting **Undo Delete** from the context menu. If it's too late for that technique, you can also undo deletions using the Recycle Bin folder.

Begin

1 Find Your File

The first step in manipulating a file or folder using folder windows is to drill down through the folder hierarchy until you reach the window that contains the associated icon.

2 Select Your File

Next, select the file or folder. To select one item, just click its name or icon. If Web-page view is on, you can point to items to select them in folder windows and on the desktop. Don't click or you'll open the folder or document unintentionally! The selected item will be "highlighted" in a different color.

3 Selecting Multiple Files

To select multiple items, click one and then hold down **Ctrl** while you click others. If Web-page view is on, you should hold down **Ctrl** while pointing (not clicking) when you're working on the desktop or within folder windows. If the items you want to select are contiguous, an easy way to select them is to click the first (highest or leftmost) one you want to select and then hold down **Shift** while you click the last (lowest or rightmost), or vice versa. (Again, if Web-page view is on, point rather than click.)

4 Selecting by Dragging

You can select several adjacent items by "lassoing" them. Move the mouse pointer to a spot slightly above and to the left of the group of items and then drag to a point just below and to the right of the items. As you drag, Windows displays a dotted rectangle around the group of items you are lassoing. As soon as you release the mouse button, all the items inside the rectangle become selected. If you're using Web-page view, make sure that the mouse pointer looks like an arrow (not a pointing hand) when you begin to drag. And no matter which window style you're using, make sure that you're not pointing directly at a file or folder when you begin to drag.

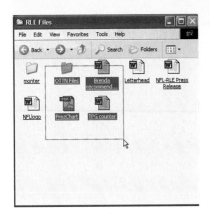

5 Selecting Everything

To select everything in the window, choose **Edit** from the menu bar and then choose **Select All** (or you can use the shortcut key **Ctrl+A**).

6 Renaming Files and Folders

You can rename a file or folder by right-clicking the icon and choosing **Rename**. Then type the desired name. This technique works whether or not single-click mode is on. If single-click mode is *not* on, you can click the file or folder's label once to select it and a second time to display an insertion point inside the label. (Be careful not to click too quickly; if Windows interprets your action as a double-click, it will open the file or folder.) Now you can type the new filename; again, make sure to leave the file extension intact. (F2 is a shortcut for renaming.)

7 Deleting Files

To delete one or more files, start by selecting the items and then press Del, drag them to the Recycle Bin icon on your desktop, or issue the **File, Delete** command. Windows asks you to confirm that you want to send the items to the Recycle Bin. Click **Yes** to go ahead and do so.

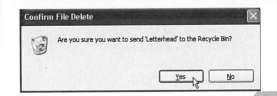

End

Copying and Moving Files and Folders

Learning to copy or move files and folders from one disk to another or one folder to another is one more crucial part of maintaining your computer's filing system. This section describes how to copy and move files using menus and using a mouse technique called drag and drop. Later in the chapter, you'll learn how to accomplish some of the same things from within Explorer.

Begin

1 Select the Items

The easiest and safest method to copy or move selected files or folders involves four steps. The first step is to select the items you want to copy or move in a folder window. If you want to copy files from a floppy disk, insert the disk in the drive, open a folder window for My Computer (from the Start menu), double-click the icon for your floppy disk drive , and select the desired files.

2 Cut or Copy

Second, issue a command to "cut" the items if you plan to move them, or "copy" them if you plan to make duplicates. You can do this either by opening the **Edit** menu and choosing **Cut** (for moving) or **Copy** (for copying) or by using shortcut keys: **Ctrl+X** cuts the selected items and **Ctrl+C** copies them. You can also just right-click the selected item and choose **Cut** or **Copy** from its context menu. (If more than one icon is selected, right-click any one of them.) Or, you can use the **Cut** and **Copy** buttons that appear in folder windows. When you cut items, the icons don't disappear right away; their outlines become dotted. As soon as you paste the items in their new location, these ghostlike icons disappear.

3 Open the Destination Folder

Third, open a folder window for the folder into which you want to copy the items. (You may need to root around in your folder hierarchy again to find the folder.)

4 Paste Them In

Finally, either right-click a blank spot within the window and choose **Paste** from the context menu or open the **Edit** menu again and choose **Paste** (or use **Ctrl+V**). You can also use the **Paste** toolbar button. You'll immediately see the items you pasted appear in the window. Alternatively, you can locate the icon for the folder into which you want to copy or move the items, right-click the icon itself, and choose **Paste** from the context menu.

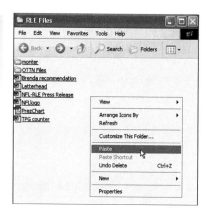

5 Copying to a Floppy

If you want to copy files from your hard drive to a floppy disk, there's an easier method. Select icons for the file(s) you want to copy. Right-click any one of the selected icons and choose **Send To**. When Windows displays a menu of places you can direct the file(s) to, choose the floppy drive option.

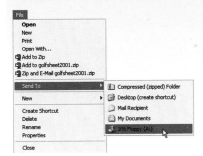

6 Moving or Copying with Drag and Drop

You can also move and copy items between folders using a feature known as *drag and drop*—that is, by using your mouse to drag selected items from one folder to another. It's safer to drag using the right mouse button rather than the left. That way, when you release the mouse button, Windows asks whether you want to copy or move the selected items. (If you drag using the left mouse button, Windows decides whether you intend to copy or move depending on whether you're dragging between folders on the same disk or on different disks.)

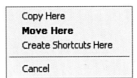

7 Be Careful When Dragging

Be wary of dragging icons within folder windows that are in List Details view; it's all too easy to rearrange your folder hierarchy by mistake. If you accidentally drag one folder on top of another, you make it a subfolder of that folder. You might want to avoid dragging icons around inside a folder window, particularly if you're using one of the views that displays large icons. If you want to move a folder, use any of the cut or copy and paste methods described previously. You're much less likely to make a mistake.

8 Using Undo

If you do drag something to the wrong place by accident, right-click a blank spot in the folder window or on the desktop and choose **Undo Move**. If you misplace either a file or folder, you can also use the **Find** command to ferret it out.

Notes

Files with the Same Name

If you try to move or copy a file to a folder that already contains a file of the same name, a dialog box asks if you want to replace the other version of the file. If you selected multiple files, your choices will be **Yes** (replace this file and then ask me about any others), **Yes to All** (replace all files of the same names), **No** (don't replace this file, but ask me about the others), and **Cancel** (stop moving or copying altogether).

End

TOPIC *16*

Using the Recycle Bin

The Recycle Bin icon on your desktop is a folder icon, even though it's not decorated with the familiar folder image. When you select one or more files or folders and either press Del or drag those items to the Recycle Bin icon, Windows does not actually erase them. It simply stores them in the Recycle Bin folder. If you have a change of heart, you can open that folder and retrieve some or all the items you previously recycled. By the same token, if you decide you really do want to delete the files and free up the space they occupy on your hard drive, you can empty the Recycle Bin.

Begin

1 What Is Not Stored in the Recycle Bin

Items deleted from either floppy disks or network servers are not stored in the Recycle Bin—they are gone for good. When you delete such items, Windows asks you to confirm the deletion. If you delete a file from within an application program, it may or may not get stored in the Recycle Bin—you'll need to try deleting one and then check.

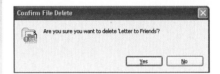

2 What Is Stored in the Recycle Bin

In contrast, when you delete items from your hard disk (by selecting them and pressing the Delete key, by dragging them to the Recycle Bin, or by right-clicking them and choosing **Delete**), you'll see a message asking whether you want to send the item or items to the Recycle Bin. (The message will be a little bit different from the one shown here if you're deleting several items or deleting a folder.)

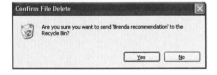

3 Finding Items in the Recycle Bin

To retrieve items from the Recycle Bin, first double-click the **Recycle Bin** icon to open it into a folder window. This window is just like other folder windows except that it includes files slated for deletion.

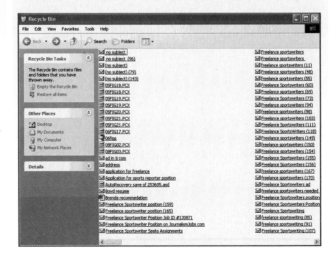

4 Restoring Files from the Recycle Bin

To recover an item from the Recycle Bin, select it, open the **File** menu, and choose **Restore**. (Alternatively, you can right-click the item and choose **Restore** from the context menu.) This puts the file back where it was when you deleted it. If you want to restore all the files from the Recycle Bin, maximize the Recycle Bin window so the tasks lists appear on the left side. Then select **Restore all items** from the task list.

5 Deleting/Restoring Folders

If you delete a folder, Windows moves the entire folder to the Recycle Bin. When you look in the Recycle Bin, you won't see any of the individual files the folder contains; you'll just see the folder itself. However, those individual files are in the Recycle Bin, too; they're still inside that folder. If you restore the folder—by choosing **Restore** from the **File** menu—Windows reinstates the folder plus its entire contents. If you just want to retain part of the folder's contents, you'll need to then individually delete the items you don't want to keep.

6 Emptying the Recycle Bin

If you are running low on disk space, you may want to empty the Recycle Bin by right-clicking the **Recycle Bin** icon and choosing **Empty Recycle Bin** from the context menu. If you're already in the Recycle Bin window, choose **Empty Recycle Bin** from the **File** menu (or the task list, if the window is maximized). You might also empty the Recycle Bin if you want to make sure that no one can easily retrieve some of the items inside. (This is almost like paper shredding, although someone with a little know-how and an undelete program could possibly get them back.)

End

Notes

How Big Is the Recycle Bin?

By default, Windows enables you to keep adding items to the Recycle Bin until it's full. (By default, the Recycle Bin is considered full when it consumes 10 percent of the space on the hard disk on which Windows was installed.) Then Windows automatically empties the Recycle Bin, freeing up that space on your hard disk for reuse.

17

Exploring Windows Explorer

Windows Explorer is a utility program that is part of Windows. You can accomplish the same tasks in Explorer as you do in folder windows—launching programs, opening documents, and copying, moving, deleting, and renaming folders and files. The main advantage of using Explorer is that it features a graphical representation of your computer's filing system. Some people find this representation a little confusing or overwhelming at first. After you get used to it, however, you'll discover that it affords a useful and coherent overview of the folder hierarchy. By giving you the big picture, Explorer makes it easier for you to see what's where and how to navigate from one location to the next.

Begin

1 Launching Explorer

To launch Explorer, either click the **Start** button, highlight **All Programs, Accessories,** and then choose **Windows Explorer,** or right-click the **Start** button and choose **Explore** from the resulting context menu. If your keyboard has a Windows logo key, you can start Explorer by holding down that key and pressing **E.** When you've launched Explorer, in the title bar, you'll see a window with the name of the folder you're in. Unlike most other windows you encounter in Windows programs, the Explorer window is divided into two sides, or *panes.* The left pane contains the diagram of your folder hierarchy; the right pane looks much like a folder window.

Name of the currently selected folder.

2 The Folder Structure

When you first start Explorer, you'll see at least four levels in the folder hierarchy: the desktop itself, the folders and other icons on the desktop (such as My Computer and the Recycle Bin), subfolders of the folders on the desktop (underneath My Computer, for example, you'll see icons for the various drives on your computer), and subfolders of the subfolders of the folders on the desktop (such as the folders on drive C).

The selected folder is usually highlighted.

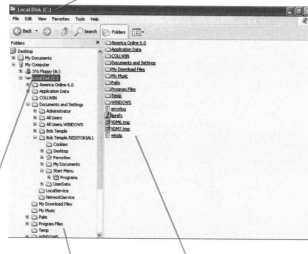

The left pane shows the folder hierarchy.

The right pane shows the contents of the folder.

3 Expanding and Contracting the Folder Hierarchy

You can expand and contract levels by clicking the plus and minus signs that appear next to some of the icons. Any icon that contains additional folders not currently shown in the hierarchy will be preceded by a plus sign. Clicking the plus sign reveals the folders inside. Any icon preceded by a minus sign has already been expanded to reveal its contents. You can contract it (hide its contents) by clicking the minus sign. Icons that have neither a plus sign nor a minus sign don't contain any additional folders.

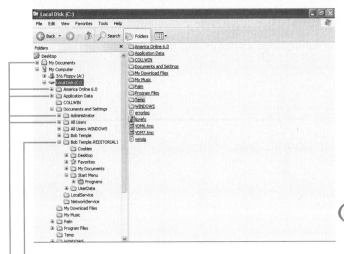

The subfolders of this folder are displayed

These folders contain hidden subfolders

5 Moving Through the Explorer Window

Each pane has its own scrollbar if it contains too much material to display all at once. You can also click somewhere in the pane to select it, and then press the Page Down or Page Up key to move down or up a windowful at a time. In addition, you can press the End key to move to the bottom of the list and Home to move back to the top.

4 Explorer's Right Pane

The right pane of the Explorer window shows the contents of the currently selected folder. The selected folder is highlighted in the folder hierarchy and its name appears in the window's title bar. As soon as you select a different folder in the left pane, the contents of the right pane change to reflect that folder's contents.

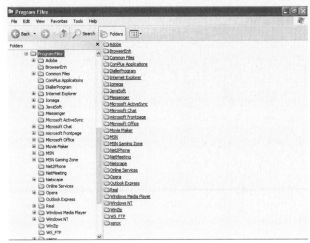

6 Opening Files and Folders in Explorer

To open files or folders within Explorer, double-click them. (If Web-page view is on, you have to double-click items in the left pane, but can single-click items in the right pane.) To launch programs from Explorer, you first need to track down the .exe file for the program. (If you don't see the file extensions, it's easy to turn them on, as described in "Rules for File and Folder Names" earlier in this chapter.) When you find the file, double-click it.

End

Notes

Changing the View

You can change your view of Explorer's right pane by making selections from the View menu. The options are the same as in any folder window: Thumbnails, Tiles, Icons, List, and Details.

Copying and Moving Items in Explorer

Windows Explorer is an excellent environment for copying and moving files and folders. The procedure is almost identical to the one you use for copying or moving items between folder windows. In Explorer, however, you have the advantage of seeing the entire folder hierarchy, so it's easier to visualize where you're copying things from and to.

Begin

1 Select the Folder

To copy or move files, in the left pane, select the folder that contains the items you want to manipulate.

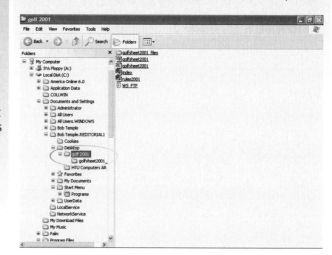

2 Select the Items to be Copied or Moved

In the right pane, select the items themselves. (You can review the techniques for selecting icons under "Selecting, Renaming, and Deleting Files and Folders" earlier in this chapter.)

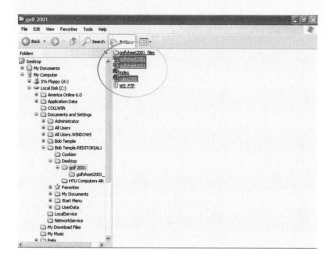

3 To Copy or Move Items

If you want to copy the selected items, issue the **Edit, Copy** command (or press its **Ctrl+C** shortcut key), or right-click one of the selected items and choose **Copy** from the context menu. If you want to move rather than copy the items, issue the **Edit, Cut** command (or press its **Ctrl+X** shortcut key), or right-click one of the selected items and choose **Cut** from the context menu. You can also click the **Copy** or **Cut** toolbar button to copy or cut the selected items.

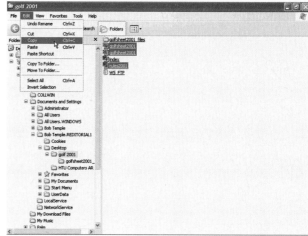

4 Find the Destination Folder

Scroll the folder hierarchy in the left pane until you can see the folder into which you want to copy the files. (Expand any folders you need to.) Select the folder and then select **Paste** from the **Edit** menu (or press Ctrl+V), right-click that folder and select **Paste**, or press the **Paste** toolbar button.

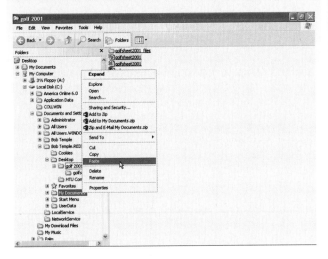

5 Copying Files to a Floppy Disk

To copy files from your hard drive to a floppy disk, just select icons for the files you want to copy. Then right-click any one of the selected icons and choose **Send To**. When Windows displays a menu of places to send the files, select the option for your floppy disk drive.

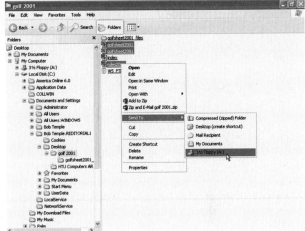

6 Copying with Drag and Drop

If you're adventurous, you can also copy or move items using drag and drop. To do this, select the items you want to copy or move from the right pane. If necessary, scroll the folder hierarchy in the left pane until the folder into which you want to paste the items is visible. Then right-drag any one of the selected items from the right pane to the desired destination folder in the left pane. Release the mouse button and, when you see the context menu, specify whether you want to copy or move the items.

End

Notes

Be Careful When Dragging

Unless you know exactly what you're doing, avoid dragging icons around in the left pane of an Explorer window; by doing so, you are actually rearranging the folder hierarchy.

Renaming Files and Folders

You can rename a file or folder in an Explorer window just as you would in a folder window: right-click its icon, choose **Rename** from the context menu, type the new name, and press Enter. Another approach is to use the **F2** shortcut key.

Creating New Folders

To create a new folder or file in an Explorer window, select the folder where you want the new file or folder to reside. Then right-click a blank spot in the right pane and select **New, Folder**.

Creating and Using Shortcuts

As you know, shortcuts are icons that provide you with quick access to a program, document, or folder, usually from the desktop. You'll most likely want to create shortcuts for programs that you use frequently. If you have an elaborate hierarchy of folders, you may want to create shortcuts for frequently used folders on your desktop—so you don't need to burrow down to get to them.

Begin

1 Creating a Shortcut

The easiest way to create a new shortcut is to right-drag an icon from a folder or Explorer window to either the desktop or the folder where you want the shortcut to reside. When Windows displays a menu of options, choose **Create Shortcut(s) Here**. (Make sure to drag using the *right* mouse button, or Windows will either move or copy the item you dragged—depending on the circumstances—without asking for your input.)

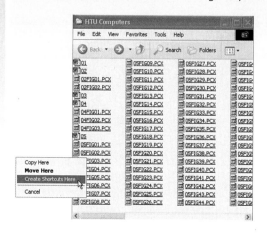

2 Shortcuts Versus Files

There's a big difference between creating a shortcut to a file on your desktop and actually moving that file to your desktop. A shortcut is nothing more than a set of directions to a file. The file itself lives elsewhere. If you delete a shortcut, you're deleting only this set of directions; the file itself stays intact and in its usual location. If you copy a shortcut, you're copying just that set of directions, you're not copying the actual file.

This is a shortcut to the Internet Explorer program, not the program file itself.

3 Shortcuts for Programs

If you want to be able to access a program quickly, it's generally better to create a shortcut than to move the program's icon to the desktop. Leaving the program in its own folder makes it easier for you to upgrade the program when a new version comes out. It's also just plain neater. The folders for most programs contain other files in addition to the main program file, including last-minute documentation files and sometimes additional utility programs, and it makes sense to leave the main program files in with these subsidiary files. Sometimes, programs won't run if the location of some of their support files changes.

4 Shortcuts for Documents

In the case of document files that you use all the time, there are arguments to be made for both creating shortcuts and moving the document itself to your desktop. The advantage of creating a shortcut is that the document itself stays in a logical place within your folder hierarchy. This can make it easy to find files and manipulate files as a group. (If all your word processing documents are in one folder, you can easily copy the entire folder to a floppy disk for backup purposes.) The one advantage of actually placing the document on the desktop is that this makes it easy to copy the file without opening any folders.

This is a shortcut to a Word document.

5 Printing Documents from the Desktop

To print a document on the desktop, you right-click its icon—either the file or the shortcut icon—and choose **Print** from the context menu. You can also use this method to print any document from its folder without opening the document first. (If you've created a printer shortcut on your desktop, you simply drag the icon of the document to the shortcut for your printer.)

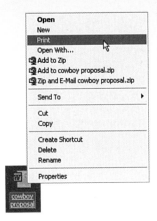

End

Notes

Searching for Files

If you can't find the particular file you're looking for, use the Search button in Explorer. (It's also available from the Start menu and in any folder you open.) You'll be able to search for the file by name, date, and a variety of other criteria. Even if you only know part of the name, you can use an asterisk for the part of the filename you don't know, and you'll probably find it. For example, if you know the filename contains the word "letter" but you don't know the rest of the name, you could search for "*letter*" and you'll get a list of all files that have "letter" at the beginning, middle, or end of the filename.

Adding Programs to the Start Menu

Another way to provide easy access to programs you use often is to add a shortcut to those programs to the Start menu. To do this, locate an icon for the program in question in either a folder window or an Explorer window. Then drag the icon over to the **Start** button. As soon as you release the mouse button, the shortcut to the program is added to the top section of the Start menu, above most recently used programs. You can also drag shortcut icons for programs to the Start button to accomplish the same thing.

Removing Items from the Start Menu

If you add something to the top of the Start menu and then change your mind, you can just right-click the item and choose **Remove from This List** from the context menu that appears. This approach only works for items at the left of the Start menu. You can't delete items such as My Computer, My Documents, and Control Panel from the right portion of the menu.

Using the Clipboard

Whenever you copy or move items from one location to another, you are using a Windows feature known as the Clipboard. Think of the Clipboard as a temporary holding pen, where you put things that you want to transport from one spot to another. Whenever you cut or copy an item in a folder window or Explorer, you are placing it in the Clipboard. Then you paste that item from the Clipboard to its new home. You've already learned to use the Clipboard to copy files and folders. You can also use it to move or copy selected data within application files to another location within the same data file, to a different document within the same application, and to a document in another application.

Begin

1 Selecting Your Data

Before moving or copying data via the Clipboard, you must select the data to be moved or copied. In most Windows programs, you can select data by dragging across it with your mouse. To select discrete items on the screen, you select one by clicking and then hold **Ctrl** while you click others.

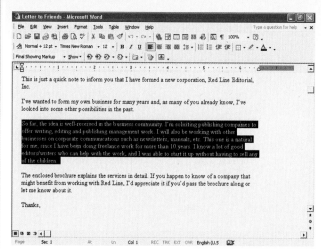

2 Selecting Data with the Keyboard

If you prefer to select data by using your keyboard, try any of the following: **Shift+End** selects from the insertion point to the end of a line. **Shift+** an arrow key selects from the current position of the insertion point to wherever you move the insertion point. If you hold **Shift** while you press the **Down** Arrow key three times, for example, you'll select from your original spot to a spot three lines down. **Shift+Ctrl+End** selects from the current position of the insertion point to the end of the document.

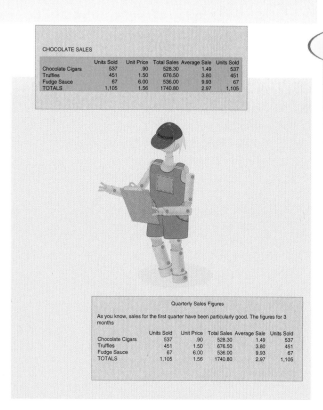

3 Issuing the Cut or Copy Command

After you've selected the desired data, you either copy or "cut" (move) that data to the Clipboard, using the **Edit, Copy** or **Edit, Cut** command or its **Ctrl+C** or **Ctrl+X** shortcut key. The data will be copied to the Clipboard automatically, so you can paste it somewhere else.

4 Move to the Destination

Next, you move to where you want to place the material you've cut or copied—be it in the same file, a different file, or a file in another application. Here is a brand new file into which to place the Clipboard contents.

5 Paste in Material from the Clipboard

Paste the data from the Clipboard using the **Edit, Paste** command or its **Ctrl+V** shortcut key.

6 Using Buttons

Most Windows programs offer Copy, Cut, and Paste toolbar buttons that speed up your work.

Copy

Cut   Paste

End

Getting Help

Windows features a very extensive and easy to use Help and Support system—a series of informational screens and a set of tools for navigating them and finding the information you need. Not only is there a Help system for Windows itself, most Windows programs have Help systems of their own that function in much the same way as Windows Help.

Begin

1 Getting Help

To get help, open the **Start** menu and select **Help and Support,** or open the **Help** menu in any folder window or Explorer window and choose **Help Topics.** To get help with an application program, select the **Help** option on the application window's menu bar.

2 The Help and Support Screen

The Windows Help and support screen you see when you first enter the Windows Help system has been completely revamped for Windows XP, so if you have an earlier version of Windows, it will look quite different. Across the top of the window are several different types of Help functions to choose from. In the main window, Help items are available by topic.

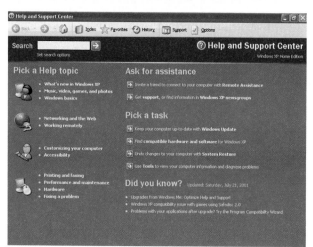

Notes

Getting Help in Dialog Boxes

Many dialog boxes offer Help systems of their own. If the dialog box provides this feature, you'll either see a question mark button in the upper-right corner or a What's This option on the Help menu. Clicking the question mark button or selecting the What's This option turns your mouse pointer into a question mark with an arrow. To display a description of an item in the dialog box, just point to it and click.

Context-Sensitive Help

In some application programs, the F1 key leads to what is known as *context-sensitive help,* meaning a screen with information about whatever operation you are performing or object you are manipulating at the moment.

3 Pick a Help Topic

Down the left side of the main Help window, you see a number of categories under Pick a Help topic. Here you'll find different topics of interest, divided into major categories such as Printing and faxing or Windows basics. When you choose a topic from this list, you are presented with a two-paned window similar to an Explorer window. The difference here is that as you drill down the categories on the left side, you can pick an article or tutorial from the right to help you answer your question.

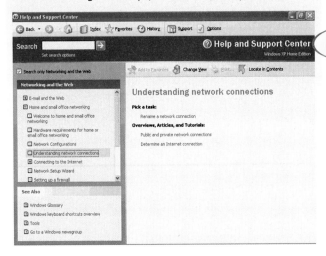

4 Getting Support

The right side of the main Help and Support window is for support—that is, Microsoft's customer support. Here you can get updates to your Windows software, get technical assistance from Microsoft, research hardware and software compatibility issues, and work with system tools.

6 Searching for Answers

You use the Search box to search for words or phrases contained within a Help topic. To use the Search function, type a keyword or phrase in the text box at the top of the dialog box. Then click the **Search** button. If you see the topic you want in the list of topics, click it once and the information will appear in the right pane.

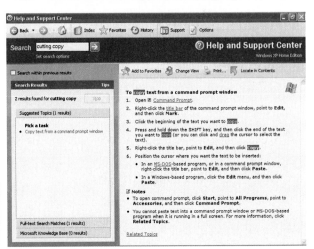

5 The Index

The Index is one of the most popular ways to get Help in Windows. You access it by clicking Index at the top of the Help and Support window. It opens an index into which you can enter a keyword, and you'll jump right to topics of interest that relate to the keyword. Highlight the topic that most closely matches your question, click the Display button at the bottom of the window, and your answer appears on the right.

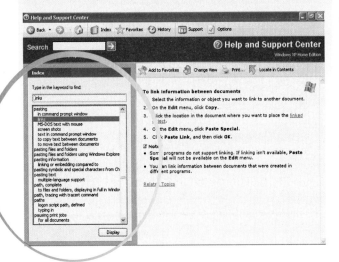

End

Customizing Windows

One of the satisfying things about Windows is that you can customize it to suit your fancy. You've already learned how to turn on and off single-click mode. That's just one of literally dozens of modifications you can make to the Windows interface to make it better fit your work style and your sense of aesthetics. Among other things, you can change the look of the desktop—adding wallpaper or patterns or changing the color scheme. You can also use the Control Panel to adjust your system to meet your needs—adjusting mouse click speed, monitor resolution, and much more.

Begin

1 Changing the Way Windows Looks

For the interior decorators among you, Windows provides some simple tools for dressing up your desktop and changing the Windows color scheme. To customize the desktop, right-click an empty spot on the desktop and choose **Properties** to invoke the Display Properties dialog box.

2 Setting Your Background

From the **Desktop** tab of the Display Properties dialog box, the **Background** list enables you to select a graphic. Using the **Position** drop-down list, you can either tile (repeat across the desktop), center, or stretch (expand to fill the desktop) the selected graphic. Use the **Color** list to choose a different color for a plain background.

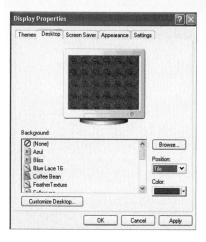

3 Changing the Color Scheme

To change the Windows color scheme, right-click an empty spot on the desktop, choose **Properties**, and select the **Appearance** tab in the Display Properties dialog box. This is where you can change how windows look when they pop up on screen.

4 Changing Your Theme

Use the Themes tab to change the overall look of Windows. If, for example, you prefer the traditional Windows look (as it was in Windows 95 and 98), you can choose the Windows Classic theme from the Theme drop-down list.

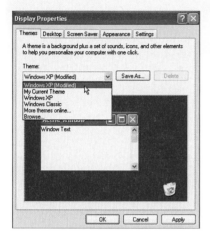

5 What Is the Control Panel?

You can also make use of the Windows Control Panel to modify your system to suit your needs. The Control Panel is a special folder that contains tools for customizing the Windows environment. You can use these utilities to do everything from adjusting the speed at which your mouse moves across the screen, to resetting the date and time, to adding new hardware or software to your system. To access the Control Panel, click the **Start** button and select **Control Panel**.

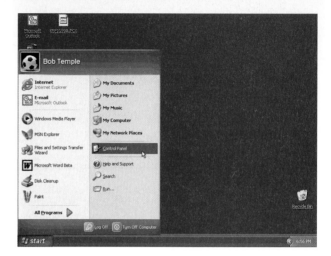

6 Using the Control Panel

After you're in the Control Panel folder, you'll need to pick a category from the list. For example, if you want to modify your mouse settings, you would click Printers and Other Hardware, and then click Mouse. (Feel free to explore the various tools; you can always bail out by either closing the resulting folder window or clicking a Cancel button.)

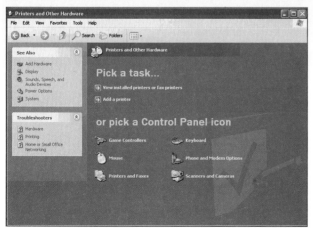

End

TOPIC *23*

Shutting Down, Logging Off, or Restarting Windows

You need to exit from Windows properly before you turn off your computer. In addition, in some cases you may want to restart your computer—if you've just installed a new program, for example. Or, a different user may want to log on under their user account. Luckily, this is a simple matter of choosing a few menu and dialog box options. First, you should save all your data and exit any applications you're running.

Begin

1 Turning Off the Computer

Before you turn off your computer, you should always open the **Start** menu and choose **Turn off computer.**

2 The Various Shutdown Options

You'll see the Turn Off Computer dialog box with the options **Stand By, Turn Off, and Restart.** Click the appropriate button for the operation you're trying to perform.

3 Logging Off

If you are sharing your computer with other user accounts or you are on a network, you may just want to log off, but leave the computer running. That way, the next family member who wants to use the computer doesn't have to power it up. To log off, just open the Start menu and select Log off. You'll get a dialog box in which you can choose Switch User of Log Off.

4 If You Forgot to Close Applications

If you forgot to close any open application windows and have any unsaved documents, Windows asks whether you want to save your data. After you have either saved or discarded any unsaved documents, you will see a screen informing you that it is now safe to turn off your computer. On some computers, it automatically shuts off the CPU for you.

End

Topic

6

Application Software

*I*n a sense, application programs are the most important part of your computer system. They're what enables your computer to actually do something useful, like create documents, perform calculations, or play games.

There are dozens of types of application programs available. In this chapter, I'll delve into three of the most commonly used types: word processing programs, spreadsheet programs, and database management programs. I'll tell you what these programs do, what they look like, and how you use them. I'll also provide some pointers on how to choose one from the many on the market.

What I won't tell you is the exact series of steps needed to accomplish particular results in particular programs. (You won't learn how to underline a word in the WordPerfect word processing program or copy a set of data in the Excel spreadsheet, for example.) Instead, I'll focus on the basic concepts and metaphors used in all word processing, database, and spreadsheet programs and the range of feats each of those programs can perform. I'll give you the foundation you need before you get to the "which keys to press" or "which items to click" stage—a foundation often overlooked in the manuals. ●

Word Processing

At its simplest, word processing on a computer is just electronic typing. Instead of pressing keys on a typewriter, you press keys on a computer keyboard that looks much like a typewriter. But there is one essential difference. In word processing, the process of composing a document is separate from the process of printing. For many people, the separation between composing a document and printing it takes some of the anxiety out of the writing process itself. Because you can start typing without committing yourself to paper, the move from thinking about writing to actually starting may feel less intimidating. Knowing that your work is so easy to fix can make it easier to start.

Begin

When you type something on a typewriter, the characters are immediately recorded on paper. If you change your mind or notice mistakes, you need to erase characters or retype a page or more of text.

1 Typing Is Separate from Printing

This separation of typing from printing, of electronic document from printed copy, makes all the difference in the world. It lets you erase, amend, and rearrange your document without retyping any of the existing text.

2 Erasing and Inserting Characters

If you erase characters, the program automatically closes any gaps left behind. If you insert characters, it pushes existing characters to the right or down to make room for the new text.

Newly inserted text—

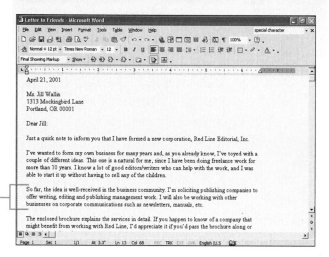

3 Moving Text

If you decide that a particular sentence or paragraph really belongs somewhere else in your document, you simply move it to the desired spot and let your program rearrange the rest of the document (including your page breaks) to accommodate the change.

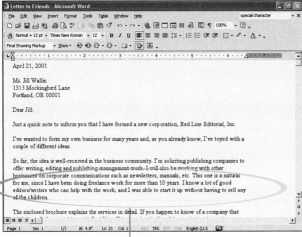

It's simple to move text to a new location.

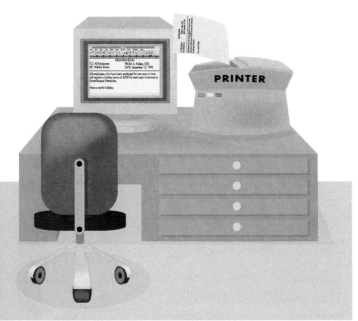

When you type something using a word processing program, the characters you type are simply stored in your computer's memory. You can make any changes you like and print whenever (and as often as) you want.

4 Undoing and Redoing Actions

Word processing programs even let you change your mind about such editorial changes, providing you with an undo or an undelete command that reverses the effects of the last deletion, move, or other action. In fact, now you can usually reverse many actions, and, if you change your mind about something you undid, you can just as easily "redo" it.

5 Printing Your Document

When you are ready to print your document, you simply issue a print command. In almost all Windows programs, this involves opening the **File** menu (by clicking the word File on the menu bar), selecting **Print**, and clicking **OK** in the dialog box that appears. In many Windows programs, you can also click a Print icon (with a picture of a printer) near the top of the screen to print a single copy of your document without going through the dialog box.

End

TOPIC **2**

What Can Word Processors Do?

The capability to insert, delete, and rearrange text without retyping is word processing's main selling point, and this alone is worth the price of admission. But word processing programs offer other features that typists never dreamed of. For starters, most word processing programs can perform the basic tasks described here.

Begin

1 Using Different Typefaces and Text Styles

Word processors can display and print characters in a variety of typefaces and sizes, with attributes such as boldfacing, underlining, and italics.

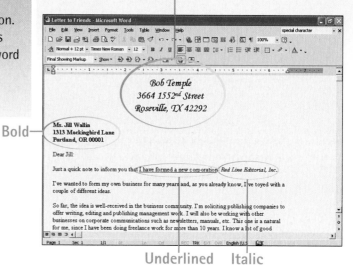

2 Searching for and Replacing Characters

Word processors can search for and replace a specified set of characters. This feature is useful if you find that you've misspelled someone's name throughout a document. You can also use it to save yourself typing. You can, for example, type some obscure character like the ~ every time you want to display your company's name and then later replace every occurrence of ~ with the name itself.

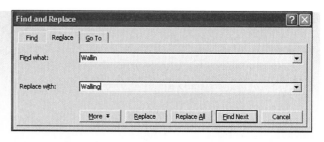

All word processing programs include a search and replace feature that lets you replace each occurrence of one set of characters with another set of characters.

3 Aligning Text

Word processors can also automatically center text, align it with the left or right margin, or full-justify text, so that characters line up at the right as well as the left margin.

4 Numbering Pages

You can have a word processor automatically print page numbers at either the top or bottom of each page. This saves you the trouble of entering page numbers within the text and then moving them around when your editing causes the page breaks to move slightly.

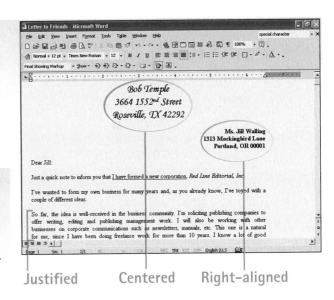

Justified   Centered   Right-aligned

5 Adding Headers and Footers

You can print headers and footers—specified sets of text at the top or bottom of each page. These headers and footers can include the current page number. Some programs let you specify different headers or footers for the first page of your document or for odd and even pages. (You won't always see page numbers or headers and footers in the onscreen version of your document. However, they should show up when you do a print preview or print your document.)

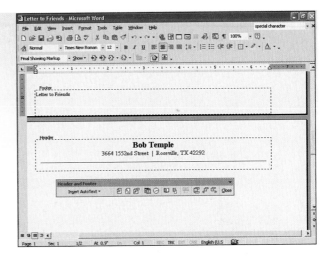

6 Using Footnotes and Endnotes

Another thing you may want to do is to format and manage footnotes and endnotes. Most word processing programs let you attach footnotes or endnotes to particular spots in your document. If you add more footnotes or rearrange text, the program automatically moves and renumbers the notes as necessary. If you use footnotes (rather than endnotes), the program automatically figures out how much room is required for notes at the bottom of each page and prints the footnotes exactly where they belong.

7 Hyphenation

Word processors can automatically hyphenate words at the end of a line. Most programs use their built-in dictionaries to break words between syllables and ask you to specify a location for the hyphen in words not found in that dictionary.

Continues

8 Columns

You can arrange text in two or more columns (as many leaflets and most periodicals do).

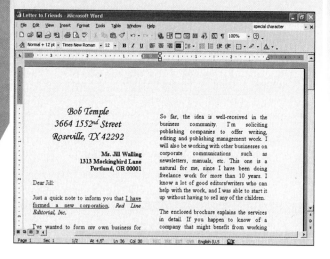

9 Spell Checking

You can have your word processor check your document for misspelled words, a process known as *spell checking*. Spell checkers can prove invaluable. (Never send out a resume without using one.) They are, however, no substitute for human proofreading. For one thing, spell checkers only check whether a particular word exists; they don't tell you if it's the right word for a particular context. If you type "here" when you mean "hear," for example, or "major" instead of "mayor," the spell checker will not blink.

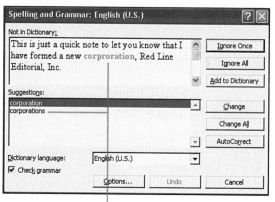

Most word processing programs can automatically check your document for misspelled words and suggest alternatives.

10 Using the Built-in Thesaurus

You can locate synonyms for a selected word. This thesaurus feature can prove invaluable if you find yourself using the same word over and over, or when you can't quite pinpoint the word you want.

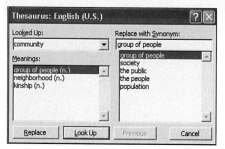

Many word processing programs include a thesaurus feature that lets you look up synonyms for a specified word.

11 Inserting Special Characters

Most word processors let you enter special characters and symbols that you can't generate on most typewriters, including foreign language characters, bullets, and mathematical symbols.

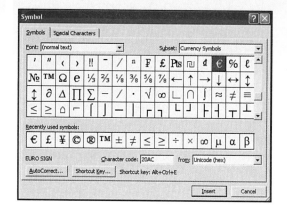

12 Creating Personalized Output

This feature, commonly known as *mail merge*, lets you generate documents, each of which includes, for example, a different individual's name and address.

Almost all word processing programs let you generate "personalized" form letters (a feature known as mail merge).

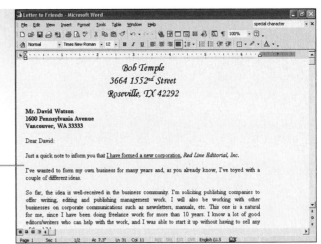

13 Adding Graphics and Formatting

You can incorporate lines, boxes, and pictures within a document. This capability is particularly useful for producing newsletters or fancy reports.

Welcome to AquaWorld!!

You and your kids will enjoy the special thrill that comes from sitting only inches from our great white shark Toby.

14 Printing Envelopes and Labels

You should be able to print envelopes and mailing labels. Some word processing programs can even print envelopes by pulling the name and address from the top of your letter, which means you don't have to retype it.

15 Using Tables and Grids

Many word processing programs have tools for creating and managing tables of information (that is, text entered in a grid of rows and columns). Most programs allow you to adjust the width of columns after you enter your text, and some let you apply special formatting—such as shading every other row. In some cases, you can even drag a table from a spreadsheet program and drop it into a word processing program.

Animal Species	Name	Age
Anteater	Agatha	2 ½ years
Baboon	Bubbles	6 months
Coyote	Caldwell	5 years
Duck	Darryl	2 months
Elephant	Erin	3 years

16 Checking Your Grammar

Some programs let you scan your document for grammatical problems, such as incorrect punctuation and double negatives, and for stylistic problems, such as overuse of the passive voice or use of redundant expressions.

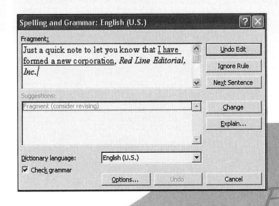

End

TOPIC 3

Advanced Word Processing Features

Almost all word processing programs include spell checking capabilities, a thesaurus, a grammar checker, and the majority of the other features discussed in the previous section. In addition, many word processing programs offer some of the more esoteric features described here.

1 Special Editing Tools

Several word processing programs provide a variety of special editing tools that facilitate editing or writing by committee. These tools allow you to insert or delete text provisionally, subject to the author's approval, or to insert comments into the text that are visible onscreen but skipped over when you print.

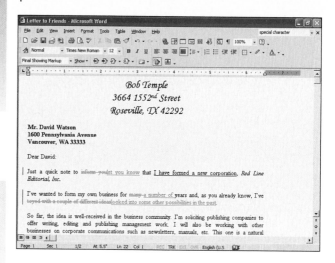

2 Using Styles

Most word processing programs allow you to create and use *styles*—stored collections of typographic, margin, and line spacing formats. Many high-end word processing programs allow you to create styles for various types of documents. Some include preset styles—for bibliographies or legal pleadings, for example.

3 Outlining Features

Some programs include outliners that help you sketch and then refine the overall structure of a document. You can create a preliminary outline with headings and one or more levels of subheadings and then rearrange these headings, often simply by dragging with your mouse. Some outliners also let you expand part or all of your outline—to display sub-headings and descriptions—and collapse them so that you see only the headings themselves.

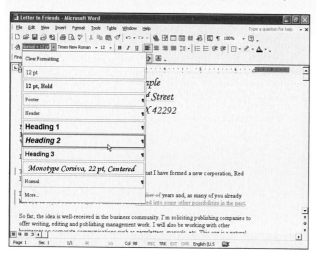

4 Generating an Index

Many programs permit you to mark words or phrases that you want included in an index and then generate an index of all those words, with their page numbers, on your command.

5 Creating a Table of Contents

In some programs you can mark section headers in the document and then automatically generate a table of contents, with section names and the pages on which they appear. These page numbers are conveniently updated when you revise your document.

6 Automatic Line Numbering

Certain programs can automatically number the lines in a document, a feature that can prove particularly useful in producing legal documents.

7 Creating Macros

Some word processing programs allow you to create *macros*, recording a set of keystrokes and playing them back whenever you like. You can use macros to automate any set of steps that you repeat frequently—for example, to enter the closing for business letters.

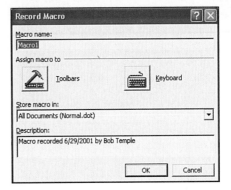

Notes

What Is a Font?

Font means a specific combination of typeface and point size (although some people use the term to mean typeface, regardless of size). Arial 12-point font means the Arial typeface and a size of 12 points. (A point is 1/72 of an inch.) People frequently use fonts with a larger point size for titles or headings within a document and sometimes use different typefaces for different elements within the document. In this book, for example, the typeface used in the header at the top of each page is different from that used in the text itself.

You Don't Need to Learn Everything

Few people actually learn or use all the features their word processing program has to offer. Within the vast collection of bells and whistles commonly offered by word processing programs, most people identify a few features they can't live without and ignore the rest. (I, personally, am hooked on the thesaurus. For you, the best thing about word processing may be the spell checker, or the capability to mix and match fonts.)

More About Macros

Some word processing programs let you use a macro programming language to create more sophisticated macros than you could create by recording.

End

Notes

AutoCorrect

Some word processing programs have a nifty AutoCorrect feature that can correct typos and misspellings as you make them. (It seems like magic, *and* it's incredibly addictive!) You can even add words that you misspell frequently to the list of words that are corrected automatically.

Using a Word Processing Program

Explaining how to use every word processing program, or even the major few, is beyond the scope of this book. But I can tell you something about what your word processing program will look like. I can also describe the central metaphors and concepts involved in word processing—topics that are often skipped over in manuals and books on the subject. Knowing a bit about the lay of the land will also help if you decide to try out a few word processing programs at your local computer store before you buy.

Begin

Menu bar

Toolbars (sometimes called button bars or speed bars)

Status bar

Insertion point

Work area

1 A Tour of the Screen

When you first start up a word processing program, your screen is largely blank—the electronic equivalent of a blank sheet of typing paper. As soon as you start typing, this page starts filling with characters. Word processing screens also contain a menu at the top of the screen and in some cases one or more sets of icons—generally called *toolbars*—representing additional choices. (You'll need to refer to your software manual for information on what each of the menu options and icons do.) There will also most likely be a status bar at the bottom of the screen telling you such things as how many pages your document contains and which page you're on.

2 The Insertion Point

Every word processing screen also contains a symbol that serves as a "you are here" marker. (When you start the program, this symbol appears in the upper-left corner of the typing area.) If you are entering text, this symbol indicates where the next character will appear. If you are deleting text, it tells you which character you are about to erase. If you are using a Windows-based word processing program, you will see a blinking vertical line (the insertion point).

3 The Insertion Point Versus the Mouse Pointer

The insertion point is not the same as the mouse pointer. To move the insertion point, move the mouse pointer to the desired spot and click, or use the cursor-movement keys. If you have trouble distinguishing the pointer from the insertion point, remember that the insertion point blinks and the pointer moves when you move the mouse.

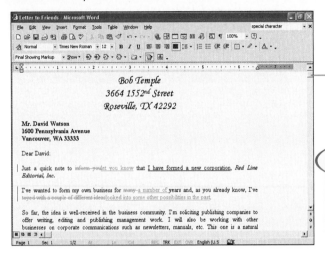
—scroll bar

5 Word Wrap

A central feature of all word processing is a feature known as word wrap. *Word wrap* means that as you type, the program "wraps" the text to the next line when you reach the right margin. There's no need to press the Enter key. In a sense, the computer handles your entire document as one long ribbon of characters that wraps from one line to the next. If you erase some characters (removing a section of the ribbon), the program pulls the rest of the ribbon leftward or up a line to close the gap. If you add characters in the middle (inserting a new section of ribbon), the rest of the ribbon is pushed forward and/or down.

7 When to Press Enter

The moral of the story is that you should only press Enter at the end of a paragraph, at the end of a line that you want to be abnormally short (like an address line), or when you want to insert a blank line at the top of the page or between paragraphs. If you want blank lines between "Sincerely" and your name at the bottom of a letter, press Enter several times. The rest of the time, just keep typing and let the program handle the line breaks for you.

4 Scrolling Your Document

One of the first things to understand about word processing programs is that as soon as you fill up the screen with text, the program starts scrolling lines off the top to make room for additional characters. To get used to this, think of your document as one long scroll or piece of paper. As you move up or down within it, part of your document may disappear from the screen, but it's not erased from memory. You can always scroll up or down to bring it back into view.

6 How Hard Returns Work

If you learned to type on a typewriter, you'll have to train yourself not to press the Enter key when you get near the right margin (the right side of the screen). Not only is pressing Enter unnecessary, it can actually create problems. When you press Enter, the program inserts what is known as a *hard return*—a code that tells the program, "Go to the next line, no matter where you are in relation to the margins." Whenever the program encounters a hard return, it breaks the line at that spot, regardless of how few words are on the line. If you press Enter at the end of a line and later delete characters from that line, the line break will not change accordingly.

Notes

The Hard Return

Although they are usually invisible, hard returns are characters, just like letters or numbers. Each one can be deleted or moved just like other characters. To get rid of a hard return, place your cursor or insertion point on or to the left of the first character on the subsequent line, and then erase the character just before that spot by pressing the Backspace key.

End

Spreadsheet Programs

In a nutshell, a *spreadsheet* is a grid of rows and columns in which you enter numbers and text. Spreadsheet programs such as Microsoft Excel are the number crunchers of the computer world, although they can manipulate text as well. Think of them as powerful, multipurpose calculators, capable of everything from adding two plus two to calculating a loan amortization schedule to projecting the likely impact of an increase of an energy tax on your cost of goods sold. Spreadsheets excel at performing both calculations on given numbers (what's the total of these 439 expense items?) and what-if computations (how much will my monthly mortgage payment increase if I change the term from 30 years to 15 years?).

Begin

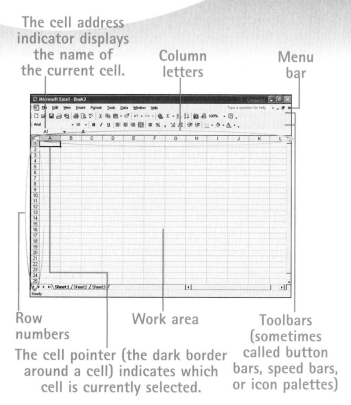

The cell address indicator displays the name of the current cell.

Column letters

Menu bar

Row numbers

Work area

Toolbars (sometimes called button bars, speed bars, or icon palettes)

The cell pointer (the dark border around a cell) indicates which cell is currently selected.

1 The Work Area Is a Grid

Although the appearance of spreadsheet programs varies a bit from one program to the next, they all have features in common. Usually, the screen is largely occupied by a grid of rows and columns, frequently known as the *work area* or *worksheet area*.

2 How Cells Are Identified

The columns within the work area are identified by letters shown at the top of the work area. The rows are identified by numbers shown at the left side of the work area. The boxes formed by the intersection of individual rows and columns are known as *cells*. Cells are identified by the combination of their column letter and row number. The fifth cell in the second column is known as cell B5, for example. (The letter always comes first.) This is known as the cell's address or cell coordinates.

	A	B	C
1			
2			
3			
4		2345	
5			
6			
7			
8			

3 The Active Cell

At any given moment, you are positioned in a single cell, generally known as the *current cell* or *active cell*. (When you enter data, it goes in this cell; when you apply formatting such as boldfacing, it is applied to this current cell.)

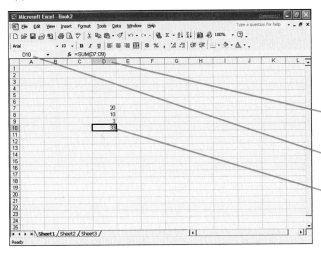

Contents of current cell

Address of current cell

Current cell

4 How to Tell Which Cell You're In

You can always tell which cell you are in by looking at the position of the cell pointer—a highlight or dark border you can move from one cell to the next using the cursor movement keys or your mouse. The address of the current cell is typically displayed on a line just above the work area, in an area usually known as the *cell address indicator*. To the right of the cell address indicator, in an area sometimes called the *formula bar*, you will probably see the contents of the current cell—whether it's numbers, text, or a formula.

5 How Big Is Your Spreadsheet?

When you create a new spreadsheet, the grid of rows and columns is empty. You start with the equivalent of a blank sheet of ledger paper—a *tabula rasa* waiting for your data. The size of this "piece of paper" is actually huge. Most spreadsheets contain hundreds of columns and several thousand rows (millions of cells). What appears on the screen, however, is a small portion of that "page," usually about a dozen columns and a couple of dozen rows. To find your way around the spreadsheet, imagine the work area as a movable window, just as you do in a word processing program. You can scroll the window sideways (to view additional columns) as well as up and down (to view additional rows).

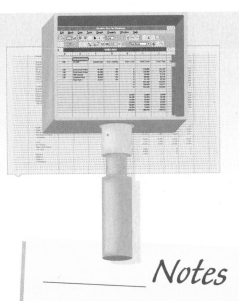

6 The Spreadsheet Screen

Most spreadsheets contain a menu bar at the top of the screen. This menu bar is typically visible all the time. The menus vary from program to program, but in general, you use menu commands to do things like moving, copying, and erasing blocks of data, inserting or deleting columns and rows, printing, saving, and changing the appearance of data. Many spreadsheets also include one or more toolbars (occasionally called button bars or speed bars). These toolbars provide you with quick (single-click) access to common commands, such as Print, Cut, and Copy.

Notes

What Are Worksheets and Notebooks?

In some spreadsheet programs, individual files are referred to as *worksheets* or *spreadsheet notebooks* rather than spreadsheets.

End

TOPIC **6**

How Spreadsheets Work

Although spreadsheets are capable of calculating almost anything you can imagine, they're not set up in advance to perform any particular calculations. It's your job to fill in the grid by entering text, numbers, and instructions (formulas) that direct the computer to perform particular calculations.

Begin

1 Using Formulas to Perform Calculations

Suppose you wanted to calculate the net income for a company. You might start by entering the numbers for total revenue in one cell and for total expenses in another. (You might also enter text identifying these numbers in two adjacent cells.) Then you would enter a formula telling the program to subtract the expenses from the revenue and display the result. You do this by moving to a blank cell and typing an instruction describing the desired calculation.

2 How Formulas Work

For example, if cell B3 contains the figure for revenue and cell B4 contains your expenses, you would enter a formula such as +B3-B4 or (B3-B4) or =B3-B4. (The exact syntax for formulas varies among spreadsheet programs.) Think of this formula as "take whatever value currently appears in cell B3, subtract the value that currently appears in cell B4, and then display the result in this cell."

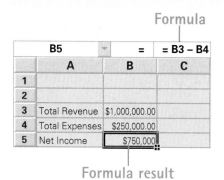

Formula

Formula result

3 Formula Results Are Recalculated Automatically

Then, whenever you change the value in cell B3 or B4, the result of the formula will be automatically—and, in most cases, instantly—updated. This feature, known as *automatic recalculation,* is one of the main advantages that spreadsheets offer over calculators. After you tell the spreadsheet what to do, you are free to change the raw data as much and as often as you like, and the program does the work of recalculating the results.

The formula stays the same.

B5		=	= B3 – B4
	A	**B**	**C**
1			
2			
3	Total Revenue	$1,000,000.00	
4	Total Expenses	$340,000.00	
5	Net Income	$640,000	

This value changed.

The formula results were updated.

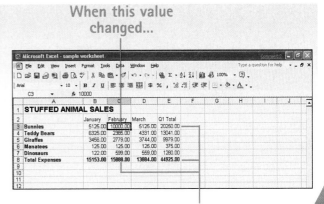

Formula in active cell

Formulas for the numbers in each column

Numbers that were typed in

Formulas for the numbers in each row

4. When Formula Results Change, Other Formulas Based on Them Are Recalculated

The advantages grow even more obvious when you have more formulas and some of them rely on the results of others, as illustrated in the "Stuffed Animal Sales" spreadsheet. If you changed the dollar amount of dinosaurs sold in January, the total for January at the bottom of that column would automatically be recalculated, as would the total dinosaur sales at the right edge of the row. (Each of those totals is based on a formula that adds up all the other values in that row or column.) Then, because the total dinosaur sales figure changed, the grand total in the lower-right corner of the spreadsheet would be recalculated as well, because that number is the result of a formula that adds up all the other values in the column (that is, the total for each type of stuffed animal). If there happened to be another formula based on the grand total, that formula would be recalculated as well.

5. What Happens When You Change Cell Values

To put this in more general terms: Every time you change the value in a cell the results of any formulas that refer to that cell, are updated. Any other cells that refer to those results are updated as well. In this way, a single change in value may set off a chain reaction, instigating changes in several cells throughout the spreadsheet.

When this value changed...

...these formula results were automatically updated.

Continues

6 Functions

Besides automatic recalculation, functions are another big advantage spreadsheets offer over calculators. All spreadsheet programs feature functions—built-in tools for performing calculations other than simple arithmetic (addition, subtraction, multiplication, and division). Most major spreadsheet programs offer around 100 different functions; you can calculate averages, square roots, depreciation, payments or earnings on annuities, and standard deviation (to name just a few).

This formula adds up all the values in cells B4 through B7.

7 Database Management Capabilities

Most spreadsheet programs offer at least a few database management capabilities—that is, tools for managing lists. At a minimum, they allow you to sort a set of rows alphabetically or numerically and to select items that match specified selection criteria. Bear in mind that if your list exceeds a hundred items or if you need to produce formatted reports or mailing labels, you are better off using a database management program. (Database management programs are covered shortly.)

These sales records are sorted by total sales but they could just as easily be sorted by monthly sales or alphabetically.

8 Formatting Tools

Many spreadsheet programs offer formatting tools, enabling you to mix and match fonts within a spreadsheet, print spreadsheets sideways, and dress them up with lines, boxes, shading, and graphical elements such as pictures and logos.

9 Macros

As described earlier in this chapter, macros are a means of automating an entire series of steps and then "playing them back" with one or two keystrokes. Many spreadsheet programs allow you to record a series of keystrokes and store them in a macro. Creating more sophisticated macros requires typing commands or even learning a scripting language.

10 Linking Files and Three-Dimensional Spreadsheets

Many spreadsheet programs offer tools for linking multiple spreadsheet files so that a formula in one file can refer to cells in another file. Others let you store multiple sets of information within a single file. (This is called a *three-dimensional spreadsheet, spreadsheet notebook,* or *workbook.*) Such features can prove extremely useful for consolidating information from several departments or time periods, or organizing several distinct but related sets of information.

	A	B	C	D	E	F	G
1	STUFFED ANIMAL SALES						
2		January	February	March	Q1 Total		
3	Bunnies	5125.00	10000.00	5125.00	20250.00		
4	Teddy Bears	6325.00	2385.00	4331.00	13041.00		
5	Giraffes	3456.00	2779.00	3744.00	9979.00		
6	Dinosaurs	122.00	599.00	559.00	1280.00		
7	Manatees	125.00	125.00	125.00	375.00		
8	Total Expenses	15153.00	15888.00	13884.00	44925.00		
9							
10							

1st Quarter / 2nd Quarter / 3rd Quarter / 4th Quarter /

Ready

Clicking these tabs takes you to a different "page" within the same file, in which you can enter a different set of data.

11 Graphs and Design Elements

Most spreadsheet programs offer some means of representing the numbers within your spreadsheets in graphical form, as a bar chart, line chart, or pie chart (among others). Some offer sophisticated graphing features that let you create dozens of different types of graphs and dress up your graphs with lines, boxes, ellipses, text, and other design elements.

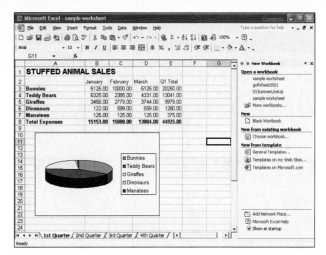

End

Notes

Experimenting with the Numbers

Another advantage of automatic recalculation is that it lets you "play" with numbers. If the Stuffed Animal Sales spreadsheet represented budgeted rather than actual sales amounts and you wanted to get your total sales up to $23,000, you could try adjusting various numbers to see exactly what it would take to get the desired total.

Database Management Programs

Most offices are teeming with files and filing systems, not to mention stacks of paper waiting to be filed. Database management programs are designed to help you manage such masses of data. Their purpose is to turn the names, notes, facts, and figures involved in running a business, a nonprofit organization, or a research project into manageable and useful information. Think of database programs as a cross between filing clerk and research assistant: They help you store and retrieve information and make some sense of it all. In other words, database management programs help you manage and use databases. A *database* is simply a structured collection of information about people (such as customers, vendors, members, or employees), things (such as products on hand, documents on file, or properties to rent), or events (orders received, services provided, sales calls made, or student registrations).

Begin

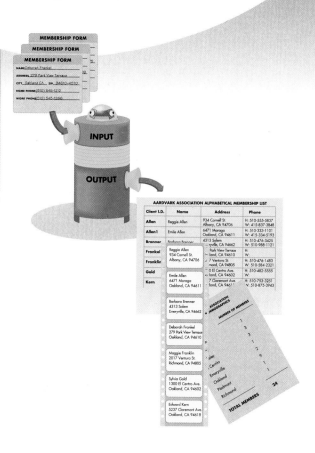

1 Managing Databases

Managing databases involves the same basic processes as library card catalogs, inventory systems, and Rolodex files, regardless of whether you perform them with the aid of a computer. Those operations include: Entering new data; locating previously entered data; changing and deleting existing data; selecting portions of your data, such as all the customers in San Francisco; arranging the data into different sequences, such as in alphabetical order by last name; and producing reports and other printed output, such as form letters and mailing labels. All these operations can be accomplished without a computer. In this sense, maintaining a shoe box full of index cards can be called database management.

2 Computerized Databases

One of the main advantages of computerizing is speed. In general, putting a database on computer won't save you much time on the input side of things. (It will probably take about the same amount of time to type in the data as to scribble it on Rolodex cards.) The time savings occur on the output side of the equation—after the information is in the computer, you can "massage" the data in any way you like with relatively little time or effort: sorting it 12 different ways, printing it in a variety of formats, or selecting all the customers who live in Cincinnati and like to order red plaid hiking shorts.

3 More Accurate Calculations

Another advantage of a computerized database is increased accuracy in calculations. Assuming they receive the right instructions, computers are generally more reliable at performing calculations than people are. You'll probably experience fewer errors and greater consistency in the data. If you have a lot of data, you want some way to ensure its accuracy. Many database programs let you prevent simple data entry errors by defining rules for what data is acceptable (a list of valid cities, for example). Some programs also let you define particular items as mandatory or fill in default values whenever an item is left blank.

4 Planning Your Database

Most database programs don't allow you to just jot down whatever information you want on each customer or inventory item. Instead, they make you decide, in advance, exactly which items of information you're going to collect. (You can change your mind about this structure, but it takes a little time and effort.) You will also need to define clear-cut rules about issues such as when old customers should be deleted from your mailing list, whether you want to allow the entry of overpayments, or what codes you will use for departments in your personnel list. (If you don't standardize, it will be difficult to find everyone in a department later.)

5 A Sample Database

To take a simple example, suppose you will use a database program to manage a personnel database. The first step is to set up a structure for your data, specifying what categories of information you intend to include for each employee.

6 Fields and Records

In database terminology, each individual category of information is known as a *field*, and the entire set of information related to each person, thing, or event is known as a *record*. When the data is laid out in a tabular or spreadsheet-like form, fields occupy columns and records occupy rows.

7 What's in a Record?

In a personnel database, the fields might include first name, last name, address, phone extension, home phone number, Social Security number, supervisor, date hired, department, position, and salary. The entire collection of data for each employee—the full set of fields—is one record. You may leave one or more of these fields empty in some records, but every record has the same set of fields. You cannot have fields in some records that don't exist in the others. Besides specifying the number of fields and their names, you often need to specify the type of data you will enter (numbers, text, dates, or pictures) and, in some cases, the amount of space you want to reserve for each field.

Fields

Records   Table or database file

End

What Can Databases Do?

Unlike word processing and spreadsheet programs, database programs do not share a common metaphor or a similar look. All they have in common is a comparable set of standard features. Most database programs include the following tools.

Begin

1 Creating New Tables

All database programs have a feature for creating and structuring new tables. Usually, when you issue the command for creating a table, you see a screen with columns for field name, type of data, and, in some cases, the field size.

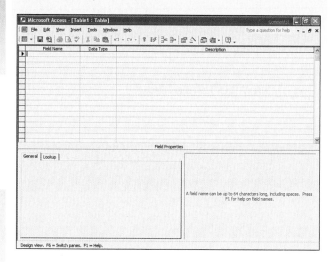

2 Viewing and Modifying Data

Most database programs allow you to view and modify data in tabular form—with a single row for each record and the fields arranged in columns. Some also provide a means of viewing and editing data in a single-record format. In most cases, after your data is displayed, you can change it by simply typing over existing values. You can also issue commands for locating, adding, and deleting records.

3 Entering Data

If your database is fairly small, with relatively few fields, you may find the standard data entry forms sufficient. If you're going to be entering a lot of data, you may prefer to design a customized form. Most high-end programs let you design your own forms—placing fields where you like, including descriptive text or instructions, and adding lines or boxes to make the data easier to read.

4 Designing Reports

All database programs have tools for producing reports. Most have features known as report designers that allow you to select and arrange the fields you want to include, perform calculations such as totals or averages, and in most cases, group records into some meaningful order. You might, for example, print a list in which employees are grouped by department, including a count of employees in each department and the average salary at the end of each departmental group. Some programs also feature report wizards or experts to automate the report design process.

	A	B
1	Home Composting Program Bins Per City	
2	Date>=1/1/97, Date<=12/31/97	
3	**City**	**Quantity**
4	Alameda	299
5	Albany	48
6	Berkeley	336
7	Castro Valley	334
8	Dublin	37
9	Emeryville	38
10	Fremont	349
11	Hayward	184
12	Kensington	2
13	Lafayette	1
14	Livermore	164

5 Constructing Queries

All database programs provide tools to help you select subsets of your data. Probably the most common selection tool is something called query-by-example (QBE). (You use QBE to pose questions about your database—what are the names of all the customers with a past due balance?, for example, or how many clients are there in each city?) Some programs include special wizards or experts to help you construct queries.

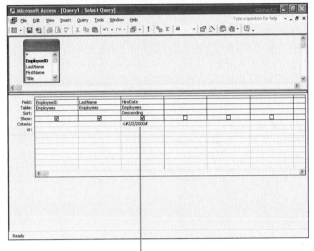

This query selects all empolyees hired before 2/02/2000.

6 Using Macros

Some database programs include macro features or even full-fledged programming languages that allow you (or a professional programmer) to automate repetitive tasks.

End

Notes

Getting Organized

Before you get too enthusiastic about how a database management program is going to change your life, keep this in mind: Database management programs do not turn you into an organized person. If you can't keep your desk in order, you may not fare much better with a database program. But if you're serious about setting up a database, the transition to computers can force you to standardize the way you structure and manage information.

Free-form Database Programs

Some database programs—known as *free-form database programs*—are more open-ended, allowing you to enter data in whatever format you like.

Choosing Software

Often computers come with much of the software you need already installed. In some cases, however, you will need to buy a program to meet your needs.

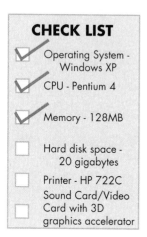

CHECK LIST

☑ Operating System -
    Windows XP

☑ CPU - Pentium 4

☑ Memory - 128MB

☐ Hard disk space -
    20 gigabytes

☐ Printer - HP 722C

☐ Sound Card/Video
    Card with 3D
    graphics accelerator

Begin

1 Does the Program Work with Your Hardware and Software?

When evaluating a program, you need to determine whether it will work with your hardware and operating system. Before you go shopping for software, make sure you know the answers to all these questions: Which operating system are you running and which version? What kind of CPU chip does your computer contain? How much memory does your computer contain? What's the capacity of your computer's hard disk, in megabytes or gigabytes, and how much of that space is currently available? What type of printer do you have? What type of sound card and video card do you have?

2 Write Down This Information Before You Shop

If you might forget the answer to any of these questions, write down all the answers and bring them with you (or have them handy when you pick up the phone). Then, before you buy, make the salesperson swear that the program will work with your hardware and that you can return the program for a full refund if it doesn't.

3 Determining the Features You Like and Need

When choosing a particular type of program, try asking friends and colleagues what they like and don't like about the programs they're using. Then you can take the top contenders for test drives by visiting the home or office of an advocate of each program or spending an hour or two at a computer store. Bear in mind that the ease with which you can accomplish mundane tasks—like changing fonts in a word processing program or entering dates in a spreadsheet program—may be more important than the high-powered extras. Also determine which special features you need, if any, and be sure to pick a program that meets those requirements.

4 Software Suites

Several of the larger software companies now sell "suites" of Windows-based business software: special bundles of software that include at least a word processing program and spreadsheet program. Most suites offer other software as well, such as programs for managing databases, maintaining an electronic personal calendar, designing business presentations, and sending and receiving electronic mail on a network. The major contenders in this arena include Microsoft Office, Lotus SmartSuite, StarOffice, and Corel's WordPerfect Office Suite.

5 Is a Suite Right for You?

If you need both a word processing program and a spreadsheet program—and especially if you need word processing, spreadsheet, and database capabilities—purchasing a suite can prove very economical. Although the programs within each suite are designed to work well together and share similar menu structures, this alone is not reason enough to buy a suite. (Well-designed Windows programs usually share and exchange data easily and have fairly similar user interfaces.) Only buy a suite if you're happy with all the programs it contains, or at least the major ones, and with the price. Otherwise, pick and choose programs individually.

6 Existing Software

If your computer came with a software suite, try using it for a while to see whether it meets your needs. Then, if you don't like one of the components (the spreadsheet, for example, or the word processing program), you can always buy a substitute for that piece, without necessarily replacing all your software.

End

Notes

Microsoft Works

In addition to its Office suite, Microsoft makes a program named Works aimed at home PC users, which contains stripped-down versions of its word processing, spreadsheet, and database programs, plus drawing and communication tools. If you're not planning on doing anything fancy, Works might prove sufficient; it can also be less intimidating for beginners than the full office suites. Many new PCs are sold with either Works or one of the major office suites already installed.

TOPIC 10

Choosing a Database Program

When choosing a database program, you need to determine whether your database is likely to include one table or many. If your database is a list of customers, for example, and you just need to maintain their names and addresses so you can periodically send out product or sales announcements, a single customer table is all you need. However, if you are running a mail order business, and many of your customers place multiple orders, you might have one table for customers and a second one for the individual orders they place. The customer table would include name, address, phone numbers, and other information that is the same for each order. The order table would include the dates of the orders, the amounts, the quantities, product codes, prices, and so on—items that vary from one order to the next. You might even have a third table for products and their prices, and a fourth for payments received.

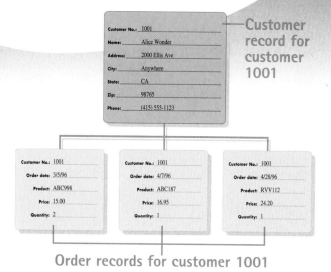

Begin

Customer record for customer 1001

Order records for customer 1001

1 Using Multiple Tables

If you are dealing with events (such as letters sent or services provided) or transactions (such as invoices or payments), your database should probably include at least two tables: one for the people or things involved in the transactions/events, and a second for the transactions/events themselves. Typical examples include Patients and Visits, Donors and Donations, Clients and Services Provided.

2 Relational Databases

Not all database management programs are designed to manage multiple-table databases. Those that do—and let you find and display matches between tables—are known as *relational database management programs*. Relational database programs let you do the following: match up data in two or more tables; transfer data between tables (posting data from an orders table to a balance due field in a customer record, for example); ask questions related to multiple tables (such as what is the name and address of each customer who placed an order for *x*); and display related data from two or more tables in reports and data entry forms.

3 Maintaining the Consistency of Your Data

The better relational database programs also help you maintain consistency between tables, preventing deletion of a customer who has orders on file, or making sure that changes happen in all related orders records.

4 Does the Program Support Your Data?

Also make sure the program supports the type of data you have. Almost all database programs let you enter text, numbers, and dates, but not all can handle graphics (pictures), free-form text fields (fields capable of accommodating any amount of text), and other types of data.

5 Database Performance

If you have a relatively small database—say, 2,000 records or fewer—speed is not likely to be much of an issue. But if you have a database of 20,000, 60,000, or 200,000 records, it will be. You may want to see results of performance tests (often called *benchmarks*) or have someone demonstrate the program on a large database.

6 Importing and Exporting Data

Decide whether you need to move data back and forth between your database program and another program—like your spreadsheet or word processing program. If so, make sure either that your database program can export data in a form the other program can read, or that the other program can read data in your database program's own file format.

7 Queries

Check whether the program has a QBE (query-by-example) feature or something comparable that makes it fairly easy to select subsets of your data and generate statistics.

8 Automation Tools

Find out if the program includes tools for automating operations, such as macros/scripts, application generators, or a programming language.

End

Notes

If You'll Need Help

If you think you may need expert help, don't buy an obscure package. You'll have a lot more trouble finding someone to help you out with Joe Blow's Database Manager than with a major database program such as Access, FoxPro, Paradox, or FileMaker Pro.

Installing Programs

Installing a program usually only takes a few minutes, especially if you're installing from a CD-ROM.Most programs come with their own installation program, designed solely to copy the main program onto your hard disk and, in most cases, acquire some informa- tion about your hardware. With luck, your manual will explain how to use the installation program. Look for an installation section in the manual or a separate manual called Installation or Getting Started. Occasionally, the program's installation instructions are printed on the box the program is sold in or the envelope containing the disks or CD-ROM.

Begin

1 Locate Your Disk or CD-ROM

If you are installing from disks, the first step in installing a program is locating the installation disk. Look for a disk labeled **Install**, **Installation Disk**, or something similar. If no such disk exists, try looking for one labeled Disk 1. Insert that disk into your disk drive. If you are installing from a CD-ROM, insert the disc into the drive.

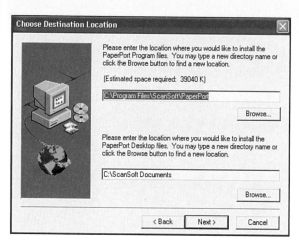

2 Beginning the Installation

With some CD-ROMs, the installation process starts automatically when you put them in the drive. If the installation doesn't begin automatically and you're using Windows, open the **Start** menu and select **Run**. Type **d:setup** in the box labeled Open, where d: is the name of the floppy drive or CD-ROM drive you're installing from. Then press Enter or click **OK**. If this doesn't work, try **d:install**.

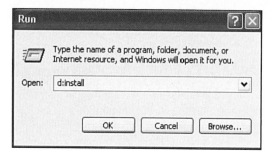

3 The Installation Process

After you have started the installation program, that program takes over. Typically, the instal- lation is a several-step process that involves going through a series of dialog boxes like the one shown here.

4 The README File

Most programs are shipped with a file named README.TXT or README.DOC that contains late-breaking news about the program. Sometimes it contains information on anomalies or bugs in the program. Sometimes it contains minor corrections to the manual. If you are using Windows, you can double-click the file (single-click if you're using the Web-page view) to open it in the Windows program it was created in. For example, TXT files will open in the Windows Notepad; DOC files will open in Microsoft Word.

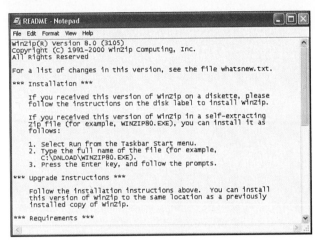

5 Modifying Your Configuration

The installation programs for some Windows programs like to modify various configuration files on your hard disk. Polite programs ask whether this is okay with you before proceeding. (Others make the changes without your permission.) If you do see a message asking if it's okay to modify AUTOEXEC.BAT, CONFIG.SYS, or WIN.INI, select **Yes**.

End

Notes

Copying Programs to Your Hard Disk or Running Them from the CD-ROM

Some programs that come on CD-ROM are not meant to be copied to your hard disk in their entirety. (This is especially common in the case of multimedia programs, which tend to consume a huge amount of storage space, often more space than you'll have or be willing to use up on your hard disk.) When you install such a program, you may be asked whether you want to copy all or just some of the program to your hard disk. (The more of the program you copy, the faster it will run, but the more space it will consume.) In other cases, you're not given a choice: A small portion of the program is copied to your hard disk and the rest remains on CD-ROM. If you copy less than the entire program from a CD-ROM to your hard disk, you'll need to insert the CD-ROM whenever you want to run the program.

Using the Installation Dialog Box

With luck, the questions in these dialog boxes will be at least somewhat comprehensible. In general, you should just accept the program's suggestions on where to place the program files or what to call things. If you are offered a choice between a standard or quick installation and a custom installation, pick the standard/quick one.

TOPIC *12*

Learning an Application Program

After you've chosen and installed a new program, you still need to go about learning it. As described here, there are several approaches you can take. Which of these approaches will work best depends on your own learning style—some people learn best on their own; others need the enforced discipline or camaraderie of a class.

Begin

Use the tools that come with the software—namely the manuals, the online tutorial (if there is one), and the built-in Help system (if any).

1 Buy a Book

Buy a book on the subject at your local bookstore or computer store. Many bookstores carry several different books on the major software packages. Some of these books are very helpful, and some, to say the least, are not. Here's a good strategy for judging a book by more than its cover: Start by looking in the index for any operation that you know you'll need to perform. If you can't find your topic in the index, choose another book. (Because much of the time you'll be using the book as a reference, the index may be its most critical feature.) Assuming you can find your topic, read what the book says about it. If the explanation seems clear and complete, keep the book under consideration and try out a few others. When you're done, buy the book with the explanation you liked best. A great place to start is at Sams' Publishing's Web site at www.samspublishing.com.

2 Take a Class

Take a class at a computer school or community college. (Check local computer magazines, computer stores, and your local yellow pages for computer school locations.)

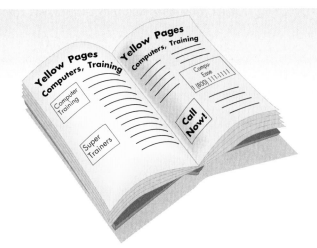

3 Ask a Friend

Find a friend who is willing to help you get started. (Most programs take more than an hour or two to master, so don't expect to have your hand held the whole time.)

4 This Book Will Provide the Basics

After you've read through this book, you should know enough buzzwords and have enough understanding of computers to manage either a book or a basic class. (If you have trouble with either, you can probably assume there's something amiss with the author or teacher.)

5 Get Your Bearings

The one general piece of advice I would offer on learning a new program is to take some time to get your bearings. As you've seen throughout this chapter, most programs work with some kind of metaphor—that is, they treat your screen "as if" it were something more familiar, like a piece of typing paper or an accountant's ledger. One way or another, they present you with a little world. Your first step is to discover what kinds of objects populate that world, how to move around in it, and what tools—like menus or sets of icons or function keys—you can use to make your mark. In other words, when you first approach a new program, don't get immediately caught up in accomplishing a specific task. Instead, picture yourself as Alice stepping through the looking glass. First explore the terrain. You can worry about how to get to the next square later.

End

_____ *Notes*

Computer Users Groups

Users groups are organizations of people who use or are learning to use computers. Most users groups have members who range from absolute beginners to professional programmers and computer consultants, although some groups lean more toward one end than the other. Such groups can be a tremendous source of free advice and technical support. The larger users groups usually have several special interest groups (commonly known as SIGs) on various types of software or computer-related topics. Many computer users groups also feature a question-and-answer period or mailing lists where confused or frustrated members can pose questions to the membership at large. Someone in the audience may know exactly where the problem lies and how to solve it. To find a users group in your area, look for listings in local computer magazines, ask at local computer stores, or look on the Internet.

Topic

7

More About Hardware

*B*ack in Chapter 2, "Anatomy of a Computer," you were introduced to the basics of computer hardware. In this chapter you'll go a little further, learning some of the finer points about peripherals (namely, monitors, printers, modems, and storage devices) that I didn't want to overwhelm you with earlier in the book. You'll also learn a bit about multimedia computing, portable computers, and networks.

In many cases, this chapter will be discussing some piece of hardware that you already have, either at work or at home. If instead you're in the market for either a new computer or new peripherals, there are several ways to research which model is best. Computer magazines regularly review various types of hardware, presenting articles on the latest printers or newest storage devices. These are excellent sources of comparative information since they frequently present tables comparing price, features, speed, and other criteria. Friends and coworkers can also be a good source of information, or at least a source of information on which models to stay away from. You can also shop online by calling up the Internet sites for various computer manufacturers and comparing features and prices yourself. You can also compare computers at online review sites such as CNET (www.cnet.com). ●

Monitors

The *monitor* is your computer's primary output device—it's a tool for displaying information, soliciting information, and responding to your requests. It's also likely to be the center of your attention most of the time you are using the computer. As a result, it's hard to overestimate the importance of a good monitor, meaning one that's clear, easy to read, and free of glare and flicker. A good monitor can make staring at the screen for eight hours bearable. A bad one can cause headaches, fatigue, and eye strain (not to mention grumpiness).

Begin

Monitors come in all shapes and sizes.

1 Varieties of Monitors

New PCs have color monitors. Most are enclosed in a large box, similar to a small TV. Some desktop computers now use flat-panel displays, which use LCD (liquid crystal display) technology similar to that used by laptops. Flat-panel displays can be expensive, but they do save space.

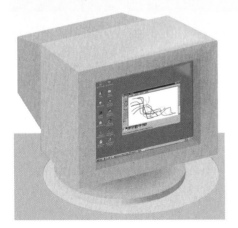

2 Monitor Sizes

Monitors also come in a wide range of sizes. (Monitor size is almost always measured diagonally across the screen.) At the small end are the standard 14-inch screens found on most low-end PCs. At the large end are 21-inch screens. Some specialty screens are even larger.

3 The Video Adapter

The monitor works with a *video adapter* that translates instructions from your computer into a form your monitor can use. Many systems now have the video adapter embedded on the motherboard. In others, the video adapter is an expansion board that fits into a slot on your computer's motherboard. Video adapters are also called display adapter cards, video cards, or video hardware. You might also hear the acronyms for various types of video cards, such as VGA and SVGA.

4 What Comes with Your Computer?

When you buy a new computer, it almost always contains a video adapter. (You probably will only need to buy a new video adapter if you buy a larger monitor or start running more graphics-intensive programs, either of which may require a more powerful and expensive video adapter.) The monitor itself may either be sold as part of the system or purchased separately.

5 What's a Cathode Ray Tube?

The monitors for most desktop computers work just like television sets: They use something called a *cathode ray tube* (CRT) to project images onto a screen. A CRT is essentially a vacuum tube with an electron gun at one end and a flat screen at the other. The electron gun "shoots" a single stream of electrons at the screen. The inside of the screen is coated with special particles, known as phosphors, that glow when struck by the electrons.

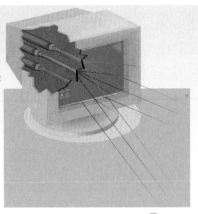

Inside a CRT, one or more electron guns at the back of the monitor shoot electrons toward the screen. When the electrons hit phosphors on the inside of the screen, the phosphors glow, creating patterns of dots on your screen.

6 How Monitors Work

In color monitors, there are three electron guns, and each screen dot consists of three phosphor dots: one red, one green, and one blue. The color of the dot onscreen depends on the intensities of the various electron streams. In both types of monitors, each of the electron beams is directed at one spot at a time, but the beams themselves move, scanning horizontally across a single line of the screen, then dropping down a line and scanning across that one, and so on. As various phosphors are struck by the electron beam(s), they glow for a fraction of a second and then fade again. To keep the image from fading or flickering, the monitor must hit the same phosphors with electrons dozens of times in one second. The term *refresh rate* means the amount of time it takes the monitor to scan across and down the entire screen, "re-zapping" all the phosphors.

_____ *Notes*

Refresh Rates

If you are shopping for a new monitor, you'll want to compare the highest refresh rate that your monitor can support at various resolutions. (You'll learn all about screen resolution and how to change it shortly.) The higher the refresh rate, the better.

Check the Display

Never buy a monitor until you see it running the software you plan to use. Some monitors are great at displaying color photographs and horrible at displaying text, and vice versa. Make sure your monitor is well-suited to the particular task you have in mind.

End

Video Standards and Screen Resolutions

Most new monitors and video adapters are capable of displaying images at various resolutions by using different numbers of dots per inch. When you use a lower resolution, the image expands: You see less on the screen but everything you do see is larger, as if you were looking through a magnifying glass. When you use a higher resolution, everything on the screen shrinks, allowing you to see more information at once. Screen resolution depends on three things: your monitor, your video adapter, and your software. As you already know, the monitor determines whether you can display images in color. It also sets the upper limit of the screen resolution—that is, how many dots per inch you can display onscreen. Some older monitors were designed to display images at only one resolution. Most newer monitors are *multisync monitors,* meaning that they can display images at various resolutions.

Begin

A spreadsheet at 800×600 resolution.

The same spreadsheet at 1024×768 resolution.

1 Pixels

Resolution is described in terms of number of pixels. A *pixel,* which is short for *picture element,* is a dot used to construct screen images. In the PC world, resolution is usually described in terms of the number of pixels displayed horizontally by the number of pixels displayed vertically across the entire screen.

2 Video Standards

The video adapter you are using determines whether you can display graphics and, if so, which of several video standards and resolutions you can use. There are several standards for PC video cards including VGA (Video Graphics Array). A regular VGA adapter displays images at 640×480 resolution (meaning 640 dots horizontally by 480 vertically). Super VGA is an enhancement of the VGA standard. It allows for higher resolutions (800×600, 1024×768, and in some cases 1280×1024). Virtually all computer systems sold today feature Super VGA adapters.

3 The Default Windows Resolution

By default, Windows displays information in 640×480 resolution. Increasing the resolution can dramatically increase the amount of information you can see at one time. However, because more pixels mean more work for your computer, you may notice a corresponding decrease in performance, particularly on slower systems. Additionally, the higher the resolution, the smaller the individual characters and pictures on the screen.

5 Changing Your Screen Resolution

To change the resolution of your screen display, right-click the desktop, choose **Properties** from the context menu to open the Display Properties dialog box, and click the **Settings** tab. Drag the **Screen Resolution** slider to the right for higher resolution (more pixels per inch) or to the left for lower resolution (fewer pixels per inch); the precise resolution setting (640×480 pixels, or whatever) will appear below the slider. Then click **OK**. (A few video adapters have their own utility programs for changing screen resolution, which you use instead of the Windows Display Properties dialog box.) If Windows asks you to restart your machine, go ahead and follow the instructions.

4 How Many Colors Should You Use?

There is a similar trade-off with colors. Windows displays images using a 16-color palette by default. You can increase the number of colors (sometimes called the *color depth*) to 256 colors or, if your display adapter allows, to as many as 16.8 million colors (referred to as *true color*, and sometimes also called 24-bit color). The greater the number of colors, the clearer your graphic images will be. The downside, again, is speed. The more colors your computer has to display, the longer it will take to display images on the screen. If you are displaying pictures, photographs, or videos, you'll probably want to use at least 16-bit color. But if all you're doing is word processing, manipulating a database, or creating spreadsheets, 256 colors may be adequate and may give you better performance.

6 Adjusting the Number of Display Colors

To adjust the number of colors used in your display, open the **Settings** tab of the Display Properties dialog box (as described previously) and use the **Colors** drop-down list to select the number of colors. Remember that the more colors you use, the greater the demand on your system. The range of choices you have for resolution, font size, and color density depends on your monitor, your display adapter, and the video drivers you have. If you are unable to drag the Desktop Area slider, for example, then either your monitor or display adapter only supports a single resolution, or you only have a video driver for that one resolution.

End

Notes

If You're Running a Special Version of Windows

If your computer is running an OEM version of Windows (that is, a version of Windows specifically designed to work with your computer), the Display Properties dialog box may differ a bit from what I've described. In this case, you may need to refer to your system documentation for more information on adjusting the color palette and resolution.

TOPIC 3

Taking Care of Your Monitor

Although monitors tend to be fairly low-maintenance machines, there are a few basics you should know about their care.

1 Power Saving Monitors

Some monitors feature an energy-saving mode, which both reduces the monitor's power consumption and minimizes wear and tear on the monitor itself. If you have a "green" monitor—that is, a monitor that features an energy-saving mode—whenever you haven't touched the keyboard or mouse for a while, the screen goes blank and only a bare minimum of electricity continues to flow to the monitor. As soon as you touch your keyboard or mouse, the monitor returns to normal mode (and the normal amount of energy consumption).

2 Using a Screen Saver

Whether or not you have a green monitor, you might elect to use a screen saver, a special program that either blanks out the screen or displays a moving image (like fish swimming or toasters flying) whenever you haven't touched the keyboard or mouse for a certain amount of time. After the screen saver image appears, you can always restore the previous screen image by moving your mouse or pressing any key. Screen savers got their name because they used to help prolong the life of a monitor. With today's monitors, that's no longer necessary; now they are mostly for fun!

3 Configuring Your Screen Saver

First, right-click the screen and select Properties. Next, select the Screen Saver tab. Use the pull-down menu to select the particular screen saver that interests you. With some screen savers, you can adjust settings such as how fast the image moves. Do this by clicking the Settings button and making your selections.

4 Taking Care of Your Monitor

Another way to pamper your monitor is to clean the screen periodically. Most monitors pick up an inordinate amount of dust, not to mention fingerprints. You can often get rid of both by wiping the screen with a soft, dry cloth. You can also safely clean most monitors with a glass cleaner, provided you spray the cleaner on a cleaning cloth rather than directly on the screen. A few monitors have special coatings, designed to cut down on glare, that may not take kindly to cleaners. If you have an expensive monitor, be sure to check the monitor manual for warnings and advice before you apply anything but a dry cloth to the screen.

5 Taking Care of Yourself

Then there's the issue of taking care of yourself while you use a monitor. Most monitors have contrast and brightness controls, usually on the front of the monitor but sometimes on the side or back. Use these to make the image as clear and easy on your eyes as possible. And remember that a badly positioned monitor can be, literally, a pain in the neck. As mentioned in Chapter 4, "Up and Running," you can minimize neck strain by positioning the monitor so that its upper edge is at or just below eye level. Most monitors also have swivel stands that you can use to adjust the angle of the screen to eliminate glare and/or neck strain. Finally, to prevent eye strain, look away from your monitor every few minutes, letting your eyes settle on a person or object that's further away.

_____ *End*

Notes

Using Power-Saving Measures

In an effort to save electricity and reduce wear and tear on your monitor, you can set it to shut off automatically after a certain amount of time without use. Right-click the screen and select Properties, then select the Screen Saver tab. Click the Power button, and you'll be able to create settings for when the monitor should automatically power down.

Screen Saver Options

In addition to the screen savers that are included within Windows, there are a large number of commercially available screen saver programs and some that can be downloaded for free off the Internet.

Printers

For years, people have predicted that computers would make paper obsolete. Although this may be true in the long run, in the short run they seem to be having the opposite effect. By giving people the power to endlessly manipulate and analyze their data, computers have facilitated the production of mountains of reports and memos that we had somehow previously managed to live without. For most of us, printing is still the final step in any project we undertake on the computer. When you finish the letter, you print and send it. When you get done calculating how much money you could make if only you did X, you print the spreadsheet and show it to your spouse, boss, or coworkers. Sooner or later, you'll want a hard copy, if for no other reason than that it's easy to carry around and show to others.

Begin

There are several types of printers used with personal computers; by far the most common types are laser and inkjet printers, with dot-matrix printers running a distant third.

Laser printer

Inkjet printer

Dot-matrix printer

1 Laser Printers

Laser printers print better, faster, and more quietly than other printers, producing output that looks close to typeset. Laser printers are also more expensive, ranging from about $300 all the way up to $6,000 (with most falling in the $400 to $1,000 range). Like photocopiers, they produce images by electrically charging a metal drum that then attracts particles of toner in a specific pattern. The drum rolls across a piece of paper that has an even greater electrical charge, causing the toner to jump from drum to page.

2 Benefits and Drawbacks of Laser Printers

Laser printers involve no impact—that is, there are no wires or other moving parts that strike the paper, making laser printers extremely quiet. Laser printers also cannot print on continuous forms of any kind, including sticky mailing labels. The advertised speeds for laser printers typically range from 12 to 24 pages per minute. Take these ratings with a grain of salt, however, since they measure the speed it takes to print a single page of text (sans graphics) over and over. When you're printing different pages, and especially when you're printing graphics, you can expect less speed.

3 Laser Printer Resolution

The quality of laser printer output is typically measured in terms of resolution. *Resolution* refers to the density of dots used to construct characters or symbols on the page. Laser printers typically print at a resolution of somewhere between 300 and 1800 dots per inch (dpi.) (Typesetting machines typically print at 1270 dpi and up.) Bear in mind that 300 dpi means 300 dots per inch horizontally by 300 dots per inch vertically, for a maximum of 90,000 dots in any square inch of a page. This is more than adequate for most business correspondence. You may want a higher resolution for desktop publishing or printing graphics.

4 Inkjet Printers

Unlike laser printers, which print an entire page at once, inkjet printers have print heads that move horizontally across the page, applying ink one line at a time. Although the resolution offered by inkjet printers is similar, the ink tends to spread through the fiber of the paper as it dries, giving characters a slightly fuzzy quality. Inkjet printers also tend to be a bit slower than laser printers, producing 1–12 pages per minute, and cheaper ($75 to $500 as of this writing, with the higher prices reserved for high-end color inkjets). Most color printers currently sold are inkjets. There are some color laser printers as well, but they are generally too expensive for use in homes or small offices.

5 Dot-Matrix Printers

Dot-matrix printers work by striking a cloth, nylon, or mylar ribbon with a set of small wires. The resulting characters are composed of a pattern of dots, just like characters displayed on a monitor. Because dot-matrix printers are impact printers—that is, they have components that actually strike the page through an ink-laden ribbon—they are perfect for printing multipart forms. They can print labels, checks, and other continuous forms designed to be fed through a printer in a single stream. (Such forms have little holes on the edges that fit over sprockets in the printer's tractor feed mechanism so they can be pulled through the printer.) Dot-matrix printers aren't often used by individuals anymore, but they are still used in some businesses, particularly in accounting departments.

End

Notes

Specialized Printers

There are several less commonly used types of printers. Label printers are small, specialized printers designed solely to print labels—directly from the screen, from a mailing list file, or from the printer program's own built-in database. If you use a laser printer for most of your work, you might consider buying a label printer as a relatively low-cost means of printing labels.

Printing in Windows

As you might expect, there are several ways to print a document in Windows. The process is equally easy whether you're printing an open document from within an application or printing an unopened document from within Explorer or a folder window.

Begin

1 Printing Open Documents

If the document is already open, just open the application's **File** menu and choose **Print**. (Typically, you can also use the Ctrl+P keyboard shortcut.)

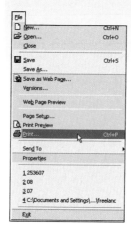

2 The Print Dialog Box

When you initiate printing by selecting Print from your application's File menu, you'll usually see a Print dialog box. You can use this dialog box to customize printing—for example, printing only the current page, printing specified pages, or printing multiple copies.

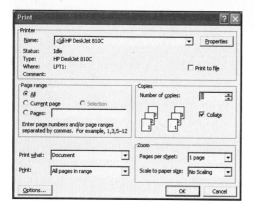

3 Printing Options

If your computer can print from several different printers, you can choose which printer to use from the **Name** drop-down list box. All pages are printed by default, but you can also print just the current page (click the **Current Page** option button), or pages that you specify (click the **Pages** option button and enter the page numbers in the text box to its right). If you want to print more than a single copy of your document, simply specify how many copies you want in the **Number of Copies** box.

4 Using the Print Button

An alternative way to print is to click the **Print** button on your application's toolbar, if it has one. When you initiate printing using a Print button on an application toolbar, Windows usually prints a single copy of your document, without displaying a dialog box or awaiting any further instructions.

5 Printing Unopened Documents

It's also simple to print documents that are not already open. To do this, start by finding and opening the folder that contains the document (you can do this either in Explorer or in a folder window). After you find the file you want to print, right-click it and choose **Print** from the context menu that appears.

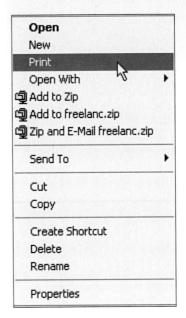

End

Notes

Getting Help on the Print Dialog Box

For additional information on using the Print dialog box, click the **?** button in its upper-right corner and then click the item you want to know more about, or look up Printing in the application's Help system.

Exiting the Print Dialog Box

If you want to leave the Print dialog box without printing, click the **Cancel** button rather than the OK button.

Printing: Behind the Scenes

In general, printers are far slower than computers. Your computer can send data to a printer much faster than the printer can print it. There are two different ways of preventing a potential bottleneck: printer buffers and print spooling. Chances are you won't have to do anything to make them go into effect. But you do need to understand them to interrupt a print job already in progress.

Begin

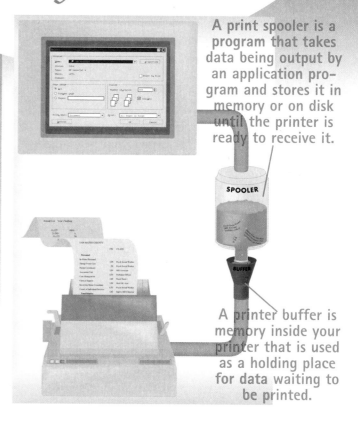

A print spooler is a program that takes data being output by an application program and stores it in memory or on disk until the printer is ready to receive it.

A printer buffer is memory inside your printer that is used as a holding place for data waiting to be printed.

1 Printer Memory

Most printers have some built-in memory that serves as a printer buffer—a kind of holding pen for data that is waiting to be printed. This is one reason that, if you interrupt printing, your printer keeps going for a while. In this case, you can often stop the printer more quickly by turning it off and then on again. This effectively erases the printer's memory.

2 The Printer Buffer

In most cases, the printer buffer is quite small—enough to hold a few pages on laser printers. As soon as the printer buffer fills, the computer needs to stop and wait before sending the next chunk of data. If you are printing a very long report, this could tie up your computer for several minutes or even hours.

3 Print Spooling

By default, Windows solves this problem by sidetracking data en route from your computer to your printer and storing it on disk temporarily until your printer is ready for it. In the meantime, you're free to get back to work in your application program. This process is known as print spooling or background printing, and the program responsible (in this case, Windows itself) is known as a print spooler.

4 The Spool File and the Print Queue

The temporary file that Windows usually creates during printing is called a *spool file*. When finished, the spool file takes up residence in a temporary holding pen known as the *print queue*. If no other print jobs are already waiting in the print queue, the new spool file is routed directly to the printer. Otherwise, it has to wait its turn. In either case, the actual printing occurs in the background, and you are free to do other work.

5 Checking the Print Queue

You can check the status of a printer's print queue by double-clicking the printer icon in the tray on the far right-hand side of the taskbar. (If you have the clock displayed, the icon appears just to the left of the clock.) You can also double-click the printer's icon in the Printers folder or, if you have a shortcut for the printer on your desktop, by double-clicking the shortcut. Windows displays a list of all the documents in the queue in the order in which they'll be printed, and the progress of each job.

6 Canceling a Print Job

To remove a single document from the queue, select it and then choose **Cancel** from the **Document** menu. (If Windows was in the midst of printing the canceled document, this will effectively stop it in its tracks. If there are other documents in the queue, Windows will move on to printing them.)

7 Purging Documents from the Print Queue

To remove all documents from the queue, choose the **Cansel All Documents** option from the **Printer** menu. You can also purge all print jobs from a local printer (that is, one that's attached to your computer rather than accessed through a network) without opening the print queue, by right-clicking the printer's icon and choosing **Purge Print Documents** from the context menu.

Notes

Other Ways to Check the Print Queue

If you point to the printer button that appears near the right edge of the taskbar when a document is printing, Windows will tell you the number of documents in the print queue. If you right-click the button, you'll see a menu with an option titled Open Active Printers and an option for each individual active printer. Select your printer to display its print queue.

End

Selecting Printers

Unless you're on a network, chances are you only have one printer attached to your computer. If you have a fax modem, you'll still need to deal with selecting printers, however, because Windows "thinks" of your fax modem as a printer as well. (You'll learn more about sending faxes from your computer later in this chapter.) If your computer is part of a network, you may also need to switch back and forth between your local printer and the network printer, or between different printers on the network.

Begin

1 The Default Printer

The first thing to know about selecting printers in Windows is that there's always one device designated as the default printer; this is the device to which Windows directs print output unless you specifically request otherwise.

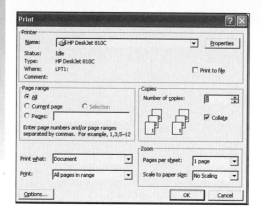

2 Selecting a Different Printer

To direct print output somewhere else other than the default printer, you select **Print** from the **File** menu inside your application and then, in the Print dialog box, select a different printer in the **Name** drop-down list.

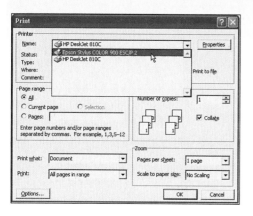

3 Which Printer Is Used?

The printer you select will become the default for the current work session only; Windows assumes you want to print to this printer unless you specify otherwise, up until you leave the application. As soon as you close the application and then open it again or load or switch to another program, Windows resumes printing to the designated default printer.

4 Changing the Default Printer

To designate a different printer as the default printer, right-click the icon for that printer in the Printers folder, and choose **Set As Default Printer**. The specified printer becomes the default printer for all your Windows applications.

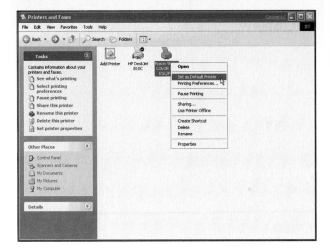

5 Adding a Printer

What if you want to choose a new printer but it doesn't appear in the Name drop-down list in the Print dialog box? In this case, you need to add the printer to the list. To do this, use the Add Printer Wizard, which you open by double-clicking **Add Printer** in the Printers folder (under My Computer). The wizard asks you a series of questions about your new printer. You may also be asked to insert your Windows disk or a disk that came with your printer.

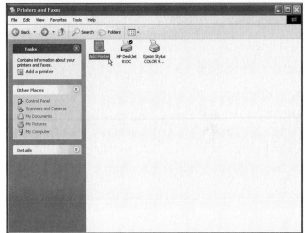

End

Notes

Quick Printing

If you have only one printer installed or you are sure you want to use the default printer, you can print documents with one click in most applications. Just click the Print icon or a toolbar (it usually looks like a printer) and the document will start to print.

TOPIC 8

Storage Devices

Most computer hard disks contain too much data to back up onto floppy disks easily. (A modest 1GB hard disk would require almost 100 disks to back up in its entirety, even if you use a backup program that compresses data as it goes.) If you're going to make regular backups of your data and programs (and you definitely should), you'll need some other mechanism for storing data long term. This section discusses some of the possibilities, including tape drives, magnetic removable-media drives, CD-Recordable drives, and magneto-optical drives.

Begin

Floppy disks

Zip disks

DAT tape

Jaz disks

1 Tape Drives

DAT tape drives (that is, tape drives that use Digital Audio Tape) can record up to 8GB or more on a single cassette tape. Just like more conventional tape recorders, however, they access data sequentially and are therefore suited for backup rather than regular data storage.

2 What Are Magnetic Removable Drives?

Magnetic removable-media drives combine the best features of floppy and hard drives. Like floppy drives, they use disks that are removable. Like hard drives, they store anywhere from dozens of megabytes to over a gigabyte on a single disk. This makes them perfect for backing up data and transferring large amounts of data from one computer to another. In addition, removable-media drives allow you to keep expanding your computer's storage capacity at a relatively low cost. Every time you run out of space, you just buy another cartridge.

3 The Types of Magnetic Removable Drives

Magnetic removable-media drives can be grouped into two categories: small-format and large-format. The most popular small-format drives are Iomega ZIP drives. These drives store a relatively small amount of data per cartridge (the smallest ZIP stores 100MB) and are rela-tively inexpensive (under $200 these days). They are well suited to transferring large files or groups of files

from one computer to another—from home computer to office computer, for example, or between friends or colleagues. (You might think of these drives as high-capacity floppy disk drives.) The most popular large-format drive is currently the Iomega Jaz drive. A good middle ground is the 250 MB

4 ZIP Drives and Small-Format SyQuest Drives

ZIP drives are becoming extemely popular and common. They have the additional advantage of coming in a parallel port version, meaning a version that can be plugged into the parallel port you usually use for your printer. This means that if you're working with someone who doesn't happen to have a ZIP drive, you can potentially take your own drive over to their home or office and plug it into the parallel port on their computer to transfer the files. Other ZIP drives use a SCSI port connection, which is less commonly used on home or small office PCs but which allows you to save and retrieve files faster. SyQuest EZ135 drives are faster than ZIP drives, which makes them more suited to storing programs and data you use often.

5 Difficulties in Backing Up Your System

The low-capacity drives don't store a lot of data per cartridge, so you cannot easily use them to back up your entire hard disk; most new computers have hard drives that hold far more than 100MB of data. (They are sufficient if you're willing to back up just your data, in 100- or 135MB chunks, and reinstall all your software from scratch should your hard drive fail.)

6 Jaz Drives and Large-Format SyQuest Drives

If what you need is a drive you can use both for backup and as an extension of your hard drive—one that is capable of running your favorite programs at the speed to which you've grown accustomed—you're better off with a large-format drive, such as the Jaz drive or high-end SyQuest drives, or even with a PD/CD drive or a magneto-optical drive (described shortly). Most large-format drives are almost as fast as most hard drives and can store between 540MB and 1.3GB per cartridge. (This means that even if you can't back up your entire hard drive onto one cartridge, you probably can fit it on two or three.) The prices for these drives run from about $300 to $700, with car-tridges costing between $50 and a little over $100.

7 CD-Recordable Drives

Another technology, called *CD-Recordable* (*CD-R* for short), lets you create CDs in a format that can be read by a regular CD-ROM drive (as well as by a CD-R drive). CD-R drives cost more than regular CD-ROM drives, although their prices have been dropping rapidly. (CD-R drive prices are now starting to dip below $500.) Although most CD-R drives only let you record data once on a CD, some let you add more data in separate sessions, adding to what's been previously recorded. One of the main attractions of this type of drive is that discs you record on using a CD-R drive can be read in any regular CD-ROM drive.

Continues

8 Using CD-R Drives for Backups

CD-R and CD-RW drives are a viable mode of backing up data. Because they are much slower than hard disks, however, they're likely to be used primarily for backup and long-term storage rather than for storing data or programs that will be used regularly. Another advantage is the cost of discs themselves—usually less than $1 each.

9 Magneto-Optical Drives

Magneto-optical (*MO*) *drives* use both a laser and an electromagnet to record information on a cartridge, the surface of which contains tiny embedded magnets. These cartridges can be written to, erased, and then written to again. They are slightly more expensive than CD-R drives but hold more data (typically in the 1–2.5GB range, although sometimes less). The drives can range anywhere from $500 dollars to thousands of dollars.

10 DVD Drives

DVD is a type of disk destined to replace videotape as the medium of choice for recording and distributing movies for home viewers. They're also expected to supplant CD-ROM drives in the coming years. The first DVD players, released in mid-1997, can read existing CD-ROM discs as well as DVDs, which range from 4.7GB to 17GB. Prices range from $200 to $1500. The first applications for DVDs are things like countrywide phone and address listings.

End

_____ *Notes*

Make Your Own Music CDs

Perhaps the most popular use for CD-R and CD-RW technology is to make music CDs. After you've downloaded songs from the Internet, you can copy them to a CD you can take with you.

Disk Prices

Another think to consider is the price of the disks themselves. CD-RW disks can be purchased for pennies, while ZIP disks cost a few dollars. So, if you have lots of data to back up or share, a CD-RW drive might be the best bet.

Modems

To send or receive data via regular phone lines, you need a device called a *modem*. The main purpose of a modem is to translate data from a form palatable to a computer into a form palatable to a telephone and vice versa. Most computers are digital devices. They store and manipulate information by turning on and off sets of tiny electronic switches. (When turned on, a switch represents the number 1; when off, it represents the number 0.) Transmitting digital data is therefore a bit like sending Morse code: At any given instant, the signal must represent either a dot or a dash. There are no gradations. Telephones, in contrast, transmit data as an analog signal (sound wave) that varies in frequency and strength, rather like the line drawn by an electrocardiograph machine.

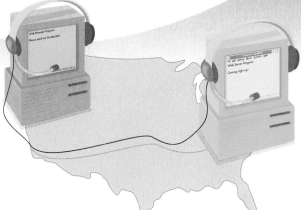

For two computers to communicate, they must both have modems and be running some form of communication program. After your modem has successfully established a connection to another modem, you are said to be online. When no such connection exists, you are offline.

1 How Modems Work

Modems translate digital signals into analog ones and vice versa. When you send data, the modem converts the digital information from the computer into analog signals that can be transmitted over phone wires: a process known as *modulation*. When you receive data, the modem converts the analog signals received from the phone into digital codes that your computer can manage (a process known as *demodulation*). The term *modem* is a hybrid of the terms *modulate* and *demodulate*.

`0101100010011110001001011`

FROM/TO COMPUTER

FROM/TO PHONE LINE

The purpose of modems is to transform digital information generated by a computer into an analog form that can be transmitted over phone lines (modulation) and to transform analog signals received over the phone line into digital codes that your computer knows how to use (demodulation).

Continues

2 Internal Modems

There are basically two types of modems. *Internal modems* are expansion boards that are installed in expansion slots inside your system unit. Internal modems are often cheaper and consume none of your precious desk space. Most new computer systems are sold with internal modems already installed.

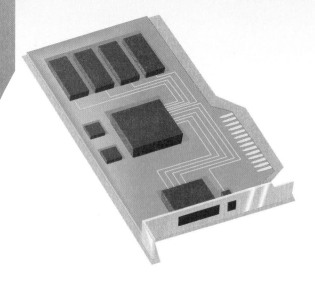

3 External Modems

External modems look like flat plastic or metal boxes (about the size of a rather thin hardback book) that usually plug into the back of your computer with a cable. External modems offer the advantage of visible status lights—little lights on the front end of the device that can help you (or the expert you get on the phone) figure out where the problem lies if you have trouble establishing a connection with another computer. External modems are also easily transferred from one computer to another, and they are usually faster than a comparable internal modem.

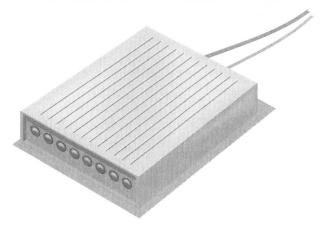

4 Data Transmission Speed

Aside from living quarters, what distinguishes one modem from the next is the speed at which it can transmit data. The speed at which modems send and receive data is typically measured in kilobits per second (Kbps). Most modems now in use transmit data at a maximum of 56Kbps. (It takes 8 bits to represent each byte of data. There is more information on bits and bytes in the Notes section.) Another type of modem, Digital Subscriber Line (DSL), transfers data many times faster. Cable modems, offered through cable television companies, are also faster. These high-speed connections can range from 500Kbps to 1,000Kbps.

5 Determining How Fast a File Will Transfer

As a rule of thumb, you can multiply the Kbps rate by 100 to determine the number of characters (bytes) transferred per second. A 60K (60,000-character) file will take approximately 10 seconds to transmit at 57.6Kbps (60,000 divided by 5,760). This rule of thumb is only approximate because the actual transmission rate varies slightly depending on the amount of interference on the phone line (if any) and other factors.

6 When You Need Speed

Modem speed doesn't matter that much if you are using your modem strictly to send short messages via email or carry on online conversations with friends or colleagues. Speed does matter, however, when you are sending or receiving files. It takes almost twice as long to transmit a file at 28.8Kbps as it does at 56Kbps. Try transmitting a file that's 1MB or more and the difference will be very noticeable. Modem speed also makes a big difference when you're accessing the Internet, particularly if you're using the graphics-intensive World Wide Web.

7 The Fax Modem

A final factor to consider when choosing a modem is whether it has fax capabilities. See the upcoming section on fax modems for details.

End

Notes

How Computers Store Information

As mentioned in Chapter 1, "The Basics," computers store and manipulate information as numbers, regardless of whether that information consists of numbers, letters, pictures, or any other type of data. Internally, computers represent all numbers using base 2, a numbering system that employs only two digits—0 and 1. (Humans, in contrast, like to think in base 10, which involves ten digits: 0 through 9.) Base 2 is often referred to as *binary notation* or a *binary numbering system*. The reason computers "think" in base 2 is that they represent information in terms of the presence or absence of an electrical or magnetic charge. The number 1 is used as the numeric equivalent of on, or charged. Zero means off, or uncharged.

Bits and Bytes

In computer terminology, the electronic representation of a 0 or a 1 is known as a *bit* (short for binary digit) and there are eight bits to each byte of information. (That is, it takes eight 0s and/or 1s to represent a single character.) For example, the pattern used to represent a lowercase "a" on a personal computer is 01100001. As mentioned, when bits are stored inside a computer, they are stored as electrical or magnetic charges. When information is transmitted from one part of the computer to another or from a computer to a modem, bits are represented by small bursts of electricity—where a single burst represents an on bit (a number 1) and a pause between bursts represents an off bit (a number 0). A lowercase "a," for example, is represented by a pause, two bursts of electricity, four pauses, and another burst of electricity.

Plugging In Your Modem

As mentioned, modems come in two basic flavors: external and internal. External modems come with an intimidating number of connectors. There are at least three connections to be made: You need to connect your modem to a power source. You need to connect your modem to your computer. And you need to connect your modem to the telephone line. If you are using a single phone line for both the modem and voice communications (that is, if you plan to talk on the same line that you use to telecommunicate), you may want to connect your modem into your telephone as well. Internal modems only need to be connected to phone lines.

Begin

The modem is connected to an electrical outlet with a power cord that has a transformer.

The modem is connected to a phone jack with a regular modular phone cord.

The modem is connected to your computer with a serial cable.

If the modem will be sharing a phone line with a telephone (rather than having a line of its own), it is connected to the phone with a modular phone jack.

1 Plug In to a Power Source

To connect your external modem to a power source, you simply plug its power cord into a wall outlet or power strip. (The power cord features a little transformer box and a standard electrical plug.)

2 Connecting Your Modem to Your Computer

To connect an external modem to your computer, you plug a cable running from the modem into a serial port at the back of your system unit. As explained in this chapter and Chapter 2, ports are data channels designed to carry data and instructions between your computer's memory and an I/O (input/output) device. Most computers feature two types of ports: serial ports, which are generally used for external modems, sometimes mice, and occasionally for printers; and parallel ports, which are always used for printers; and the USB ports, which allow you to connect a variety of exernal devices such as drives and printers. At the back of the system unit, you will usually find one or two serial ports that serve as gateways into the computer's internal communication channels.

3 How Serial Ports Work

Serial ports are always "male" (that is, have pins sticking out) and have either 9 or 25 pins. Most PCs have either one or two serial ports, but it's possible to have neither. (If you don't have a serial port, you either need to buy a circuit board that includes a serial port or use an internal modem.)

Serial port

Serial cable

9 to 25 pin adapter

4 Using Adapters

If the connector on the end of your modem cable has the wrong number of holes for your particular serial port (say your modem cable has 25 holes and your serial port has only 9 pins), you'll need to get a special 9 to 25 pin adapter from your computer store. This is rather like buying an adapter that lets you plug a three-prong plug into a two-prong electrical outlet.

5 Connecting to a Phone Line

Finally, connect your modem to a phone line. If you have a separate phone line for your modem, you will generally run a modular phone cord from a phone jack on the wall to the back of your external modem, or to the piece of your internal modem card that protrudes from the back of your computer. If you don't have a separate phone line, you run one cord from the modem into the phone and another from the modem into the phone jack. This way, you and your modem can share the same line— although not at the same time. (In most cases, there are specific spots on the modem for plugging in cables to the phone line and to the telephone itself. Sometimes they are identified. If not, check your modem documentation to determine which is which.)

End

Notes

Call Interrupt

Try not to attach a modem to a phone line that has call interrupt in effect. Otherwise, an incoming call may either break the connection between modems or introduce a signal that your modem will not know how to interpret. (If you happen to be in the middle of transmitting a file, such errant signals can ruin the file transfer or make it necessary for you to retransmit the file from scratch.) In most cases, you can disable call waiting by dialing *70.

Fax Modems

Many of the modems currently being sold are fax modems—they not only let you send and receive data, they let your computer double as a fax machine. Like regular modems, fax modems come in both internal and external varieties. They also have advantages and disadvantages relative to regular fax machines, in terms of both sending and receiving faxes.

Begin

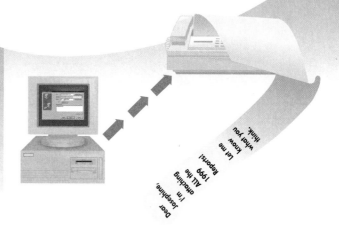

1 Sending Faxes

Fax modems are particularly useful for sending documents and graphics created on your computer because they eliminate the need to print the data first. On the other hand, if you want to use a fax modem to transmit data that you have only in "hard copy" (that is, on paper), you need to first scan it into your computer using a scanner.

2 Receiving Faxes

Fax modems let you read incoming faxes on your computer before deciding whether they're worth printing. However, you can only receive faxes when your computer is turned on and your fax software is running, which means that you either have to tell your associates to send faxes only during your regular hours or leave your computer on during off hours.

3 Fax Software

When you buy your fax modem, it will come with fax software. Windows includes a built-in fax program named Microsoft Fax.

4 How to Send a Fax

In Windows, after you have installed a fax modem and a suitable communications program, sending faxes from your computer is simply a matter of "printing" a document to your fax software. Just open the document you want to fax, select the **Print** command from the **File** menu, and then choose your fax program from the drop-down list of available printers. As soon as you select **OK**, your fax program takes over long enough to request information on the intended recipient and the cover page you want to use, if any. You can also create and send faxes directly from within most fax-capable communications programs. You may choose to do this if you just want to fax a quick note and have no need to create it in another application (or to save it to disk).

5 What Happens When You Receive a Fax

When you receive a fax, it generally goes into something called a *fax queue*. To view it, load your communications program (if it's not already loaded) and issue a command for viewing received faxes. Even if a fax consists entirely of text, your fax modem will usually receive it as a graphical image. This means that you usually can't load it into your word processing program and edit it afterwards. There are several exceptions to this rule, as described next.

6 OCR Software

Some fax sp;fware [rpgra,s om;ide WinFaxPro includes optical character recognition (OCR) capabilities that allow you to translate some or all of a received fax into a text file that you can import into a word processing program or other application. OCR will not work on all faxes: It does best with sans serif fonts in a fairly large typeface and requires a fax image with good print quality.

_____ *End*

_____ *Notes*

Fancy Faxing Stuff

If you want to do the fancy stuff—like OCR, scheduling faxes to be sent at a later time (when the phone rates drop, for example), sending faxes to lists of recipients, or retrieving newly received faxes from your laptop or other remote computer—you'll probably need to buy a specialized fax program such as WinFaxPro. (If you're shopping for a program, make a list of all the features you need and then all the features you'd like, and take it with you to your local computer or software store.)

Quick Faxing

If you have Microsoft Fax set up, it should be easy to fax an existing document without opening it first. Right-click the document, choose **Send To**, and choose **Fax Recipient** from the Send To menu that is displayed. If you're using another fax program, you can add it to the Send To menu. To do so, open the SendTo folder (it's inside the Windows folder). Then add a shortcut to your fax program to this folder. (Find your fax program in Windows Explorer or in its folder window, right-drag it into the SendTo folder, and choose **Create Shortcut(s) Here** from the context menu.)

Multimedia Computing and Sound

A few years ago, *multimedia* became one of the biggest buzzwords in the computer industry. Computer systems are regularly advertised as "multimedia PC," games are touted as being multimedia, and so on.

By themselves, most PCs are only capable of beeps and a few whirring sounds. Today's computers come equipped with sound and video cards designed to maximize your enjoyment of the Internet and software programs. They allow you to hear the music, speech, and other sounds and see the images clearly.

Begin

1 What Is a Multimedia Program?

A *multimedia program* is a program that communicates in more than one medium. In practical terms, this means any program that employs any combination of text, pictures, sound, and full motion video. The first multimedia computer programs were encyclopedias that mixed text and graphics. Today's multimedia applications often feature full-motion video and sound and range from elaborate and visually stunning games to sophisticated interactive training programs.

2 What Is a Multimedia Computer?

A *multimedia computer* is any computer that can take full advantage of multimedia programs—that is, it can generate sounds, display pictures, and store large quantities of data. (Both sounds and pictures consume a great deal of disk space.) In terms of hardware requirements, this means a computer with a reasonably fast processor, a color monitor, plenty of memory, a sound card, speakers or headphones, and a CD-ROM drive. Virtually all packaged computers sold today are multimedia computers.

3 What Is a Sound Card?

A *sound card* (also known as *sound board*) is a circuit board that is capable of translating program instructions into sounds. When you hear sound from a CD-ROM program (such as a game) on a PC, the sounds are actually being generated by the computer's sound card. The CD-ROM is simply delivering instructions to the sound card about what sounds to produce and when.

4 Using Sound Cards

A sound card fits into an expansion slot inside your computer's system unit. If your computer doesn't already have a sound card, you can add one (if you're not afraid to open up your computer and if your system unit has an available expansion slot). Sound cards range in price from about $50 dollars to several hundred dollars. As you might guess, the more expensive boards can produce richer, more complex tones.

5 Speakers

If you want your computer to communicate in sound, you'll probably want speakers as well. Although it is possible to hook up the sound card to your stereo system, for most people a pair of inexpensive computer speakers is adequate and more convenient. A pair of computer-compatible speakers will cost you anywhere from $25 to several hundred dollars.

6 3D Graphics

The latest video cards are 3D graphics accelerators that allow you to see objects and moving pictures in 3D. These are great for serious game players who want a more "realistic" experience.

End

Notes

Keep Disks Away from Your Speakers!

Speakers contain magnets that can destroy the data stored on floppy disks. Unless your speakers are designated as "magnetically shielded," keep them at least a few inches from your floppies. You don't have to worry about CD-ROMs, because information on CD-ROMs is recorded with lasers rather than magnets.

Playing Audio CDs

All CD-ROM drives can play audio CDs (the music CDs you play in your stereo system) as well as CD-ROMs. Playing CDs on a computer lets you listen to your favorite music at work without installing a stereo in your office. After you start playing an audio CD, it keeps playing while you work. If you're worried about disturbing coworkers, you can always listen through headphones. (Just be wary of humming along too loudly.)

1 Plugging in Speakers

Any pair of speakers should work with any sound board, so choosing speakers is simply a matter of deciding how much you care about sound quality and how much you're willing to pay for it. To set them up, you just plug them into a jack at the back of your computer, which is, in turn, attached to your sound card. (Look for a jack labeled something like Speaker in or Spk in.)

2 Listening to CDs with Headphones

If you don't have a set of speakers or if your speakers are not connected to your CD-ROM drive, headphones are your only option for listening to audio CDs. You can use regular stereo headphones, which you can purchase at most stores that sell stereos or home electronics, and just plug them into the headphone jack on the front of the drive. If your CD-ROM drive has a volume control knob on the front, you can use it to control the headphone volume. Volume can also be controlled by the application that plays the CDs on your computer.

3 Troubleshooting Speakers

If you do have speakers but they don't make a peep when you play an audio CD, your CD-ROM drive is probably not connected to your sound card. You can either try to make the connection yourself (if you're adventurous and have both the sound card documentation and an audio cable) or get a technician to do it for you.

4 Playing an Audio CD

If you're using Windows, as soon as you insert an audio CD into the drive, Windows starts playing the disc. It also launches a utility program named Windows Media Player that allows you to jump from track to track, create "play lists" that determine which tracks are played and in what sequence, or direct the drive to play tracks in random order.

5 Using Windows Media Player

Windows Media Player allows you to play and manage all your entertainment activities through one program. You can play DVD movies and audio CDs, and organize your media files. You can also build custom playlists and use the program to make your own CDs (assuming you have a CD-R or CD-RW drive).

End

Notes

Using Drag-and-Drop in Windows Media Player

Windows Media Player also allows you to rearrange the order in which a CD is played. You can have the program "shuffle" the track and play them in random order, or you can drag individual titles in the list and drop them to a different location.

Portable Computers

In the world of computers, the smaller the package, the larger the price tag. If you compare two computer systems—one a desktop system and the other a portable—with the same CPU speed, hard-disk capacity, amount of RAM, and extras (CD-ROM drive, sound card, speakers), the portable will generally cost much more. (The portable's price can be as much as double the desktop's.) However, if you travel a lot or if you want a computer you can easily carry from office to home and back, the convenience of a portable may outweigh the price.

1 Running on Batteries

For travelers, portable computers not only offer the advantage of coming in a small, lightweight package, they can also run on batteries, for at least a few hours. This means you can write a report or a couple of letters on your coast-to-coast flight or do your homework in your favorite café. Most portable computers provide you with some kind of warning when your battery is running out of juice—either a warning on the screen or a continual beeping. This gives you a chance to save your work and turn off the computer before it runs out of power. You can easily recharge a portable's battery by plugging it into an electrical outlet for an hour or two.

2 Laptops and Notebooks

The term *laptop computer* used to indicate a subcategory of portable computers—those that were small enough and light enough to fit on your lap. Then the term *notebook computer* was invented to mean laptop computers that were almost as small as a notebook. These days, just about all portable computers are notebook sized, and the terms *portable computer, laptop,* and *notebook* are used almost interchangeably.

3 Handhelds

There are even smaller computers known as *handheld computers* that typically weigh about 1/2 lb. These tend to be used primarily for scheduling programs and address books and often come with hardware and software that enables you to synchronize the scheduling/address data on the palmtop and your desktop PC. (This allows you to make changes from either computer.) Most of the higher-end handheld designed to talk with PCs use an operating system called Pocket PC. Pocket PC-based computers can run special Pocket PC. versions of standard Windows software, such as word processing, spreadsheet, and presentation programs.

4 PDAs

There's yet another term for pint-size computers: *PDA*, for *Personal Digital Assistants*. Some people use the terms palmtop and PDA interchangeable; others reserve PDA for devices that combine limited computing capabilities with other talents, including the capability to act as a cellular phone and send faxes. Most PDAs use a pen and stylus rather than a keyboard for input, and feature handwriting recognition and, in some cases, voice recognition.

5 Portable Screens

If you're shopping for a portable computer, you'll want to consider screen type and size. Portable screens vary widely in both size (from about 12 inches to slightly over 15, measured diagonally) and clarity. They also support different ranges of screen resolutions: Some support regular VGA resolution only (640×480); others can go as high as 1024×768. (If you're thinking that high resolution seems impractical for a small screen, bear in mind that you may want to plug a full-sized desktop monitor into your portable when you're not on the road.) Be aware that some, but not all, portables can power both the portable screen and either a full-size desktop monitor or overhead display simultaneously. This feature is a must if you plan to use your portable to deliver presentations.

6 Portable Speed

You also need to take speed into account when hunting for a portable. At any given moment, the fastest desktop computers are always faster than the fastest portables. (As of this writing the high end for desktop computers is 1.7GHz for a desktop PC and 7.0GHz for a portable.) As with desktop computers, the faster the CPU, the higher the price. If you already have a desktop computer and plan to use the portable only when traveling, you may be willing to compromise on speed, unless you plan to use the portable to do demanding multimedia presentations. If you plan to use it as your one and only computer, however, you may need to pay the extra price.

Continues

7 Storage and Memory

Storage space and memory are also important in a laptop. The size of hard disks in portable computers varies quite a bit. You're more likely to need more disk space if you're using a lot of graphical images or different programs or are planning to use your portable as your sole computer. As in a desktop computer, the amount of RAM you have will impact the speed of your computer and the number of programs you can comfortably run at once. (64MB to 128 PBs becoming standard on new computers. 32MB may be sufficient if you don't run graphics-intensive programs or use multiple programs at once.)

8 Battery Life

Battery life is another important consideration. All portable computers sport batteries that let you use your computer when there's no electrical outlet in sight, a feature that's especially important when you're in transit. (When an electrical outlet is available, you can also plug into that, sparing your battery.) If you spend a lot of time working on long airplane flights, you might want to invest in a second battery pack so you can swap batteries when the first one gives out halfway across the Atlantic. (Some models make it easier to swap batteries than others.) Two types of batteries are commonly used in portables: nickel hydride batteries and longer-running lithium-ion batteries. Most batteries can power from one to three hours of continuous computer use before they need recharging.

9 Pointing Devices

Different laptops have different pointing devices. Using a mouse is impractical when traveling, because mice require a fairly large flat surface. (On a plane, you'd probably knock over your neighbor's drink trying to click the Close button!) All portables therefore feature an alternative pointing device that you can use on the road; some have trackballs, some pointing sticks, some touchpads, and a few offer both a pointing stick and a touchpad. (All these pointing devices were described in Chapter 2.) Most portables also have either a mouse port or a regular serial port into which you can plug a mouse when you're not traveling.

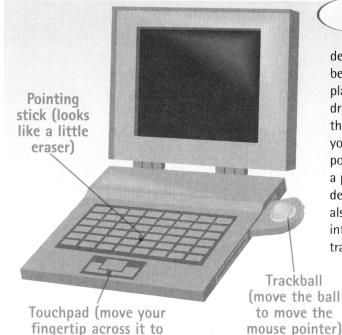

Pointing stick (looks like a little eraser)

Touchpad (move your fingertip across it to move the mouse pointer)

Trackball (move the ball to move the mouse pointer)

10 Weight

Portable computers weigh from under two pounds for mini-portables to over eight pounds. Weight makes a lot of difference if you plan to frequently lug your computer, along with all your other bags, through airports. It makes less difference if your computer will mostly travel from home to work and back.

11 Keyboards

All portable keyboards differ a bit from desktop keyboards. At the least, they usually forego a numeric keypad and rearrange some of the cursor-movement keys. On some keyboards, the keys are slightly closer together than on regular desktop computers. Some portables let you have your cake and eat it too, by featuring a fold-out keyboard that fits inside a small case when closed but that opens to a more comfortable and familiar size when in use.

12 Portable Extras and Accessories

You should also investigate which components and accessories a laptop has. These days, most portables feature a modem and a CD-ROM drive; some come with a sound card and speakers. Some include DVD players, so you can watch a movie while on the go. In some cases, you can pick and choose the extras you want, like buying a car. Bear in mind that extra features usually mean at least a little extra weight. Some portables keep their weight down by foregoing an internal floppy disk drive. On these systems, there's usually an external floppy disk drive that you can plug in when needed. Some portables let you replace the CD-ROM drive with other components, such as the battery, a floppy disk drive, or a second hard drive.

13 Ports and Port Replicators

Most portable computers have ports that allow you to plug in a regular desktop monitor, keyboard, and mouse. Some have only a few ports; if you want more, you need to purchase a separate *port replicator,* a device that lets you connect to several peripherals at once. Rather than plugging all your peripherals back in every time the portable returns to your office, you can leave the peripherals plugged into the port replicator and then simply plug in your portable.

14 Docking Stations

Docking stations are port replicators with some extras—often providing additional components, such as a CD-ROM drive, speakers, or network card, and sometimes including a hutch where you can stash the portable (the monitor sits on top), leaving your desk free for a full-size keyboard and a mouse. Some portable computers are equipped with an *infrared port,* which allows you to connect with an infrared-equipped printer or network without using cables.

Continues

15 Liquid Crystal Displays

The screens on most laptop computers use a technology known as liquid crystal display (LCD). In LCD screens, liquid crystals (a fluid that reflects light) are sandwiched between two polarized pieces of glass or plastic. These polarized sheets shut out all light waves except those that are parallel to their particular plane. Inside the display, tiny electrodes pass current through the crystals, causing them to form spirals that bend the light to a greater or lesser degree. The amount of current determines the amount of spiraling, which in turn determines how much of the light actually makes it through the front of the screen. (In areas where the light is not bent at all, the beam is completely blocked and the screen remains dark.) In the case of color LCD screens, the light passes through various color filters.

16 Active Versus Passive Matrix Displays

LCD screens are often characterized as either passive or active matrix displays. In passive matrix displays, groups of pixels (screen dots) share the same electrodes. In active matrix displays, which are more expensive, each pixel gets a transistor of its own. The resulting images are much clearer and easier to read. Active matrix displays also drain batteries much faster than passive matrix displays, making them less appropriate for long airplane flights and other work sessions conducted without the benefit of an electrical outlet.

End

Notes

Battery Power Check

Most portable computers display the amount of battery power remaining, either on the screen or on a panel built into the computer. If you are using Windows, check the tray at the right edge of the taskbar for a battery status utility program icon. In some cases, you only need to point to the icon to see the amount of battery life remaining.

Energy-Saving Mode

Don't panic if your screen blacks out when you haven't even touched the machine. Some portables automatically go into energy-saving mode when you haven't touched the keyboard or pointing device for a while. This feature is designed to prolong battery life. In most cases, you can turn the energy-saving mode on and off. (You might prefer to have it off when you're using an electrical outlet.) See your computer's user's manual for details.

PCMCIA Cards

PCMCIA, which stands for Personal Computer Memory Card International Association, is a standard often used in portable computer expansion slots and accessories. PCMCIA cards (also known as PC cards) are credit card-sized devices that fit into slots in your portable and add additional memory or extra capabilities, such as sound. If possible, purchase a computer that has one or more PCMCIA slots so you can easily upgrade the system later. There are three types of PCMCIA cards available—Type I, Type II, and Type III—with Type I being the thinnest and Type III the thickest. (Type I cards are typically used to add RAM or ROM to a computer; Type II cards are most often used for modems or fax modems, and Type III cards can be used for disk drives.) Most new portables have a PCMCIA slot that can accept either a Type II or Type III card.

Installing New Hardware in Windows

One of the big selling points of Windows 95 and 98 is a feature known as *Plug and Play (PnP)*. Plug and Play is a standard developed by Microsoft and various computer hardware manufacturers that's aimed at taking the pain out of installing new hardware devices on PCs. Prior to PnP, installing new hardware meant finding and installing special *drivers* (programs designed to let your computer talk to your peripherals) and making sure the new device didn't try to use various communication channels and memory locations already claimed by another device. PnP was designed to eliminate such problems.

Begin

1 Using Plug and Play

Theoretically, if you have a computer designed for PnP and are using a PnP operating system (like Windows), installing a PnP printer, sound card, modem, CD-ROM drive, or other peripheral is a simple matter of plugging in the device.

2 Adding New Hardware

It's not always quite this simple. Assuming you are using a PnP computer, when you attach a PnP device, you may see a message indicating that Windows has recognized the new device—either immediately or the next time you start up your system. If Windows needs a driver that is not currently installed, you may at that point be asked to insert a disk or the Windows CD-ROM. If you don't see a message but the device appears to be working, you can assume that everything is fine.

3 The Add New Hardware Wizard

If the device is not working properly, try using the Add New Hardware Wizard. To run this wizard, open the **Start** menu, choose **Control Panel**, and double-click the **Add Hardware** icon (or single-click, if single-click mode is on). Then follow the instructions on your screen.

Continues

4 Working with Legacy Peripherals

When you install what Microsoft calls a *legacy* peripheral (that is, an older device that is not Plug and Play compatible), you'll need to use the Add Hardware Wizard, as described previously, to let Windows know about the new device. (Computer people use the term *legacy* to refer to anything that's left over—no longer on the cutting edge.) You'll need to install drivers for the device. They are typically provided on a disk from the manufacturerr.

5 Removing Legacy Peripherals

Whenever you remove a legacy peripheral from your system, you need to let Windows know that the device is gone. This enables Windows to reuse the resources (places in memory and internal communications channels) that it previously allocated to that device.

6 Removing Legacy Devices Within Windows

To tell Windows that you've removed a legacy device, follow these steps: Right-click the **My Computer** icon and choose **Properties** from the context menu to display the System Properties dialog box. On the Hardware tab, lick the **Device Manager** button. The Device Manager displays a list of your hardware devices organized by type. Right-click the name of the item you have removed from your system. (If you don't see the item, look for a category heading that describes the type of device you removed, and click the plus sign to its left to display a list of items in that category.) Click the OK button to close the System Properties dialog box.

7 Parallel, Serial, and USB Ports

As you know, computers usually pass information to and from peripherals using ports: parallel, serial, and USB. Parallel ports transmit units of data simultaneously, like a set of soldiers marching abreast. Serial ports pass information on a single wire, one unit of data at a time. If you look at the back of your PC, the parallel ports are the ones with 25 holes in them. Serial ports have pins sticking out—either 9 pins or 25 pins. There's a another of port known as a SCSI (pronounced scuzzy) port that is sometimes used to connect devices like external CD-ROM drives, tape backup units, or external hard disks. It contains holes, like a parallel port. Many newer computers also sport round ports, known as PCI ports, for connecting the mouse and keyboard. (Often you'll see little pictures next to the ports indicating which type of device plugs in there.) USB ports are like fast serial ports that allow you to add multiple peripherals.

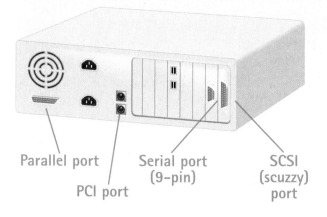

Parallel port   Serial port (9-pin)   SCSI (scuzzy) port

PCI port

8 Which Type of Port Do You Need?

Most PC printers are parallel printers, meaning they are designed to be connected to a parallel port. But a few are serial printers, meaning they need to be connected to a serial port. You can tell which type you need to plug the printer into by looking at the connector at the end of the printer cable: If it has holes rather than pins, you need to plug it into a serial port. Some printers are also USB printers, so they need to connect to a USB port. If your printer is on a network, your computer will communicate with it through your network connection (usually Ethernet).

9 Installing a Legacy Device

When you install a legacy device, you may be asked the name of the port to which it is connected. In most cases, your printer will be connected to LPT1, which is the name of the first parallel port (or, more precisely, the name of the internal communications channel which is connected to that parallel port). If you have two printers connected to your computer, the second one will probably be connected to LPT2. Your mouse will probably be connected to the first serial port, which is usually referred to as COM1. (Again, technically speaking, COM1 is the name of a communication channel inside your computer rather than the name of the port itself.) Your modem, if you have one, will probably be connected to COM2. A serial printer will probably be connected to COM2 as well. Other legacy dexices, such as keyboards, have their own ports as well.

End

Notes

Device Emulation

If you get to the point where you're asked to choose the manufacturer and model number of your device from lists and your particular device is not listed, try contacting the manufacturer of the device to see whether they've developed a Windows driver. If not, look in your manual to see whether the device emulates another type of device. Many printers can emulate Epson or Hewlett-Packard LaserJet printers, for example. If so, select from the lists the manufacturer and model of the device that your own device can emulate.

The Plug and Play BIOS

Technically, a computer designed for Plug and Play is one that uses a PnP BIOS. The BIOS, which stands for Basic Input/Output System, is a part of your operating system that is stored in a ROM chip inside your computer. (It's the BIOS that performs some of the initial hardware tests when you turn on your computer and that loads the rest of the operating system.) Most PCs created during and after 1996 use a PnP BIOS; most built before 1995 do not. PCs built during 1995 are a toss-up: Check your system documentation.

Troubleshooting Problems with Legacy Devices

If you have trouble getting a legacy device to work, look up "hardware conflict, troubleshooting" in the Windows Help index. This takes you to a wizard that steps you through the process of resolving conflicts among peripherals.

TOPIC 16

Networks

Begin

Networks are groups of computers that are linked together. There are three reasons to network computers: 1) To enable multiple computers to share peripherals, such as expensive printers, scanners, and fax equipment. 2) To allow people to exchange messages via computer (a process known as email) and to easily transfer files from one computer to another. 3) To allow computers to share data and programs so that, for example, three people in a department can write a report together or work with the same spreadsheets. This capability is particularly useful in the case of databases, which many different people in an organization may need to access and change.

Networks are groups of computers that are linked together to share data, programs, or peripherals, and to facilitate communication and file exchange within an organization.

1 Local Area Networks and Wide Area Networks

The term *local area network* (*LAN*) means a network in which the computers are all connected with wire cables. (This generally means that they're in the same part of a single building.) LANS are contrasted with *wide area networks*, or *WANs*, in which some of the links in the chain are connected by modems and phone wires or satellites.

2 How Networks Are Set Up

The details of setting up a LAN are best left to experts. (Setting up a WAN is even more intimidating.) But to make a long story fairly short, there are three essential steps in the process: 1) Special expansion boards, generally known as *network cards*, must be installed in each of the computers. 2) The computers must be connected in some way, usually via wire cables. 3) Network software designed to control the flow of information across the network must be installed on each of the computers.

3 File Servers

Most networks include one or more computers that are designated as file servers. A *file server* is a computer whose hard disk is accessible to other computers on the network. Its job is to "serve" data and program files to these other machines via cables or other network connections. When there is a dedicated file server, the other computers are usually called either *nodes* or *workstations*.

A file server is a computer that "serves" data and program files to other computers on a network.

4 Peer-to-Peer Networks

On many smaller networks, each computer can access the hard disk of any of the other computers, and there are no computers dedicated to the task of delivering goods to the others. Such networks are known as *peer-to-peer* networks because all the computers in the chain are on roughly equal footing.

In a peer-to-peer network, all computers can access all other computers in the network; there are no computers specifically designated as file servers.

Continues

5 Logging In to the Network

Even if your computer is part of a network, you need to explicitly "log in" to the network to use it. The procedure for logging in varies from one type of network to another. In most cases, you'll be asked for your username (that is, the name you're known by on the network) and then a password. Assuming that the network recognizes your name and password, it gives you access to other computers and resources on the network. Most networks have built-in security features that allow the network administrator to limit access to sensitive data (such as personnel or financial data). In such cases, your username determines which data files and programs you can use.

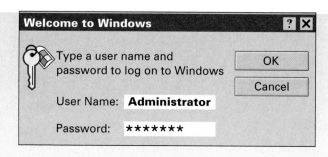

6 Accessing the File Server and Other Computer's Drives

In most cases, you will be able to access the file server's hard disk just as you would any other disk. On a PC, the server's hard disk is usually assigned one or more drive letters (just as your own hard disk is usually labeled C). In a peer-to-peer network, each computer will usually be assigned a name and you first select the computer and then the drive you want to access.

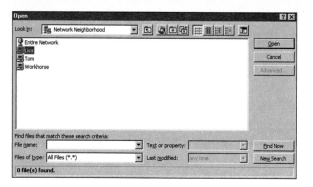

7 Logging Out

When you're done using the network, you should "log out," meaning disconnect from the network. When you shut down your computer, you should be logged out, although in some cases you may need to type logoff or something similar. Check with your network administrator for the details.

8 Network Administrators

The business of running a network can also be fairly complicated. For this reason, most networks of any size are assigned a full- or at least part-time network administrator. (If your report won't print or your computer starts displaying error messages, the network administrator is the person to see.) Nonetheless, there are a few pieces of information that everyone on the network should know, if for no other reason than to help you communicate with the network administrator. Information such as how to log into and log off of your particular network and how to access email can be provided by the network administrator. Information such as how to log into and log off of your particular network and how to access email can be provided by the network administrator.

End

Notes

Network Email

Most networks have electronic mail (email) programs that enable people on the network to send messages to other people on the network via computer. After you get used to it, you may well find this mode of communicating superior to both answering machines/voice mail and interoffice memos. It can eliminate the need for "phone tag" and make it easy to convey information that's too involved to leave on voice mail. (Email also has the advantage of being easier to store and review later.) In addition, email is easier and faster than printing and then delivering memos. In some organizations, it's the preferred vehicle for sharing ideas, making announcements, scheduling meetings, and so on.

Sending Mail

When you want to send a message to someone using email, you type in the message and then request that it be sent to a particular person's electronic "mailbox." (You can also send the same message to several mailboxes at once.) In most cases, this means that the message is stored, as a small file, in a subdirectory of the file server's hard disk that has been reserved for a particular person's "mail." In some email programs, as soon as your message has been sent, a window appears on the recipient's screen indicating that a message is waiting. He or she can then read and print the message whenever it's convenient. In other programs, the recipient finds out about your communiqué only when explicitly asking for messages. For more infomation on e-mail, see Chapter 8, Going online.

Topic

8

Going Online

These days, one of the main reasons people buy a computer is to get "online"—that is, to access the Internet, the Web, or online services like America Online. Anyone who has seen a newspaper or a TV news program in the last six or seven years has heard at least a little about the Internet. And almost everyone with a computer has received at least one free trial subscription to an online service.

The Internet is rapidly changing the way we communicate, conduct research, and do business (not to mention the way we check the weather, shop for shoes, and display pictures of pets and newborn babies). It's not only changing the face of capitalism and library science, it's changing the face of politics as well, by providing an open and, at least up to now, uncensorable forum for public discussions as well as another means for people to communicate with government officials and easily obtain government documents. This chapter will tell you everything you need to jump into the fray—from how to select your access route to the Internet, to how to find resources on the World Wide Web. ●

Online Basics

Begin

Getting onto the Internet has never been easier, but there are some basic things that you need to know before you take the big step. You have to decide who you want to get your Internet service from, what type of connection you would like to have, and so on. You also need to make sure your computer is fitted with the right kind of hardware and software for your journey online.

1 The Right Hardware

You can pay your Internet service fees and have all the right software at your disposal, but if your computer isn't ready to tackle the Internet, you won't get far. There are two key elements to your computer hardware: RAM and your modem. They both directly impact the speed at which you can view pages, download data, send and receive e-mail, and so on. The amount of RAM you need depends on the operating system you're running. If it's Windows Me, 2000, or XP, you should have 128MB of RAM on your system. If you're running an older version of Windows, such as Windows 95 or 98, you can probably get away with 64MB. As for a modem, you'll need a 56Kbps modem to experience the Internet well. A faster connection, such as a DSL or cable modem, is recommended for serious users (which you may quickly become). With prices for those services dropping, it's worth a look. (These connections are covered shortly under "DSL and Cable Connections.")

2 Browser Software

You're going to need a software program, called a *browser*, which allows you to view pages on the World Wide Web and access other Internet areas. The leading browsers are Microsoft Internet Explorer (version 6 is the newest), and Netscape Navigator (also version 6). Internet Explorer is almost always installed along with your Windows operating system, so you probably already have it on your computer. Navigator may be installed on your computer already as well. Regardless, both programs can be downloaded from the Internet for free.

3 E-mail Client

The program you use to send and receive e-mail is called an *e-mail client* (or e-mail program). Microsoft packages an e-mail client, Outlook Express, with Internet Explorer so you probably already have it installed. Netscape Messenger, a companion to Navigator, is available free from Netscape as part of a larger Internet applications suite called Netscape Communicator. In addition to sending and receiving e-mail, e-mail programs allow you to organize the e-mails you've received into different folders, send group e-mails, and so on.

Notes

Where to Get Internet Software

If you bought a computer and are using the preinstalled browser, you may be using an older version. To get the most-current version of either Internet Explorer or Netscape Navigator, all you have to do is download it from the Web. Internet Explorer can be found by going to **www.microsoft.com** and clicking on Downloads. To find Navigator, go to **home.netscape.com** and click on Downloads.

4 Internet Service Providers

In order for your computer to get onto the Internet and access the millions of pages of information available on the Web, you need to do business with an Internet Service Provider, or ISP. An ISP is a company that houses Web servers and allows individuals and businesses to connect to their computers, which are in turn connected to the hundreds of other computers that make up the Internet. In other words, you need an ISP to get access to the Internet. You can work with a national ISP, like EarthLink or AT&T WorldNet, or a local ISP in your area. You can choose an ISP that allows only dial-up connections, or you can use a DSL or cable Internet connection (all covered here). Another type of connection that is growing in popularity is wireless Internet, which is offered by some ISPs.

5 Dial-up Connections

A dial-up connection is exactly what it sounds like: a connection from which your computer dials to connect with the ISP. You do this using your modem and a phone line in your home. The ISP you work with should provide you with complete instructions as to how to make that connection. Dial-up connections are the least expensive option, but they also are the slowest. Although most people feel satisfied with their 56Kbps dial-up connection, after they've used a faster method, they seldom go back. Using a dial-up connection either ties up a phone line in your home, or causes you to add an additional line. Dial-up connections average around $21.95 per month at this writing, but if you shop around, you can probably find a cheaper rate.

Your computer

Your ISP's computer

The Internet

6 DSL and Cable Connections

Digital Subscriber Line, or DSL, connections are many times faster than dial-up accounts. They are available through phone companies and some other ISPs. DSL does require an additional line to be run to your house, so there are often setup charges involved. Cable Internet is purchased through your cable television provider, and offers very fast connections, up to 1,000 Kbps. Together, these types of connections are referred to as *broadband* connections. They are more expensive than dial-ups, but offer much faster service. Plus, they are "always on"— meaning any time your computer is turned on, you are connected to the Internet— and they don't tie up a phone line. On the low end, broadband rates are usually in the $50/month range.

7 Commercial Online Services

Commercial online services, like America Online (AOL), are different from ISPs. While they do offer full Internet access, they also offer content that is available to their member only. For example, an AOL member can see anything on the Internet, but can also see lots of things that members of other ISPs can't. AOL now boasts 30 million members, and its ease-of-use is a major reason. Lots of first-time Internet users flock to AOL. These services are covered in detail in the next topic.

End

AOL and Other Commercial Online Services

A variety of general-purpose online services, such as AOL, CompuServe, and The Microsoft Network (MSN), are available. For some people, they are the least intimidating routes to cyberspace; the software they provide makes it easy to get set up and to use the service after you're online. Traveling the huge and rather chaotic Internet via an online service may seem like taking a guided tour of the Amazon, versus heading out on your own with your trusty compass and a few Power Bars. On the other hand, you might outgrow the online services and find them more hindrance than help. In this case, you may want to use a regular Internet service provider, which are covered later in this chapter.

1 E-mail

All general-purpose online services offer electronic mail—that is, the capability to send and receive messages and files via "electronic mailboxes" (folders of files on the information service's hard disk). Whenever you call into the service, you are automatically informed if you have mail waiting and your mail is downloaded; at that point, you can either read your messages while you're still online, or disconnect first and read or print them later. E-mail is built into the software that you use for accessing the service.

2 General Purpose and Specialized Online Services

There are more than a dozen national online information services. Some, like Dow Jones Interactive (which focuses on financial information and services), are quite specialized. Others, like America Online, CompuServe, The Microsoft Network, and Prodigy Internet, are broader in scope and offer news, weather, and sports information, including Associated Press stories and, on some services, more extensive press clips from UPI, the *Washington Post*, and *Reuters World and Financial Reports*.

3 Travel Information

You'll also find travel information and services that let you find out about airline flights, hotels, motels, and car rentals and then make reservations online.

4 Financial Information and Services

Most services offer financial information and services, including current stock market price quotes, access to online brokerage firms, and access to home banking services.

5 Online Games

Many services provide games, both single and multiple player. In single-player games, you play against yourself or the computer. In multiple-player games, you play against one or more people currently online.

7 Shopping Services

In addition, you'll find shopping services for everything from clothes to cameras to computer hardware and software. You can even have gourmet food or flowers delivered anywhere in the country.

9 What You'll Pay

Most online services have fixed monthly fees, and many have additional charges for special services. A few offer discount rates for calls before or after prime time, but most online services can be accessed through local telephone numbers, saving long-distance charges.

10 Each Service Has Its Own Character

Although there is plenty of overlap among online services, each has its own personality and strengths. CompuServe probably has the most extensive research tools and databases, and the widest range of forums on computer hardware and software. America Online offers an exceptionally smooth, easy-to-use interface and has excellent resources for children. AOL is the most widely used service in the world.

11 How to Choose an Online Service

Depending on your needs and interests, you may choose a service because of the particular functions or forum topics it offers. Or it may just be a question of ambiance. For some, it's a question of where their friends are; if your friends are all AOL members, you'll be more likely to join that service.

6 Research Information

Online databases exist that include access to encyclopedias, *Consumer Reports*, dictionaries, and health-related databases that provide up-to-date information on disabilities and diseases such as AIDS and cancer.

8 Forums and Discussion Groups

Most services also provide you with access to forums (also known as *discussion groups*) that are essentially ongoing electronic conversations on a particular topic. Depending on the topic and the people involved, a forum resembles an electronic version of a clubhouse, lodge, study group, professional network, cafe[as], or singles bar. There are forums on cooking, wine tasting, religion, national politics, working from home, raising various species of pets, photography, gardening, coin and stamp collecting, sailing, genealogy, and, most important, computer hardware and software topics. Many information services offer professional forums that allow various types of professionals (including doctors and nurses, entrepreneurs, journalists, musicians, lawyers, and computer programmers and consultants) to exchange information and advice, generate ideas, and collaborate on projects.

12 Free Trial Subscriptions

If you're interested in sampling a service, keep your eyes open for free introductory offers. Many of the services provide special deals in an attempt to one-up their competition. You can pick up a free AOL CD at just about any bookstore.

Continues

13 How to Subscribe

Depending on the version of Windows you are running, you will likely have a version of AOL (and possibly other services) preinstalled on your system. To check, just open the Start menu and click the More Programs button. You'll likely see an AOL icon that you can select. If not, a free CD provided by the service will very easily walk you through the necessary steps.

14 Interfacing with an Online Service

All the online services provide software that acts as a "front end" for their service. These programs generally display a screenful of buttons you can use to access various parts of the service. They also usually let you compose e-mail and specify information you want to receive even before you go online. You can then direct the program to dial up the service, send and receive your e-mail, download any requested information, and then immediately disconnect, potentially saving you quite a bit of money in connect time charges.

End

Notes

Getting Tech Support with a Forum

As mentioned, most general-purpose online services offer forums on various types of hardware and software. Some of these forums are devoted exclusively to technical support and are monitored by the technical support staff. Others feature information sharing, conversation, and exchanging of sample files and utilities. If you post a question in such a forum, you may get an answer either from the tech support staff or from an experienced user who happened to get there first. One advantage of using forums for tech support is that you don't have to limit yourself to regular business hours. If you have a Monday deadline and a problem crops up on Friday, you can post a message and, with luck, some knowledgeable user will dial in over the weekend and offer a solution. Many software companies now have Web pages on the Internet as well, with answers to frequently asked questions (known as *FAQs*) and other technical information about their products.

The Internet and World Wide Web

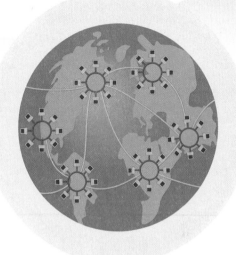

Begin

To its devoted participants, the Internet represents the true promise of telecommunications and indeed of the entire computer age. The Internet (or simply the Net) is a global federation of networks that have agreed to share information and resources across extremely fast information channels. It is simply a huge, open-ended (some would say anarchic), and rapidly expanding system for communicating and disseminating information.

1 What Is the Internet?

Much of the Net's growth can be attributed to something known as the *World Wide Web,* or the Web. As its name implies, the Web is a system that connects information, regardless of where it's stored—letting you jump from an article on orchid care stored on a computer in Dubuque to a related article on plant pruning on a system in Sydney, Australia.

2 How the Internet Started

Started as a tool to let scientists and researchers share expensive computer resources, in the last several years the Internet has grown into something far larger, more diverse, and more unpredictable. Between 1983 and the present, the number of servers (networks providing information) on the Net has grown from 500 to more than 20 million, and the number continues to increase exponentially.

3 Who Used to Use the Internet

Until the early 1990s, the only way to gain access to the Internet was through one of the participating networks. The Internet was therefore primarily the province of professors, students, and government employees (mostly at the Department of Defense).

4 Who Uses the Internet Today

Now, thousands of companies provide public access to the Internet for a fee. In addition, online services offer Internet access, along with tools for exploring and exploiting the Net's vast, and sometimes overwhelming, resources.

Private businesses, nonprofit organizations, and individuals, as well as the original collection of colleges, universities, and governmental agencies all have Web sites today. Anyone with a little cash and an ISP can put up her own site using a simple Web site creation program. Unlike the online services, the Net is neither owned nor run by any single organization or company.

Continues

5 What Can You Do on the Net?

Just about everyone's first question about the Internet is "What can I do with it?" (See "What People Do on the Net" for more on this.) Even today, the Internet is experiencing phenomenal growth, and new technologies are being developed. Given the volume of expansion and change, it's impossible to say what people will be doing on the Net in the future. For now, the most common uses are for personal entertainment, education, or shopping, e-mail, participating in discussion on newsgroups or in chat, and sharing files.

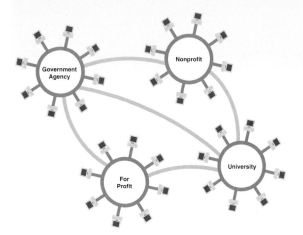

7 The Web's Graphical Interface

One of the main reasons for the Web's success is its graphical interface. In place of the text-based interfaces and arcane Unix commands that used to characterize life on the Net, the Web sports colorful typeset pages, graphics, sounds, video, and sometimes live movie footage.

8 Web Sites

Fierce competition exists among Web sites for the hippest and most innovative pages. Although you'll often hear the terms *Web site* and *Web page* used interchangeably, a Web site is actually a collection of Web pages, and a Web page is a single document within a Web site. There are even several Web sites that are nothing but catalogs of the coolest Web sites of the week, with links to each of those sites.

6 Surfing the Web

To surf the Web, you need browser software such as Microsoft's Internet Explorer. Using the browser, you can leap from one *Web page* (interactive document) to another by clicking a picture or piece of text—known as a *link*—on the screen. Such links allow users to interact with documents stored on computers across the Internet as though they were part of a single text. Using links to jump from site to site to site is commonly known as *surfing* the Web. It's important to remember that on the Net these links are for single-clicking, not double-clicking. Text links are often—although not always—underlined. If you pass your mouse over a piece of text and it changes from an arrow to a pointing hand, you'll know you've found a link.

These buttons are links.

This image is a link.

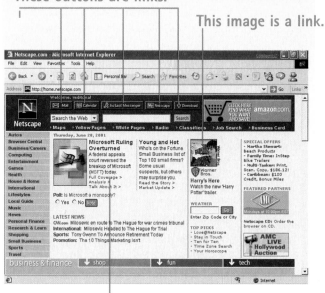

This text is a link.

9 Other Parts of the Internet

Although the Web is only one part of the Internet, it's probably the most accessible, user friendly, and fun part, as well as the fastest growing. Other pieces of the Net include the newsgroups and mailing lists, FTP, chat and instant messaging, all of which you'll learn a little bit about shortly.

End

A Brief Internet Glossary

The Internet is filled with (some might think plagued by) acronyms and obscure terminology. Here are some of the key terms you'll need to know to make sense of the Net.

1 Channels

Special Web sites that you subscribe to and that then deliver content to you on a schedule that you designate. With most Web sites, in contrast, you have to travel to the site to retrieve content.

2 Chat

A type of communication on the Internet that allows people to communicate with each other in real time, either through a one-on-one discussion or in groups. Many Web sites offer chat "rooms," which are places within the site in which these discussions are held. There also are chat programs that are available.

3 Download

The act of taking files from the Internet and saving them onto your computer. Downloading can take on many meanings; for example, every time you go to a Web page, you are actually downloading the files for that page into your computer. More strictly, however, downloading is actively copying a program or file onto your computer from a remote location.

4 FTP (File Transfer Protocol)

A protocol that provides file transfers across a variety of types of computer systems. FTP sites are Internet sites that have files you can download using FTP. To download these files, you need to use software that supports FTP. (Most Web browsers do.)

5 Home Page

The page you land on when you first access a Web site. It often contains an index and links to other pages of information.

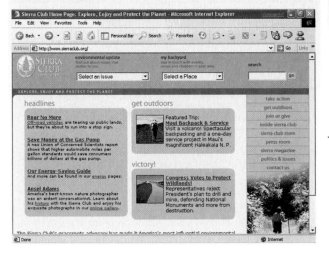

6 Hypertext

A way of creating documents that allows for interactive navigation—that is, for jumping from one place in the text to another via links within the document itself. Most Web sites use hypertext, allowing users to delve into topics or go off on related tangents by clicking a highlighted or specially formatted word, phrase, or picture.

Continues

This is the Sierra Club's home page.

7 HTML (Hypertext Markup Language)

The language in which Web pages are formatted and Web information is distributed. (Don't panic; you don't need to know HTML to browse the Web. These days you can even create Web pages without knowing any HTML.)

This is the underlying HTML code for the Sierra Club's home page.

8 HTTP (Hypertext Transfer Protocol)

The method by which documents are transferred from a Web site to your server (the computer you're logged into) and from the server to you. You'll often see this acronym at the beginning of Internet site addresses, which are known as uniform resource locators or *URLs*.

9 Instant Messages

A hybrid between e-mail and chat, instant messaging programs allow people to send messages to other users of the same software; the messages automatically appear on the recipient's screen.

10 ISP (Internet Service Provider)

A Net site that, for a fee, serves as a conduit for users to temporarily connect to the Net. Unless you have access to a Net site through your work or school, ISPs are your only access route to the Net other than the online services.

11 Plug-ins

A small program that works in tandem with a browser, adding extra features like special sound and video capabilities. As browsers become more and more capable, however, you're less likely to require plug-ins unless you have specialized needs.

12 TCP/IP (Transmission Control Protocol/Internet Protocol)

The network communications protocol used to connect diverse types of computer systems across the Internet.

13 URL (Uniform Resource Locator)

An Internet site address that begins with the transfer format (**http://** for Web documents, **news://** for newsgroups, **ftp://** for FTP sites) followed by the name of the server where the site's files are stored, the file's directory path, and its filename.

14 Usenet (USEr NETwork)

A computer network, accessed through the Internet, that consists of more than 20,000 newsgroups (online forums) on almost every topic imaginable—and is growing fast.

15 WWW (World Wide Web)

A system that allows for worldwide hypertext linking of multimedia documents so that information can be linked and accessed regardless of its physical location.

End

What People Do on the Net

So, what *can* you do on the Net, as of this moment? For starters, you can chat with people from around the world, plan your trip to Bali, send irate messages to your senator or representative, download stock quotes, and read the latest local, national, and international news. However, because no single entity runs or oversees the Net, its content is a lot more diverse than that of the online services. You'll find more of the avant garde, the innovative, the obscure, and the ridiculous. You'll also find resources you won't find anywhere else. Because it doesn't cost much to set up a Web site, any person or institution that wants to make information or ideas available is free to do so. In addition, because most academic institutions are Internet hosts, they can and often do open their library doors to the public, which provides you with unparalleled resources for research. Here are just a few of the Net's resources:

1 Government Sites

Government and legal documents including bills currently before Congress, state and federal laws, and U.S. Supreme Court decisions.

2 Educational Materials

Educational materials from several museums, such as the Smithsonian and the Exploratorium.

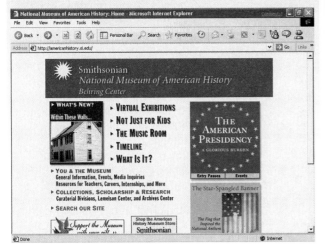

3 Radio and TV

Every major radio and television network has its own site to highlight its programs and personalities. You can even browse the TV listings at TV Guide's site.

Continues

4 Magazines and Newspapers

Hundreds of online magazines, or "zines" offer content. Virtually every major national magazine, be it a news weekly or a specialty publication, has its own site, as do most newspapers.

5 Career Opportunities

There are many national job posting sites, like Monster.com, that allow you to search for a better job. You can also search the classifieds on your local newspaper's Web site. Or, if there's a particular company you'd like to work for, go to its site and check out job postings; most companies put their openings online.

6 Online Resources

The entire text of literary classics such as *Moby Dick* and *Alice in Wonderland* are available online, as well as weather satellite photos, *Webster's Dictionary*, *Roget's Thesaurus*, and a form for looking up a ZIP code. You can get a map to the soccer field for the kids' game tonight and even get an aerial view of the field. You can find out what's playing at the local theater or download a favorite song or CD.

End

Notes

Don't Get Overwhelmed

The drawback to the profusion of information on the Net is that it's overwhelming. The challenge for new users (and even old hands) is figuring out exactly what's out there and how to extract your needles from the information haystack. (You'll learn a bit more about doing this under "Searching for Sites" later in this chapter.)

Understanding Internet Addresses

Before you get online and start firing off e-mail to all your friends or jumping around to different Web sites, it helps to understand a little bit about Internet addresses. There are two basic types of Internet addresses: those for e-mail and those for Web sites.

2 Top-Level Domains

There are six primary domains for U.S. Internet sites: com (commercial), edu (educational), gov (government), mil (military), net (network), and org (organization). Because of the large number of sites currently on the Web, some new top-level domains are now available with more are on the way. Other countries have a country-specific top-level domain; Canada's is .ca. The top-level domain comes at the end of both e-mail and Web addresses.

3 Sending E-mail

When you are on the Internet, you can address Internet e-mail to another Internet account just by using the recipient's address. In addition, you can send information between the major online services, or between online services and the Internet using the Internet's mail capabilities. This means that if you have an account with an ISP and your friend or colleague has an account on America Online, you can still exchange messages. In this case, however, you may need to refer to the online service as well as the user when you specify the address.

Begin

1 Anatomy of an E-mail Address

Internet addresses have three basic parts. First is the person's *username*—the name the user types when logging in to the computer that has her Internet account. Next is the *domain name*. The third part is called the *top-level domain*.

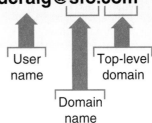

dcraig@sfo.com

User name | Top-level domain | Domain name

4 Sending Mail Within an Online Service

In most cases, sending mail within an online service—that is, one member of the service sending a message to another member— is easier that regular e-mail. In AOL, for example, you can simply type the recipient's username, and leave out the "@aol.com," and they will receive your message.

5 E-mail Addresses Versus URLs

Note that Internet e-mail addresses are different from URLs. The former are used to identify a particular user on the Net, the latter to identify a Web server—that is, a computer that makes information available via the World Wide Web. The URL is what you type into your Web browser program to tell it to go to and display a particular "page" of information. In most cases, you'll enter the URL for the home page (starting page) for a particular Web site. URLs typically start with www, for World Wide Web, and then follow with the domain name and the top-level domain, all separated by periods (which are usually called dots). For example, the *Time* magazine Web site can be found at `www.time.com`.

End

Talking to People on the Net

Begin

The millions of Internet hosts and the resources they offer are only one of the big reasons for accessing the Net. The other is person-to-person communication. There are five ways to communicate with individuals and groups of individuals on the Net: e-mail, mailing lists, , newsgroups, chat, and instant messaging.

1 E-mail

E-mail on the Net works just as it does on online services: You send a message directly to someone's electronic address and it is stored in his electronic mailbox, awaiting retrieval. For more information, see the upcoming section "Sending and Reading E-mail."

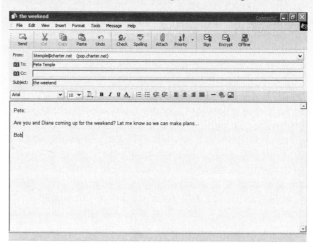

2 Mailing Lists

The Internet features tens of thousands of electronic mailing lists ("lists," for short) covering a huge range of interests, from bluegrass music to yoga, AIDS research to woodworking, home schooling to Elvis memorabilia. After you *subscribe* to (ask and receive permission to join) one of these lists, you receive copies of all the mail sent to the list and can send mail to all the subscribers. It's rather like finding a group of electronic pen pals. There are even sites, such as the List Universe site shown here, that help you track down mailing lists of interest to you.

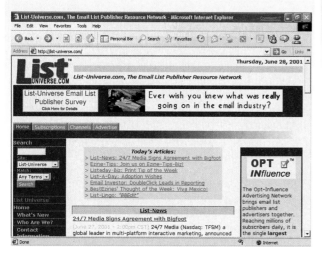

3 Finding People with Common Interests

Given the huge number of people on the Net, anyone can find others with whom they have common ground in terms of intellectual interests, professional goals, and/or lifestyle. Although there may not be anybody in your hometown or even your state who shares your interest in Chinese word processing, for example, you can be sure that there are several people on the Net who do (even if most of them are in other countries).

4 E-mail Overload!

The free-form nature of lists is both part of their charm and one of their drawbacks. Because every piece of mail goes to everyone on the list, joining even a small list can bring you dozens, if not hundreds, of pieces of e-mail every week, if the list's members are particularly chatty. Unless you are truly fascinated by the subject at hand or have an abundance of free time, you'll probably want to limit yourself to only a few selected lists. (Don't worry. It's just as easy to get off a list as it is to get on: A single e-mail message to the list administrator should do the trick.)

6 How Newsgroups Work

Unlike mailing lists, where every person on the list gets every piece of mail, newsgroup articles are stored on a computer called a *news server*. To read the articles, you need a program called a *newsreader*. (Both Outlook Express and Netscape Messenger include newsreaders.) The newsreader shows you a list of current articles in any newsgroups you choose to view, and you can decide which ones you actually want to read.

5 Usenet Newsgroups

Usenet newsgroups are electronic discussion groups through which people with shared interests exchange information and ideas. Usenet itself is actually a separate computer network, but most Internet hosts provide access to Usenet, so Internet users can participate in its newsgroups.

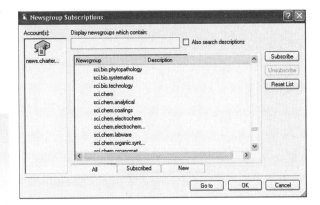

7 How to Find Mailing Lists and Newsgroups

No central registry of mailing lists or newsgroups exists, although there are a few brave souls and organizations that make some attempts to catalog them. You can get lists of mailing lists and newsgroups at the Web site **http://www.tile.net**. The List Universe site mentioned earlier (found at **http://www.listuniverse.com**) includes lists of newsgroups, as well as mailing lists. Another useful tool for searching Usenet archives is provided by Google at (**http://groups.google.com**).

8 Chat and Instant Messaging

Both chat and instant messaging allow users to communicate directly with each other in real time. Chat can be done using a chat "client" (program), but most people who chat do so by using the chat area on a favorite Web site. For example, if you are a fan of the NBA, you can chat with other NBA fans at the league's Web site, **www.nba.com**. Instant messaging requires a software program such as AOL's Instant Messenger or MSN's similar program. Instant messaging allows you to send a note directly to the computer screen of a person whose username you know, as long as she is online.

Notes

Getting a Shorter Version

You can often subscribe to the "digest" version of a mailing list. Typically, you'll receive one e-mail with all the day's messages together instead of multiple e-mails.

Internet Etiquette

The Internet has its own culture and rules of etiquette (called *netiquette*). It's good form to spend some time reading a newsgroup or list before you participate more actively. (This is sometimes called *lurking*.) Get a feel for the tone of the group before you start expressing your opinions. Some groups are friendly to strangers, whereas others are not. The experience will probably be more pleasant, not to mention more useful, if you make an effort to fit in with the particular online community.

End

Getting onto the Net

Begin

One of the simplest and least intimidating ways to try out the Net is through an online service. However, some of the larger Internet service providers (ISPs) are becoming more and more user friendly. In addition, if you feel less of a need for hand holding, it may work just as well for you to use one of the hundreds of smaller, local ISPs.

1 How You'll Pay

Online services and ISPs offer flat monthly rates for unlimited access. In most cases, you must supply a credit card for a monthly charge; some others offer prepayment as an option. Very few ISPs allow you to be billed for service after the fact.

2 What Features Are Available

Not only do the prices vary from one service to the next, Internet-related features differ as well. For example, some online services allow parents to block certain newsgroups or pages whose names contain specific words, and to place similar restrictions on Web pages. AOL offers Parental Controls, which allow you to set surfing criteria based on the age of your children. (These days, you can often block sites with your Web browser, as well.) Many of the smaller ISPs provide you with Internet access only, although some of the larger ones provide content as well.

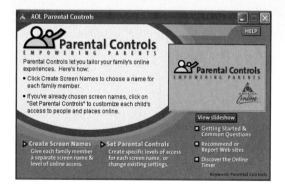

3 Search Tools and Cool Sites

The breadth and utility of search tools also vary from service to service. Some services also offer a single home page and perhaps a few pages of cool Web sites, whereas others provide dozens of Web pages, with information on a range of subjects and links to other Web pages and newsgroups.

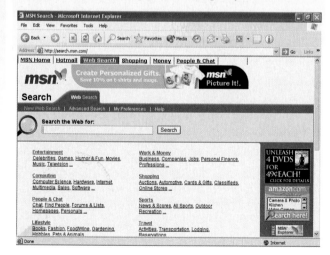

4 Comparing Services

Because each of the online services constantly offer new and improved tools and features, it's impossible to say which one is the "best" or even to give an up-to-date account of their offerings. The same is true of ISPs. There are thousands of them out there, ranging from large and user-friendly, to small and bare bones. Computer magazines, both in print and online, are one of the best sources for up-to-date information on the relative merits of online services and ISPs. If you can get online through a friend or work, you can research pricing and features on the Web.

5 How Services Organize Information

One advantage of online services over ISPs is that they do some of the work of organizing the content for you, offering tours and tutorials and their own lists of interesting sites, mailing lists, newsgroups, and downloadable software. These days, however, some of the larger ISPs also provide content and an easy-to-understand environment. There are also a large number of Web sites, such as **www.yahoo.com** and **www.netscape.com** that act as *portals* by providing news and links to other information, organized by topic.

6 When to Use an ISP

If you use the Internet more than occasionally, you may want to use a local Internet service provider (ISP) rather than an online service. This typically gives you the luxury of using the Web browser of your choice. Most accounts also include 5MB or more of storage space on the provider's server that you can use to set up your own Web site should you care to. You'll get an e-mail address (many providers offer multiple e-mail addresses) and, in most cases, unlimited access to the Internet. Many times you'll get quicker and more reliable connections. That is, you'll find it easier to reach the Internet and will be less likely to be disconnected once you're there. After you've chosen an ISP, it can assist you in configuring your computer to utilize the service.

End

Notes

Finding an ISP

If you're trying to track down information about ISPs, try The List, INT Media Group's guide to ISPs, at **http://thelist.internet.com**; currently it lists more than 4,500 ISPs. You might also want to check out the ISP Directory at **http://www.boardwatch.com/isp**.

Begin

Browsing the Web

When you first launch your browser, you'll probably land on a particular Web page. Which one will depend on which browser you're using; the company that makes the browser will connect you to one of its Web pages by default. All the major browsers offer some means of storing the names and URLs of sites you like so you can easily return to them later. In Netscape Navigator, these stored site addresses are called *bookmarks*. In Internet Explorer, they're called *favorites*.

1 Getting to a Web Page

There are two main ways to get to a page on the Web. You can enter the URL for the page and press Enter, or you can click a link (text or graphical) that leads to the desired page.

You can enter a URL here and press Enter.

You can click a link to travel to the page it points to.

2 Entering the URL

Near the top of the browser window, both Netscape Navigator and Internet Explorer feature a combo box/drop-down list labeled Address or Location. You type the URL there and press Enter. If the URL for the page you want to access begins with the characters `http://www`, you can omit that part and just enter the rest of the URL. If you click the arrow at the right of the address/location combo box, you'll see a list of the URLs you accessed most recently. Select from the list if you want to return to one of those sites.

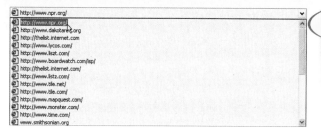

3 While the Page Transfers

While the browser is fetching the page, you'll probably see a status message at the bottom of the browser's window, indicating how much of the transfer is already complete. You don't have to wait until a page has finished displaying before you scroll through the text or move on to another page.

4 Clicking Links

If the page you are viewing contains a link that interests you, just click the link to move directly to a page on the specified topic. If you want to return to the previous page (the one that contained the link), just click the **Back** button in your browser. After you have used a particular link on a page, the link changes color. This lets you see which links you've already traveled and prevents inadvertent wandering in circles. (You can still use a previously used link, in case you *want* to wander in circles.)

6 The Back and Forward Buttons

The **Back** button redisplays the last page you viewed. (You can keep reversing your steps by continuing to click **Back**.) The **Forward** button undoes the effect of the **Back** button, taking you back to the page you were on when you clicked **Back**.

You can click these links to read more about the topic.

You can click the Back button to go back to the previous page.

5 The Home Button

Both Netscape Navigator and Internet Explorer have buttons near the top of their windows that let you accomplish common operations. The **Home** button takes you back to the *start page*—that is, the page that was displayed when you first launched the browser.

7 The Stop Button

The **Stop** button aborts the current transfer of information from the ISP to your computer. You'll find this useful if your browser is in the midst of displaying a page and you decide it's not worth the wait or decide to cancel a download in the middle of the process.

8 The Print Button

The **Print** button sends the currently displayed page to your printer.

Continues

Notes

Upgrading Your Bookmarks and Favorites

If you upgrade to a newer version of the same browser, your bookmarks/favorites will be there for you automatically. You don't need to fiddle around with transferring files or anything like that.

Organizing Your Bookmarks

If you accumulate a lot of bookmarks/favorites, you may want to organize them into folders. See your browser documentation for details.

Notes

Displaying "Live" URLs

Many e-mail programs automatically display URLs in e-mail messages as live links. You'll be able to tell because the URLs will be underlined and will often be a different color text. To travel to the site, you can click the link to launch your browser and go to that page.

9 Creating a Bookmark or Favorite

To create a new bookmark or favorite, first get to the page you want your browser to remember. Then, if you have Netscape, click the **Bookmarks** button and choose **Add Bookmark**. If you're using the Internet Explorer, click the **Favorites** option on the menu bar and select **Add to Favorites**.

10 Finding a Marked Page

You can quickly go to a bookmarked or favorite page after you've marked it. To do this in Explorer, pull down the **Favorites** menu and choose the site from there. You may need to choose the category you want from the Favorites menu, then choose your favorite site from the submenu that appears. In Navigator, just click the **Bookmarks** button and choose the desired bookmark, or bookmark category, from the menu that appears.

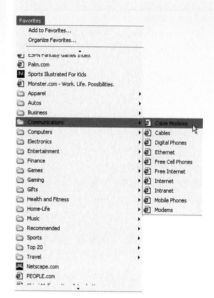

11 Changing Your Start Page

It's easy to change the page that's displayed automatically when you start your browser. To specify a start page in Netscape Navigator, select **Edit**, then **Preferences** from the menu bar to display a Preferences dialog box. Then click the **Home Page** option button, enter the URL of the desired page in the **Location** text box, and click **OK**. If you're using Internet Explorer, select **View** from the menu bar, then choose **Internet Options** to display an Internet Options dialog box. Select the **General** tab. Then enter the URL for the desired site in the **Address** text box under Home Page and click **OK**.

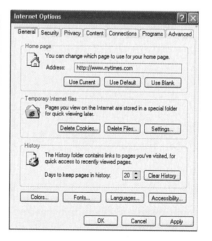

End

Searching for Sites

There are literally millions of sites on the Web, and more are created every minute. One of the great challenges of using the Web is finding sites that interest you or that contain the information you're looking for.

Begin

1 Your Browser May Recommend Sites

The major browsers provide links directly to recommended new and interesting sites. Most of the online services (and some of the larger ISPs) also help point you to interesting sites, which is one of their main selling points.. In addition, many computer magazines periodically run articles on not-to-be-missed sites.

2 Finding More Links

Plenty of Web pages consist largely of links acting, in effect, as directories to all the Web pages on a particular subject. For example, Yahoo! (`http://www.yahoo.com`) is a large directory site that contains many thousands of links, organized by topic.

3 Finding Search Engines

Dozens of specialized sites, known as search engines, are designed to help you search for resources on the Web. Some of the most popular are Google, Lycos, and Alta Vista. All the services provide search engines that let you hunt for Web pages by entering one or more keywords. Many also feature directories of Web sites so that you can search for information by category.

Continues

4 Finding Search Engines via Your Browser

In Netscape Navigator, you can access several popular search services by clicking the **Search** button. In Internet Explorer, click the **Search** button on the toolbar to display a Search bar on the left-hand side of the screen. If you find a particular search service that you like, you might want to bookmark it or declare it a favorite it so you can access it without remembering or typing its URL. You might even want to designate it as your start page, as described in the previous section.

5 Entering Keywords

To search by keyword when you're at a search site, just type the word and click the adjacent button (**GO, Search, Seek, Go Get It**, or the equivalent). The procedure for searching for more than one word varies from service to service. In some cases, you just type in the words. In others, you place a plus sign before each keyword that has to appear in the search result. You can exclude pages that contain a particular word by typing the word preceded by a minus sign. In some cases, if you want to search for a particular phrase—San Juan Islands, for example—you enclose the phrase in quotes.

6 How to Conduct Searches

Many search engine sites include a link or two to information on conducting searches using that particular page. It's a good idea to read that information because there's a lot of variation from one site to the next.

7 How Results Are Displayed

Most search sites display results a few sites at a time. You'll see the total number of matches found, then the first 10 sites, often the ones that are most relevant or that most closely match your criteria. The information shown for each site usually includes a title, (which is also a link to the site) and a brief description of the site's content. To display the next set of sites, click a button labeled **Next Results, Next Page**, or the equivalent, at the bottom of the page.

Notes

Search Site URLs

The URLs for some of the most popular search pages include **www.excite.com**, **www.google.com**, **www.lycos.com**, **www.yahoo.com**, and **www.altavista.com**.

Other Types of Searches

Most services let you search for FTP sites and for newsgroup messages, as well as Web pages. Many search services also provide tools for looking up e-mail addresses, displaying road maps, or getting a local weather report.

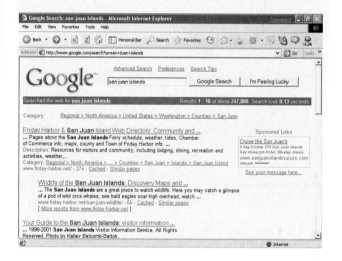

End

Downloading and Installing Software

Many fans of the Internet claim that the real reason for accessing the Net is to download software, especially free software. As you'll soon discover, the Net is loaded with software of every price and purpose.

Downloading means receiving a file from a remote computer. The easiest way to remember the term is to think of the remote computer as hovering somewhere above you.

Begin

1 Freeware, Shareware, and Commercial Software

Some of the software available on the Net is the same type of commercial software you can find at your local computer store. Much of it is freeware (free software) or shareware (low-cost software you're allowed to try out for a period for free). If you like a shareware program and plan to continue using it, you are obliged to send a small fee to the software developer who created it. In exchange, you usually get either a more full-fledged version of the program or a version that continues working after the trial period is up. In some cases, you receive a manual and free software updates as well.

2 Downloading Upgrades

The Internet is also becoming a popular means of distributing upgrades to commercial software, because it saves the software manufacturer the cost of creating, packing, and shipping disks. It's a good idea to check software vendors' Web sites for news of upgrades to your favorite programs (including your trusty browser). Minor upgrades are often free; major upgrades usually come at a price.

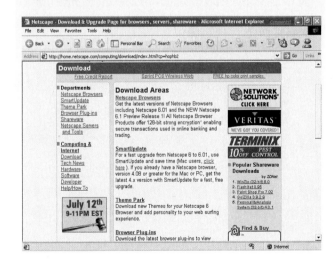

3 Downloading Beta or Evaluation Versions

Some software developers let you download beta or evaluation versions of their programs for free. An evaluation version is typically a partial version of the program that works only for a designated trial period. A beta version of a program is a program-in-progress: It more or less works but still has a few bugs and glitches. Beta software often expires after a certain date (usually about the time the software is due to be released for real), forcing its users to shell out money for the completed release version. The advantage of using beta software is that it gives you a glimpse of what's coming down the pike.

5 How File Compression Works

Many of the files you download from the Internet will be compressed. *File compression* means translation of a file into a coded format that occupies less space than the original file. The amount of space saved by compressing a file depends on the file type, but it's not unusual for compressed files to take up half the space or less of the originals. (Graphical files and database files tend to compress the most.)

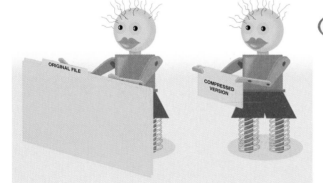

4 How to Download

When you reach a Web site that offers software downloads, the first thing you should do is read the installation instructions at the site itself. Then click the link (often labeled **Download**) that initiates the download process. In most cases, you'll see a Save As dialog box. (In Internet Explorer, you'll get a dialog box that asks you if you want to save this program to disk or run it from its current location; make sure that the "save this program" button is checked.) You'll see a suggested filename in the Save As dialog box; it's usually best not to change that name. Make sure that you know to what directory you are saving the file. Many people create a Downloads folder on their C: drive for this purpose, or just save everything to their desktop and file it later.

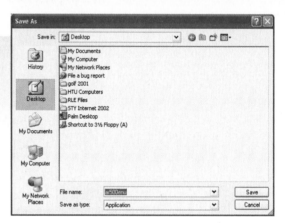

6 Why Compress Files?

There are two reasons to compress files: 1) To save room on disk. 2) To save time when sending data from one computer to another, thus keeping your computer (and phone line) from being tied up for long periods. The smaller the file, the less time it takes to transmit. Bear in mind that you cannot actually use files in their compressed form. Rather, you need to decompress (expand) them to their original size.

7 How to Decompress Files

Some of the compressed files you download will decompress and install themselves automatically while you're still online. Others will be what are known as self-extracting EXE files—meaning they have a file extension of EXE (for executable), and when you execute (run) them by double-clicking them in a folder window or Windows Explorer , they automatically decompress. Many compressed files actually contain compressed versions of multiple files. Therefore, when you decompress them, you may get several decompressed files, not just one. After you have run a self-extracting EXE file, you need to look for a file named SETUP or INSTALL and run that one to finish the installation process.

8 Zip Files

Some of the files you can download on the Internet are zip files—meaning that they employ the commonly used PKZIP format and they have a .zip extension. You'll need a special program to "unzip" such files. The most popular one for Windows is a program named WinZip. You can download a trial version of this program from the WinZip Web site at **http://www.winzip.com**. After you've downloaded WinZip, double-click the executable file (probably called winzip80.exe) it to start the installation.

End

Notes

Virus Protection

If you plan to download files, you'll want to get a virus-scanning program and you'll probably want to have it running as you download. See Chapter 4, "Up and Running," for more information on virus protection.

Online Applications

Rather than downloading the software or installing it from a CD, some software programs can be accessed over the Internet and used from a person's computer by paying a monthly fee. When a company makes its software available in this manner, it is called an Application Service Provider, or ASP.

Online or Offline?

If you plan to send a particularly long message, you might want to compose the message offline and connect to your ISP to transmit it only when you're done. For directions on how to do this, consult your mail program's documentation or online help.

The Mail Window and the Browser

When you're in a mail program, the mail window may obscure the browser window. (You are actually running two separate programs, even if one of them is actually a part of your browser.) To get back to your browser window, either close the mail program window or just select the browser window by clicking its button on the taskbar. (Remember that every program currently running is represented by a taskbar button.)

Begin

Sending and Reading E-mail

For some, e-mail is the best thing the Internet has to offer. E-mail is a communication form unto itself: often breezier than letters, a little less personal than phone calls. If you spend a lot of time at your computer, you can easily fire off your messages without leaving your desk. You can cut and paste text from documents already on your computer. You can easily copy a message to multiple recipients and can sometimes even set up ongoing groups of recipients, addressing a message to all of them with a single keystroke. And, you can "attach" files to your message. The ability to hold low-cost conversations with people around the globe is well worth the price of Internet admission.

2 Other Mail Programs

Many mail programs are available. For example, when you install Microsoft Office, you get a program named Microsoft Outlook, which is both a mail program and a general information manager. (It includes a calendar, a contact manager, and other utilities.) Internet Explorer comes with Outlook Express. In addition, Netscape and many other browsers come with their own e-mail utilities that are built into the browser. You don't need to do anything to install them. There are specialized mail programs (Eudora is the most popular) that do nothing but send, receive, and help you manage your e-mail. There are also browser-based e-mail systems such as Yahoo! Mail and Hotmail that allow you to check, send, and receive e-mail from any computer in the world that has an Internet connection. You simply log on to the appropriate Web site, login with your username and password, and view your mail. However, these services don't allow you to work with your mail offline.

1 Your Default E-mail Program

When you initially set up Internet access you are asked whether you want to set up an Internet mail account. If you said Yes and you didn't install any other e-mail programs or browsers afterwards, the browser automatically launches your default e-mail program when you choose to send or receive e-mail. Your default depends on your setup; most likely, it will be Outlook Express. You can check which e-mail program is the default, and change it in the Preferences area of Netscape Navigator or the Internet Options area of Internet Explorer.

3 Creating E-mail Messages

How you create a message depends on which program you're using. In Netscape Navigator, the simplest method is to pull down the **File** menu, choose **New**, and then choose **Message** or press Ctrl+M to open a Composition window. You can also launch your mail program (Eudora, Outlook Express, whatever) and then either click the **Compose Message** button or **New Mail Message** button, or look for a Compose option on the menu bar.

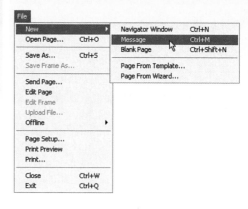

4 The Message Composition Window

Regardless of which mail program you're using, after you initiate the process of composing a message, you arrive at a message composition window. (It may be labeled **New Message**, **Composition**, or something like that.) In this window, you specify an e-mail address to send the message to and, generally, a subject. (If you were to send me a message about this book, for example, you'd enter **lisabiow@sfo.com** as the e-mail address and **How to Use Computers** or some other descriptive word or phrase as the subject.) In most cases, there's also a text box in which you can enter e-mail addresses of people you want to "cc" (carbon copy) the message to.

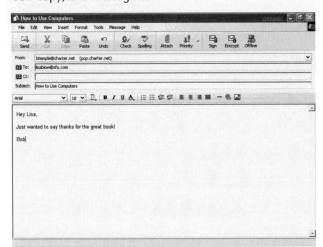

5 Sending Messages

In Netscape, when you click the Send button, your message is delivered immediately by default. (If you prefer to save the message for later delivery, choose **Send Later** from the **File** menu.) In Outlook Express, clicking the Send button places your message in your Outbox. You then need to take an additional step to actually transmit the message. To do this, click the **Send and Receive** button in the toolbar at the top of the window. However, you can set Outlook Express to send messages immediately by opening the Tools menu, selecting Options, and checking the "Send messages immediately" box on the Send tab.

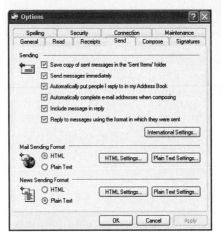

6 The Address Book

Most mail programs provide a means for you to save e-mail addresses in an *address book*. When you compose new messages, you can then choose from this list rather than racking your brain for Aunt Tillie's address. The address book is especially helpful for addresses that are very long or obscure.

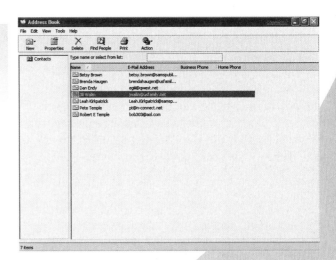

Continues

7 Reading Your Mail

To check for incoming messages from the Internet Explorer window, click the **Mail** button on the toolbar (it looks like an envelope) and select **Read Mail**. This launches whichever mail program you're using (Outlook Express, Microsoft Outlook, and so on). Enter your password if requested. Then use your e-mail program's command for checking mail. For example, in Outlook Express you can click the **Send and Receive Messages** button. The other option is to launch your e-mail program directly and go from there. For example, if you're using Outlook Express, you can launch the program by clicking the button for it from the Quick Launch toolbar on the taskbar.

8 Reading Your Mail in Netscape

You can launch the Messenger program by selecting **Communicator, Messenger** from the Netscape Navigator menu bar. Then enter your mail password if requested. (It is usually the same as the password you use to connect to your ISP.) The Messenger program automatically checks for any new messages and displays them in your Inbox.

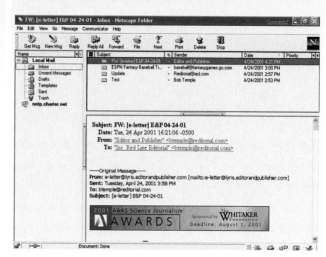

9 Printing Messages

After you're in your mail Inbox, you'll see a list of messages received. In some mail programs, you'll see the contents of the currently highlighted message in the bottom half of the window. In others, you'll need to double-click the message to display its contents. To print the message, first display the message and then look for a Print button on the toolbar.

10 Replying to Messages

All mail programs let you reply to an incoming message rather than composing a brand-new message in response. This saves you the trouble of entering the person's e-mail address or a new subject. The procedure for replying to a message varies from one program to the next. Look for a Reply button or command in the window you use to view incoming mail. In some programs, you can right-click the message in the Inbox list and select Reply.

11 Deleting Messages

After you're done with a particular message, you can highlight that message in the message list and press the Delete key or click a Delete button. In some programs, deleting a message simply moves it to a Deleted Items folder. It isn't really gone until you delete the contents of that folder. To actually get rid of such messages, get into the Deleted Items folder and delete the items by using the Delete key or Delete button.

The Reply button sends a response to the person who sent you the message.

The Reply to All button sends a response to the person who sent you the message as well as any other recipients of the message.

End

Index

HOW to USE

How to Use *provides easy, visual information in a proven, step-by-step format. This amazing guide uses colorful illustrations and clear explanations to get you the results you need.*